MONSTER GARAGE™

HOW TO
CUSTOMIZE
DAMN NEAR ANYTHING

Discovery CHANNEL

MOTORBOOKS INTERNATIONAL

This edition first published in 2003 by Motorbooks
International, an imprint of MBI Publishing Company,
Galtier Plaza, Suite 200, 380 Jackson Street,
St. Paul, MN 55101-3885 USA

Motorbooks International titles are also available
at discounts in bulk quantity for industrial or
sales-promotional use. For details write to Special Sales
Manager at Motorbooks International Wholesalers
& Distributors, Galtier Plaza, Suite 200,
380 Jackson Street, St. Paul, MN 55101-3885 USA.

ISBN 0-7603-1748-8

On the front cover: Artwork copyright of the
Discovery Channel

Endpaper: The Monster Garage lockers.

On the frontispiece: A welding helmet used on the show.

On the title page: In episode 21, a crew was assembled
to transform this Cadillac DeVille into a demolition
derby car.

On the back cover: The cast of *Monster Garage*:
Jesse James and a team of skilled, innovative
craftspeople. These two images show the team at
work on the Rock Crawler (a 1968 Ford Bronco).

**Discovery Communications/ Monster Garage book
development team:**
Thom Beers, Executive Producer, Original Productions
Clark Bunting II, General Manager, Discovery Channel
Sharon M. Bennett, Senior Vice President, Strategic
    Partnerships & Licensing
Deidre Scott, Vice President, Licensing
Carol Le Blanc, Vice President of Marketing and Retail
    Development
Sean Gallagher, Director of Programming Development,
    Discovery Channel
Elizabeth Bakacs, Creative Director, Strategic Parnerships
Erica Jacobs Green, Publishing Manager

Acquisitions Editor: Lee Klancher
Associate Editor: Leah Noel
Art directed by Rochelle L. Schultz
Designed by Brenda C.Canales

Printed in China

CONTENTS

BY THOM BEERS

Creator and Executive Producer of

Monster Garage and **Monster House**

The inspiration for *Monster Garage* came to me in dream. One particularly restless night, I awoke from a nightmare about a wicked green Mustang that could cut grass at 100 miles per hour.

That vision really stuck with me, and I started fantasizing about morphing vehicles while stuck in the L. A. traffic. I used the driver next to me as the starting point for my visions. The unkempt young man in the SUV looked like a garbage truck driver. The old guy wearing the cock-eyed ball cap and driving the school bus seemed like the type who just wanted to be vacationing on a lake in Minnesota.

From there, I took the Monster Machine thing about three steps further. I wanted to produce a crazy sci-fi Thunderdome kind of thing, where guys battle over a hot motor in a giant cage or rappel down the walls chasing after a hydraulic ram. We were going to create this omniscient character, the Mighty Metal Morpher, to be a mysterious, deep synthesized voice behind the show, passing judgment on the contestants. I wanted it to be way over the top, just like my dream about the green Mustang.

The vision changed when I did *Motorcycle Mania* with Jesse James. I was struck by how people reacted to the scene where Jesse hand-builds the gas tank. I think a big part of Jesse's appeal is that he gets down and dirty with his hands. People love to watch craftsmen work. By taking that approach to *Monster Garage,* we created a show that was less Mad Max and more a celebration of American craftsmanship.

I also found that the show's real-world garage angle really hit home for me. My dad worked at a Ford garage, and I spent one day each month hanging out with him in the parts department. I love the smell of motor oil and fuel—it's a perfume that reminds me of those workdays with Dad, and I smell it every time I go on the set of Monster Garage.

I think the garage is a very spiritual place, somewhere that people gather to work with their hands. It's totally overlooked in our society, yet so vital. Recently, a group of high-ranking executives came in to spend some time on the *Monster Garage* set. Unlike most visitors, they didn't want to see the show taped. They just wanted to weld. So Jesse spent the day with them, showing them the basics. They stuck a few pieces of metal together. They were as happy as little kids.

Thom Beers

Obviously, a big part of the appeal of *Monster Garage* is the pleasure of building something with your hands— even if only vicariously, through the show's guests—which is why I'm excited about this book. It offers people a starting point to pick up a hammer, welder, or paint gun.

I hope you learn a few things on these pages and find the inspiration to make a monster of your own.

Build it . . . don't buy it.

BIOGRAPHY

Thom Beers is the president and executive producer of Original Productions, a premiere reality-based production company that produces innovative and provocative programming content for cable and syndicated television.

Established in 1999, the company has grown into one of television's leading suppliers of popular-culture documentaries under Beers. Beers and his team have produced such shows and series as Monster Garage, Monster House, Biker Women, Turf Rockets: A Lawn Mower Racing Challenge, Impact!, Plastic Surgery: Before & After, Gut Busters, Greatest Motorcycles, Motorcycle Mania I & II, Crash Files, Harley Davidson: The Birth Of The V-Rod, Mystery Of The Alaskan Mummies, Extreme Hawaii, Vegas Weddings, Shipwrecks & Salvage, Wrestling School, and Contortionists.

Beers' productions have won a number of Emmys, Aces, National Education Awards, Cine Golden Eagles, and awards at the New York Film Festival and the Houston Worldfest Film Festival. He is a member of NATAS and IDA and also serves on the board of directors for the Telluride Mountain Film Festival.

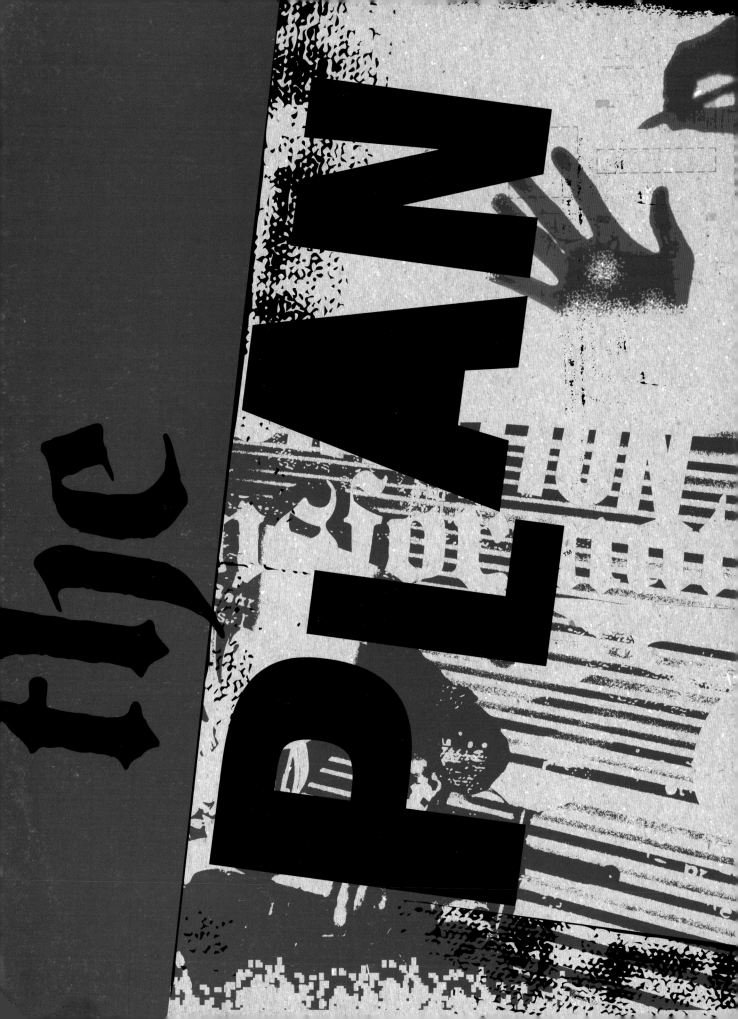

PART 1

ENVISIONING YOUR MONSTER

BY TIM REMUS

Planning for a new custom is the most important step in the whole project. Ordering parts, bolting the wheels onto the frame to make it a roller, lowering the engine into place; all those steps might be more exciting, but the task of deciding which wheels and which engine is ultimately more important than buying or installing the parts themselves.

At most professional shops and even on the set of Monster Garage, the planning comes before anything else. You need to know not only the budget but how you intend to use this new vehicle. Do you want it to be really fast or just look fast? The nostalgia trend is in full swing; anyone trying to build a car that looks like it came from another era needs to lock in that era and get all the details just right. The custom car world of today encompasses a wide variety of car types and styles. The good news is that you can build pretty much anything you want to and, with good execution,

"I really like the transformation and fabrication side of the show. It really proves what's possible with good teamwork, skills, and a vision."

–Steve Rumore, 4x4 Fabricator,
Rock Crawler team member

come out with a custom that turns heads down at the local drive-in. The bad news is that it can be hard to pick exactly what you want from such a vast menu.

Many professional shops use a rendering or formal drawing to cement the concept for the car. If customers do not have an exact idea of what they want, a designer is hired to work through a series of sketches until the customer says, "That's it, that's the car." Then the sketch is used to make a full rendering, complete with paint color and graphics.

In the case of your plan for the new custom, start by clipping magazine photos of your favorite customs, or build a photo file of machines with the look you're after. You don't have to build a clone of what you see at a show, but if something has the "look" you're trying to achieve, it makes sense to define and use the essential parts of that look.

During the early part of this process, pay attention to things like the body proportions of the vehicles you study. Note whether the top is chopped, the rake, the tire sizes front and back . . . these are all critical dimensions. As one experienced builder explained, "What's important is the proportions of the car, not just the dimensions."

In other words, you need to pay attention to the relationships between the parts of the car. How much you chop a top has a major impact on the car's looks, partly for some not-so-obvious reasons. The relationship between the height of the top and the mass of the body is terribly important and helps define the look of the car. When you chop the top, or section or channel a body, you've made a big change in this essential relationship. This is your car—you can do anything you like. Just be sure to think first and cut second.

DESIGN LIKE A PRO

Plenty of hot rodders and custom car builders sketch their projects before starting. Some of those sketches are nothing more than doodles on a napkin. To formalize the process and make it a better prediction of what the new car will really look like, you can borrow some ideas used by professional designers and car builders.

First, start out with a stock side view of the car. This can be a photograph or an image clipped from a magazine. The important thing in either case is that it be a straight side view, without any distortion. Now take the image over to the copy machine and make some big blowups and a whole series of copies.

Next comes the fun part. With scissors and tape, cut off the top and raise or lower it to your heart's content. Study the effect of a little more or less cutting. This method will also help you predict how much you need to add to the middle of the roof as you cut the posts and lower the lid.

You can use the same methods for lowering the car, trying different rake angles, or channeling the car down over the frame. When you've got the look you want, make some enlargements of the finished product and hang them on the refrigerator. Then check and see how they look in a week. You can even use colored markers to try different paint colors or graphics packages.

For the more computer literate among us, a scanner and PC can make the whole process easier. Scan the original into the computer, make some copies of the resulting file, then use a software package like Adobe Photoshop to lower the lid or change the rake angle. This might be your opportunity to finally learn how to use the PC you bought the kids for Christmas. Who knows? This could turn into a family project.

A rendering of the vehicle is the starting point of a project. The rendering ensures that the everyone involved in the project—whether you are dealing with team members, vendors, or customers—sees the same end result.

The methods don't really matter. What does matter is the end product. Just like the big shops, you want an image of the finished car—one big enough that you can stand back and appreciate its proportions and overall look.

This image will be the visual blueprint for the project. It will help keep you excited about the car when energy or money run low and it becomes hard to stay involved. The image taped to the refrigerator or toolbox will also help keep you focused. When a new set of wheels or a new fad shows up in the magazines, you won't be tempted to begin modifying the plan for the car.

CONCRETE PLANNING

You need to know more than just what the car will look like. Obviously, you need to know how much the car will cost as well. Figuring out the true cost means being brutally honest about how much of the car you can build yourself.

We all like to think we're the world's best mechanics—that there isn't anything we can't do or can't learn to do. If pressed, we could rebuild the space shuttle before the next launch. However, if this new car is going to get finished before the end of the next millennium, you may have to be more honest about both your mechanical abilities and your available free time.

We all have to farm out some of the work. Only a small percentage of us are qualified to do finish paint work, and even fewer would attempt to do any upholstery. Part of the budgeting process involves breaking the assembly of the car down into various subunits. Will you buy a complete crate engine, for example, or rebuild the one sitting in the back of the garage? If you intend to rebuild the engine, you'll need a budget for outside machine work. And if the machine shop is going to grind the crank, bore the block, and fit the pistons, maybe it makes sense to let them do the finish assembly of the entire engine.

I'm a big believer in "do it yourself," whether it's a plumbing project in the house or installing ball joints in the daily driver. In the real world, though, most of us run out of time. The classifieds are always filled with project cars and street rods that didn't get finished. Those projects started off as someone's dream, but somewhere along the line they turned into nightmares. The idea is to finish the car, and to do that, you need a

Monster Garage team members review the plan before starting. The tighter the deadline you are working under, the more crucial a good plan becomes.

The Firetruck required a Lincoln Town Car to be ripped apart so that a water pump capable of delivering 1,250 gallons per minute could be installed. At this point, the finished Firetruck is visible only in the plan because the real one is a tangle of struts, engine parts, and a pump.

Unforseen challenges are part of even the best-laid plans. When you have a good team, meeting those challenges is a snap, as the Firetruck crew demonstrated in the second episode of **Monster Garage.**

Building a Monster, like creating a custom machine, requires the ingenuity to solve the problems that arise. The more elaborate your custom, the more likely you are to encounter challenges that require cutting, fitting, and machining.

Choosing your team of people to help you create your custom is a crucial aspect of the process. Just as the Monster Garage team's success hinges on the team's ability to cooperatively problem-solve, you will need painters, engine builders, fabricators, and parts suppliers who will help you overcome obstacles rather than create additional ones.

certain momentum. Something has to get done every month—preferably every week. By farming out some of the jobs you could do yourself, more total work gets done during a given period, and the slow progress of turning a sketch on the wall into a finished vehicle is more likely to stay on track.

At some shops they use elaborate planning forms that list every part on the car, along with the price. In fact, a chassis builder's checklist is available on a few Web sites. You can also find forms that list outside labor tasks for things like sandblasting, polishing, upholstery, paint, chrome, glass cutting and installation, and even the final detailing. Before the project starts, they know exactly how much it's going to cost, how many hours of labor are involved, and how many of the operations will have to be performed by outside shops.

In the same way, you can make a list of all the parts, their cost, and the necessary labor. Now break out the labor you can't or won't do yourself, and get cost estimates. The planning should include time

estimates as well. How long will it take you to assemble and paint the frame, and how long will it take the chassis shop to narrow the Ford 9-inch rear end? Try to schedule the various labor operations so things dovetail. For example, you can't make the chassis a "roller" until that rear end is finished and painted.

IT'S GOTTA BE REAL

The planning and estimating needs to be realistic. If you underestimate either the time or money, it's easy to get disappointed when things take longer or cost more than expected. Cost overruns can also play havoc with the family budget and destroy family support for the new hot rod.

Because the finish bodywork and paint are such a big part of the project in terms of both time and money, some home builders finish everything but the body, assemble the car, and drive it in primer for one year. This strategy does stretch out the time needed to truly finish the car, but it puts it on the road that much sooner.

In the end, a good plan and a team of innovative, hardworking people put the Firetruck together right at deadline.

The biggest advantage to this method is that you can go out and have fun with the car now, instead of one year from now. Back-to-basics hot rods always have a certain allure and seem to get more popular as time goes on. You don't have to tell them it's unfinished. Just paint it primer black (or gray) and drive it proudly to the local or national event. It also gives you a chance to "debug" the car easily—disassembling an unpainted car for repairs or adjustments is easier and less stressful.

The other advantage of this program is that you allow the bank account to recover while driving the car in primer. When it comes time to pull the body off for that high-quality paint job, you can have the money already set aside in the savings account.

SPEAKING OF MONEY

The topic of money brings up a short discussion of how you pay for this car. Too often, home builders try to pay as they play. Just write a check for the frame, then the axles one month later, and the wheels one month after that. While the long-term nature of most of these projects makes this type of financing possible, there's an Achilles' heel here as well.

The trouble comes when your need for something expensive coincides with a low point in the family cash flow. Then the purchase of the engine or tranny or wheels gets put on hold until funds are available. The project stops moving forward, your own attentions are drawn elsewhere, and before long the "new hot rod" is just that pile of parts over in the corner of the garage—the one you haven't put a wrench to in six months or more.

The result of planning and ingenuity was a 5,000-pound firefighting monster machine capable of extinguishing a fire in a six-story burning building. If you apply the same recipe to the custom machine of your dreams, success is sure to follow.

When you finish the car or buy a partly finished car and complete it, it will be worth a fair amount of money. Consider various financing options before you begin construction. Simply make sure you have a source of funds so that a monetary shortfall or a hiccup in your personal finances doesn't put the project on the back burner.

THINGS YOU NEED

In addition to the rendering, you need to know the dimensions for the car and the chassis. Though this is covered in more detail later in the book, you need a working drawing of the chassis, so you know where the firewall, axle centerlines, and body-mounting holes are.

Many experts feel strongly that anyone starting from a complete car should take the time to measure everything before blowing it apart. Even if you plan major changes, it's good to know how far the stock bumper was from the ground and how much clearance there was between the frame and the concrete slab the car is parked on for the measuring session. Get out your camera and take some pictures, both close up and far away. If nothing else, these may be the basis for the clip-and-paste session mentioned earlier.

HARD PARTS

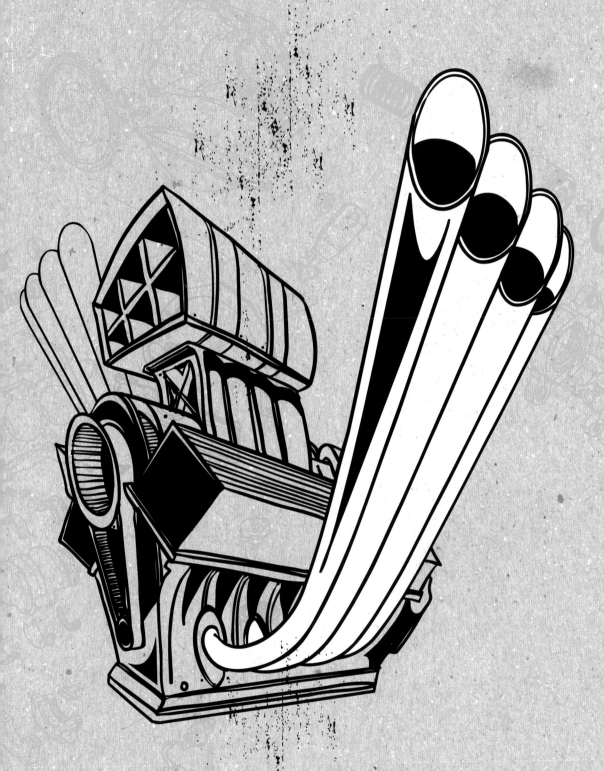

PART 2

NOTHING'S SACRED

When Jesse and the Monster team turned a Porsche 944 into a golf-ball collector in episode 6, they proved that nothing's sacred in the world of wild wheels. Although the 944 is a bit of a black-sheep member of the Porsche family, mounting a clown-face golf-ball launcher on a fine German automobile had to have a few of the faithful sleeping uneasily. The lesson? When it comes to customizing, don't forget that the result is intended for you and you alone. Don't be afraid to break rules to make the Monster machine of your dreams.

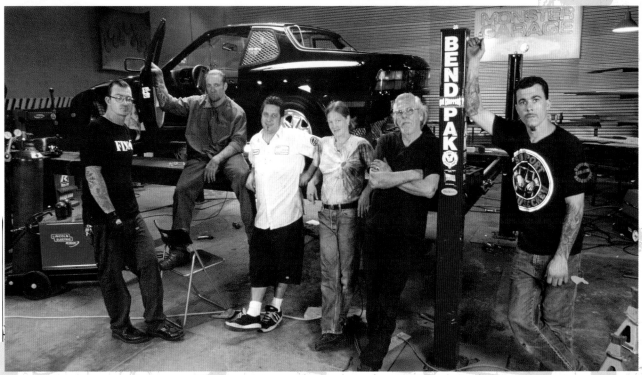

CHAPTER

2.1

POWER YOUR
MONSTER

BY JIM RICHARDSON

The heart of a custom vehicle is the motor. This section of the book focuses on the most popular engine to modify—the Chevy small-block V-8—and describes the basics of finding and modifying this staple of hot rodders, drag racers, and street machine builders.

Finding a Chevy small-block is easy. Finding precisely the right Chevy small-block is another matter. The biggest problem with finding exactly what you want is that Chevy small-block engines almost all look alike. The newest Generation III computerized, injected engines certainly have a distinctive look, but the earlier blocks, from the 1980s back to the 1950s, look so similar that it's hard to tell whether a block is a 400, 350, 327, 307, 305, or 283, unless you know them well or have access to the casting numbers.

Consult an expert or, better yet, pick up a reference book that lists casting numbers and other details that will help you make sure you get the correct Chevy small-block for your needs.

THE SHORT AND LONG OF IT

You'll hear the terms "short" and "long" block when checking around for engines. A short block includes only the bottom end of an engine—the block, crank, and pistons—but not the heads, manifolds, or accessories. If all you did was damage the block in an otherwise decent engine, the short block may be just what you need. A long block is a complete engine, including heads and valvetrain, but you still need to use your old manifolds and accessories with them.

Look for the casting number on the back of the engine, behind the head on the driver's side. The arrow and dots on the right indicate the shift on which the block was cast.

The painted numbers at the upper left indicate that the block has been bored .030 inch over. The .010 below tells you that the block is 10 percent nickel, making it stronger.

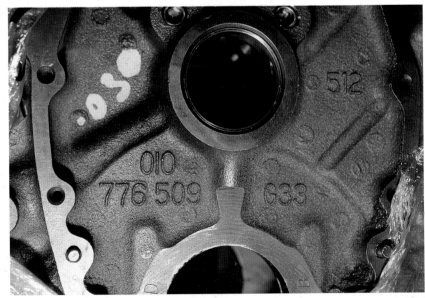

SALVAGE YARD TREASURES

Whoever said one man's junk is another man's treasure knew what he was talking about. But just to make sure you don't buy a pig in a poke, take the time to carefully examine your prospective purchase. Here are a few tips on what to look for and what to avoid:

Don't accept a junk engine that has been hit in its vibration damper or timing gear housing. Such an engine could easily have a damaged crankshaft or camshaft. You don't want an engine-and-transmission combination that has been hit hard from the rear, either because the entire driveline could have been knocked out of alignment. Also, inspect the donor car, if possible. If it appears to have been well maintained until an accident, its engine is probably sound. But if the car was sadly neglected or is worn out, the engine

will be too. It's not out of the question to buy a non-running engine, but be sure to remove the heads and inspect it before making a purchase.

Most junkyards will start an engine for you if you ask, whether it is in a car or not. But hearing it run won't tell you much more than whether there are major problems. Look for blue smoke, which is an indication of worn rings or leaking valve guides, causing oil consumption problems. Listen for rhythmic clunks, clanks, and bonks that would indicate rod or main bearing wear.

To really determine your prospective engine's condition, warm it up for 15 to 20 minutes, then shut it off, block its choke and throttle open, and run a compression check. To do that, you need to remove all of the spark plugs and ground the coil

After some tests, we discovered that this old car still had a good block in it, although the engine was tired.

Judging from the car's condition, we would assume the reading is more like 132,456.

high-tension lead, to prevent a fire from starting. Of course, you'll also need to know the correct compression spec for that particular engine, which can be found in a shop manual.

Your donor engine's cylinders should be within 6 pounds of the specification. If the compression is 10 pounds or lower all across, the engine is in need of an overhaul. If the compression is down in two adjacent cylinders, it probably has a leaking head gasket or a cracked head or block. If the compression is down in just one cylinder, it could be rings, valves, a holed piston, or a bad head gasket. If you shoot a little oil down the cylinder, re-test it, and the compression comes up, the problem is rings. If the compression stays down, it's probably valves. If it comes up only a little, both the rings and the valves need work.

Look the plugs over, too. If they're wet with oil or rusty, avoid that engine. Oil on the plugs indicates ring or valve-guide problems, and water in the combustion chambers means a leaky head gasket or a cracked block or head. Finally, look inside the cooling system and around the freeze plugs for signs of corrosion. An engine that's extremely rusty inside will need cleaning out at the very least, and it could have major problems.

Another thing to keep in mind while engine hunting is that you want the entire engine, including brackets, manifolds, valve covers, carb, and so on, if it's coming from a car that isn't the exact year and model of yours. Some items can be similar and yet not fit from engine to engine. It's also a good idea to get the throttle linkage because bending new linkage to fit is no easy task.

Small-blocks have been put into everything from Italian sports cars to modified Model Ts because they're the best American production engine ever.

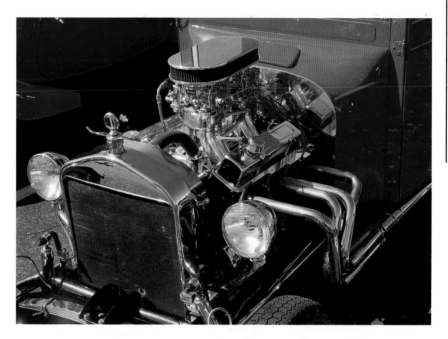

A later, super-tuned small block will drop right into a mid-1950s pickup.

HOT SWAPS

Nothing is more appealing at a show than a correct, original, restored car, but some such cars just don't make very good drivers. Sometimes, the engine for your year wasn't as good as the one in the next year's model, or perhaps your car is equipped with a six and you'd like to put in a V-8. Well, you can do it, but it might be more complicated than you think.

Plan ahead, talk to people who have made the swap you intend to make, and be sure to get all the accessories and the throttle linkage when you find your replacement engine. Just remember, the bigger and more powerful the new engine is, the more stress you'll be placing on a classic's stock driveline. Another problem is that some smaller unit-bodied cars have been known to crack from metal fatigue at their doorframes after being twisted by the torque of a big mill, making them dangerous to drive.

Even essentially stock small-blocks can kick up dust with a little tweaking.

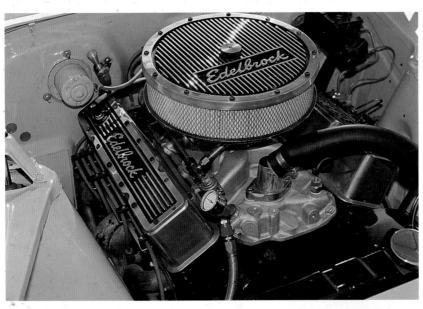

Thanks to the automotive aftermarket, you can buy all the go-fast parts with one check and easily bolt together a pretty hot street machine.

Check any prospective purchase for cracks, using a Magnaflux Spotcheck Jr. kit.

You don't want the engine out of this car. The driveline is bent and bashed, and who knows what happened to the rapidly spinning crankshaft.

This isn't such a bad deal because you can check everything out before you make the purchase. And that price probably becomes more flexible as the afternoon wears on.

If you can't hear a prospective purchase run, take a head off and look inside it before making a purchase.

HeADS

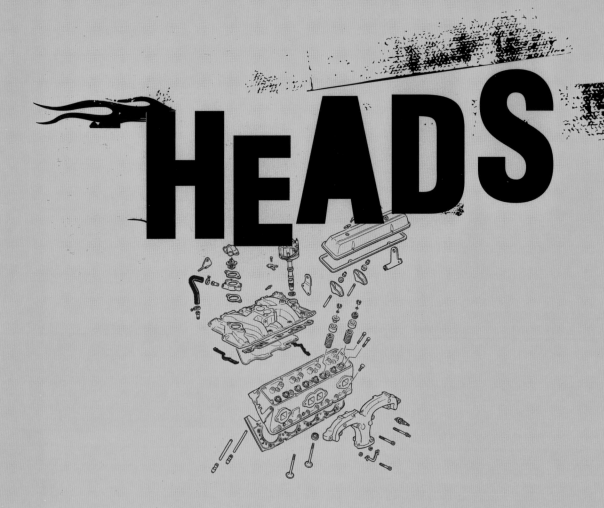

BY JIM RICHARDSON

Certain small-block heads are better for performance applications than others. You'll hear lots about 68 cc versus 74 cc heads, bigger valves versus smaller, aluminum heads versus cast iron, and "camel hump" versus other castings. All these factors have advantages under certain circumstances.

Chevrolet has developed hundreds of different small-block head configurations over the years, for all kinds of applications, so the possibilities are mind-boggling. An entire book could be written about Chevy small-block head castings alone, but many of them wouldn't interest anyone except the historians. So which heads are best for you?

That depends. Some heads lend themselves to modifications better than others, and some of them can't be used at all on cars that must meet today's air-pollution standards. Of course, aftermarket performance heads are available from a number of sources that will meet current pollution laws and give hotter performance. If you can afford them, they'll save you the time and effort you'd expend in modifying a set of stock heads.

With a little work, the heads that came on your engine, or a set of used heads you find at a swap meet or wrecking yard, can be made to perform well too. Just be careful when buying used heads. Make sure the vendor will allow you to exchange them for another set if they turn out to be defective. And use casting numbers to verify whether you're getting the heads you want.

1. A sturdy valve-spring compressor is required to decrease the tension of valve springs when removing valves.

CLOSED- VS. OPEN COMBUSTION CHAMBER HEADS

Earlier, cast-iron small-combustion chamber heads (64 cc) from the 1960s can be made to breathe well and can deliver more torque all across the rpm range. When surfaced and paired with flattop pistons, they can easily bump your compression up over 10:1. At this point, your engine would suffer from detonation on pump gas, which will ruin it in a hurry.

Because of their superior heat-conducting capacity, aluminum closed-combustion-chamber heads are better when combined with flattop pistons, but they're more expensive and harder to find. Even cast-iron small-combustion-chamber heads are becoming pricey and rare these days. Dished pistons, when combined with closed-combustion-chamber heads, will lower your compression ratio to around 9:1, so if you do find a good set of closed-combustion-chamber heads for a reasonable price, grab them while you can.

2. Once a valve spring is compressed, keepers can be removed. Keep any parts that are to be reused separate from each other and labeled.

3. Once a keeper is out of the way, let the tension off the valve spring and remove the rest of the assembly.

4. Pull the rubber oil seal off and slip the valve out of its guide.

5. If you plan to reuse the rocker studs, leave them in place. Otherwise, remove them by using spacers and a nut to press against the head.

6. One way to check for cracks is to use a Spotcheck Jr. kit from Magnaflux.

7. Clean the area to be checked using the cleaner included. Be sure to check around the valve seats and bolt holes.

8. Shoot on a light coat of the red dye and let it soak in.

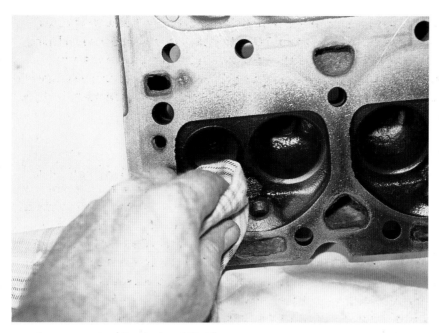

9. Next, shoot a little cleaner on a rag-not the part-and wipe off the red dye.

10. Spray on a light coat of the developing powder.

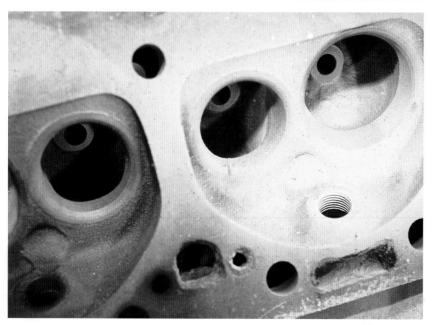

11. Cracks show up as red lines. Cracked Chevy heads aren't usually worth fixing.

Open-combustion chamber heads (72–74 cc) are not as good for all-out racing but can be made to breathe well for street use and are much more common and less expensive to acquire. Unless you live in a cold climate, you'll want to block the heat riser ports that heat up the fuel mixture during cold starts because this also makes the mixture less dense once the engine is warmed up, which cuts power. There is one caveat: these heat-riser ports were added partly to meet smog restrictions, so if you're going to put your engine in a later car that has to pass smog tests, you may not want to block them.

BIGGER VS. SMALLER VALVES

Most small-block 350 heads came with either 1.94/1.5-inch intake and exhaust valves or slightly larger 2.02/1.6-inch valves for performance situations. If you're going with a more radical cam in a 350 or are building a stroker, you'll definitely want to go with the larger valves. If you're leaving your engine basically stock, you'd be better off leaving the valves at 1.94/1.5 inches if that's how the engine w as set up originally.

The bigger valves do help you at higher rpm, but they offer a significant increase in airflow only if the intake valve is deshrouded and the head is pocket ported. The factory did this as a separate machining operation on heads in which bigger valves were installed. Otherwise, just installing bigger valves, you'll only incur added expense and might actually hurt your engine's performance.

ALUMINUM VS. IRON

Aluminum heads have the advantage of conducting heat better than iron heads. Therefore, an engine equipped with them can run a slightly higher compression ratio without detonation, but they do not add horsepower per se. Aluminum Corvette heads from engines of the late 1980s to early 1990s breathe well, but because of their small combustion chamber (58 cc), they won't accept larger valves. However, if you find a set in good shape for a decent price, purchase them. With a little judicious porting, they'll perform very well indeed.

Many people tout the weight advantage of aluminum heads. At only 20 pounds each, they weigh less than half as much as cast-iron heads, but we're talking about a savings of only about 44 pounds altogether. Unless you're putting your engine in a very light, purpose-built race car, that doesn't mean much.

This is a closed-combustion chamber head with big valves installed. They'll make mighty horsepower but will probably make your compression too high for the street.

Later on, open-combustion-chamber heads can be made to perform by pocket porting and will still keep your compression in the pump-gas range.

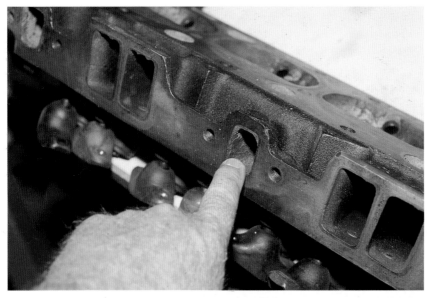

These heat riser ports can be blocked to produce a cooler air-fuel mixture, provided you don't live in a cool climate.

You can tell what kind of head you have by looking at the cast-in symbol on the end. Double-hump heads are good street rod candidates.

Head casting numbers are in the rocker arm area. The casting number tells us that these heads may be from a 400-cid motor.

This casting number indicates a later (after 1987) head. It won't take as much porting as an earlier head.

CAMSHAFTS

BY JIM RICHARDSON

You must decide what you want your engine to do and what kind of vehicle you want to put it in before you choose a cam. Just going for the most radical cam you can find is a big mistake for street use, even if you build the engine around the cam. You could wind up with big flat spots in acceleration, short valvetrain life, and a car that is not particularly fast or even fun to drive.

These days, with the advent of computers, the selection of cams is endless, so with a little thought and care you can get whatever you want, within reason. In the last 20 years, computer research has produced cams that can give you such awesome torque at low rpm that your Malibu will accelerate like a bullet from 0 to 60. You can also get cams that give you awesome horsepower at high rpm, lower those E.T.s in the quarter mile, and shut down the competition. The stock cam is in between these extremes, though nearer the low-rpm end.

The people who developed your small-block's original camshaft were no fools. They had a tough job to do. They needed to come up with valve timing that would provide a smooth idle, decent gas mileage, and low emissions. Yet it had to give you good performance at all rpm ranges and allow your engine to last for 100,000 miles and more without needing major work.

CAM BASICS

Quite simply, the camshaft in a conventional four-cycle engine opens the intake and exhaust valves at just the right time so the air-fuel mixture comes in on cue, is burned, and then the exhaust gas is cleared from the combustion chamber in time for the next event. The cam also turns the distributor, which causes the spark plugs to ignite the mixture at precisely the right moment. It turns the oil pump and drives the mechanical fuel pump, too. In a way, it's the brains of the engine.

1. Smear a little assembly lube on the cam bearings before installing the cam.

2. Screw in a long bolt at the front of the cam to use as a handle while installing the cam. Slip the cam in carefully, so you don't smear the bearings or bark the cam lobes against them.

3. Notice the special crankshaft sprocket with three keyways. One is straight up, one is 4 degrees advanced, and one is 4 degrees retarded, to help degree-in the cam.

4. Slip the timing chain around the crankshaft sprocket, then over the cam timing sprocket. Line up the timing marks, then attach the cam sprocket.

5. Timing marks must align straight across, as shown here. If they are out by even one tooth, your engine will not run right.

The challenge for cam designers is that the optimum time for each combustion event varies with engine speed (rpm). Some cams do their best work at low rpm, others at high rpm, and others, such as your engine's stock cam, are a compromise between the two. Many people would say, "Just give me the cam that makes the most horsepower." But horsepower isn't what makes it possible to hit 200 miles per hour from a standing start in a quarter of a mile. Torque does that.

A simplified explanation of torque versus horsepower is that torque is a measurement of the amount of work your engine can do, and horsepower is an indication of how quickly it can do it. An Indy Champ car engine can produce upward of 900 horsepower, but you wouldn't want to put one in your 18-wheel Peterbilt because it wouldn't make enough torque to move the vehicle, even without a load.

On the other hand, a 600-cid Cummins diesel puts out only about 400 horsepower, but it can move 10 tons of cargo with ease all day long because it makes in the neighborhood of 1,200–1,400 foot-pounds of torque. The small 900-horsepower Indy car engine can do less work, but the work it does is done *very* quickly. A huge diesel engine can do an awesome amount of work, but it does it slowly.

The cam is only one factor in the equation. Stroke, bore, displacement, and engine and vehicle weight, along with a number of other factors, are also involved.

A low-rpm engine gets most of its power in the combustion chamber because the chamber has more time to fill with the air-fuel charge. A bigger charge means a greater force exerted on the piston when the

6. You can use a magnetic base and a dial indicator to find top dead center on the piston.

7. At top dead center, zero out the dial indicator, then move your degree wheel to zero it out as well. You can tweak your pointer a little to align it precisely.

8. Install a lifter and determine lobe center on the intake lobe first. Cams are correctly installed at perfect split overlap.

charge is ignited. As rpm goes up, the cylinder has less time to fill, and less time to pump the exhaust out, so the amount of work it can do goes down. However, at high rpm, the total amount of work that gets done in a given interval goes up.

So, what's your choice? It depends on your intentions. Do you want to move a lot of weight off the line in a hurry, perhaps sacrificing a little top-end performance, or do you want a little street rod to blow through the traps in the low nines?

You need to consider other factors as well. For example, you need to decide whether you'll be running a standard transmission or an automatic, what your transmission and differential gearing will be, how many rpm your engine can handle, and how well behaved you want your car to be on the street.

You can do all the homework yourself to determine what duration and lift you might need for your application, or you can simply call a reputable cam manufacturer with your requirements.

OVERLAP

Early automotive engines were designed with no overlap. That is to say, when the piston reached bottom dead center on the induction stroke, the intake valve opened and let in the air-fuel mixture. The exhaust valve would be completely closed at this point. On the compression stroke, both valves would be closed. When the gas fired, the piston would come back down to bottom dead center, the exhaust valve would open, and the gas would be let out.

Early designers thought that having the valves even partially open at the same time would cause a loss of power. Later, it was determined that a little overlap added to the engine's power because the slug of escaping exhaust gas created a vacuum behind it that helped pull in the air-fuel mixture, providing a mild supercharging effect.

Ed Iskenderian started experimenting with this effect back in the 1940s and developed overlapping

9. Turn the engine to determine the exact lobe centers on the cam. Make sure there is no slop at the lifter.

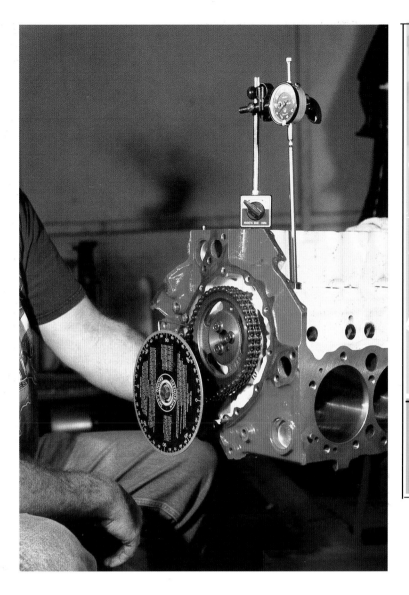

cams that increased power dramatically. Isky referred to this overlap as the "fifth cycle" and set about developing cams to make the most of it. In the 1950s, he came up with his famous Isky Five Cycle cam that made awesome horsepower. The sound alone from an engine equipped with one of these was enough to intimidate the competition.

There is a limit on how creative you can get with valve timing on a single-cam engine. There is also a limit to how long a cam with conventional lifters and pushrods can hold a valve open. Dual overhead cams permit much more flexibility. Also, a stock-grind cam has rather pointed lobes, so the valves stay fully open only for a short time.

To get the valves to stay open longer, the tips of the lobes must be made wider, but this can go only so far before it has a negative effect on valve timing. Also, the ramps on the sides of the lobes get so steep that the result is rapid cam and lifter wear unless you go to roller lifters, and even then there are limits. Finally, flat-

tappet lifter diameter is limited, which leaves only so much area to work with before the valve starts to override the lifter.

The overlap a cam can stand is also limited. Overlap is what causes that rough idle with radical cams. At low rpm, some of the unburned intake gases are passed into the exhaust manifold, where they ignite, causing that popping, rumbling sound. At higher rpm, a more radical cam comes into its own, and the engine can produce prodigious amounts of horsepower.

Most street rod applications are best set up with hydraulic lifter cams. Back in the early 1960s, hydraulic lifters could cause a dangerous situation at high rpm, called lifter pump-up, but that is largely a thing of the past if your lifters and valvetrain are fresh and properly set up and you keep your small-block below 6,500 rpm. Also, the big advantage with hydraulic lifters is that the valves are kept in constant adjustment at zero lash, so they are much quieter.

10. A more accurate way to determine top dead center is to make yourself a piston stop out of steel strap and use that rather than a magnetic base and dial gauge.

11. Holes in the cam drive sprocket can be drilled out and an eccentric washer (available from speed shops) can be installed on the locator pin, to locate the cam exactly at split overlap.

12. Finally, secure the cam with a locking device like this. Just bend up one tab on each bolt.

Disadvantages to radical hydraulic lifter cams are that they produce a rougher idle and contribute to low intake-manifold vacuum. The latter can be a problem in cars equipped with automatic transmissions and power brakes. A radical hydraulic lifter cam can actually cause you to lose your brakes unless you have an auxiliary vacuum booster tied into the power brake system.

Solid (mechanical) lifters can handle higher rpm and more radical cams and do produce a smoother idle, but the rockers must be adjusted frequently and carefully if your engine is to perform to specs. For most street applications, a hydraulic cam is the best choice, but if you really want radical performance for weekend bracket racing, go with a solid lifter cam.

MAKING IT BETTER THAN NEW

Once you've made your cam selection, buy new lifters, pushrods, and rockers to work with it. Try to buy all from the same manufacturer, to ensure compatibility. Roller lifters and rocker arms cut down on valvetrain friction because they have rotating rollers riding on the cam and valves.

Roller lifters are great for any application and allow you to run a more radical cam without durability problems. The only catch is cost. Roller rockers and lifters are many times more expensive than stock ones. Of course, the latest generations of Chevy small-block V-8s already come with roller lifters.

Roller lifters are more expensive because they're made of steel rather than iron and are much more difficult to manufacture. If you can spring for roller lifters and rockers, by all means use them, but make sure the cam you buy is designed to work with them. Solid lifter cams work only with solid lifters, hydraulic lifter cams must have hydraulic lifters, and roller lifter cams work only with roller lifters, so don't try to switch them around.

INSTALLING A CAM

You can install a cam in a small-block without tearing the engine down, and in most cases you can even install a cam without removing the engine from the car. However, the best way to put in a hotter cam is to do it when you have the engine down for overhaul. Cams (stock or hot) are not expensive, so even if you're just overhauling your stocker, replace its cam with a new one. Lobes wear flat, and your engine will never be at its best with an old cam in it. Also, always install a new timing chain, along with new timing sprockets if the

sprockets are notched or worn where the chain rides on them.

To install your cam, find a long bolt with the same threads as the hole in the end of the cam and use it to help guide the cam into place. Or you can attach the timing sprocket to the end of the cam, to make handling it easier. Coat the cam bearings and journals lightly with a suitable assembly lube.

As you slip the cam in from the front of the engine, be careful not to bark the lobes against the block or to smear or mar the cam bearings. You can turn the cam slightly to work it through, but make sure you support it at both ends with your hands as you work. Once the cam is seated in the back bearing, try turning it. The cam should turn easily and shouldn't bind.

Smear each cam lobe with assembly lube after installation. You should be able to reach the cam. Smear the lobes with lube before installation if you are only installing the new cam with the engine still in the car. This is a crucial step to avoid rapid lobe wear when the engine is in its first few minutes of running, before the oil gets up into the galleries in quantity. Lifters are held against the cam under a lot of pressure by the valve springs, so without a good assembly lube, the cam lobes will self-destruct in minutes.

Turn the crankshaft until its sprocket's timing mark is straight up, at 12 o'clock, pointing directly toward the cam. Slide on the cam timing sprocket and turn the cam until its timing mark is immediately opposite the crankshaft's timing mark, at 6 o'clock. Take the cam timing sprocket off again, smear the sprockets with assembly lube, dip the timing chain in clean motor oil, and slip it over the crankshaft timing sprocket and cam timing sprocket.

Now hold the cam timing sprocket in place with your hand while you install its attaching bolts. The keyway in the crankshaft and the locator pin in the camshaft sprocket take the guesswork out of orientation. Make sure you don't slip and get the timing marks out of synchronization with each other because if they're off even by one tooth, the engine won't run correctly.

What we've just described is the standard way to install a stock cam, and it will work fine for a performance cam most of the time. Since you're going to all this trouble, you might want to make sure your valve timing is spot on. It's not unusual for a cam to be out 1 to 4 degrees, and if they are, it won't perform to specs.

CHAPTER
2.4

CARBURETORS

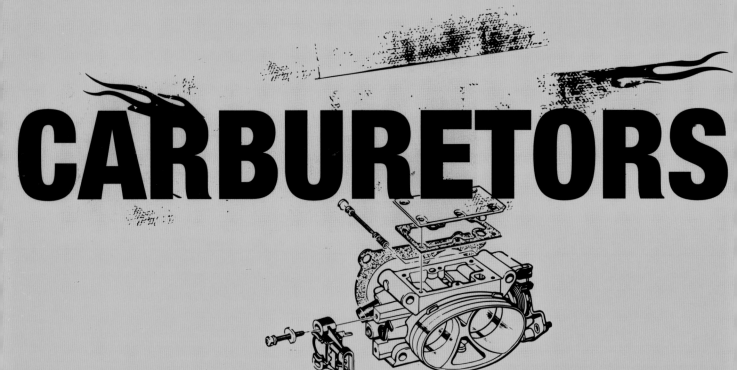

BY JIM RICHARDSON

Probably the most poorly understood aspect of engine tuning is the carburetor. Many novice street rodders think that the bigger their carburetor is, the better their engine will perform. Not true. In fact, the most common reason for customer unhappiness with high-performance carbs can be traced to overcarburetion.

People often buy a big 850 cfm carb when 600–750 cfm is ideal for their engine. Then when they install it and put their foot in it, their engine stumbles and sags before finally coming to life. They return the carb, thinking it's faulty, when in fact it's their thinking that's faulty. The problem is that the big carb gets a weak signal because of the lack of air velocity—it doesn't come on when it needs to for good midrange acceleration.

A carburetor's job is to vaporize gasoline and mix it with air. Bigger carbs can mix more fuel into more air, but that's useful only if you have a bigger engine. For routine driving with a stock Chevy small-block up to about 3,500 rpm, a stock two-barrel works fine.

Only when you jump on the gas and take the rpm up past where most people routinely drive will two more throats do you some good. When you install a jug the size of a hot tub on your small-block, air takes its time getting to where it's going, so the drop in pressure from piston suction isn't enough to pull much fuel into the slow airstream of a too-large carb.

A small carb gives great performance until the engine gets up into the higher rev ranges, where it then starves for air. Coming up with a good compromise between low-end oomph and high-end

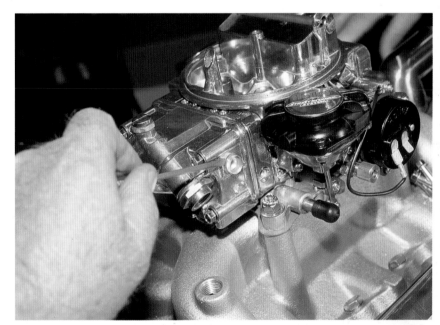

Holley carburetors provide solid performance and are easier to tune than comparable carburetors from other manufacturers.

On most Holley four-barrels, you can check the float level through this sight glass without removing the float bowl cover.

If you need to change the float level, you can adjust it right on top of the carb.

Idle mixture screws are conveniently located so you can get at them without contorting yourself.

Here is a Holley float. The chamber comes off the end of the carb with four screws.

horsepower is the key to a great street rod engine, and it's harder to accomplish than setting up a constant-throttle racer.

So how do you determine which carburetor your small-block needs? It's simple. We'll get to that in a minute, but first, let's look at how a carburetor works.

DEEP BREATHING

Did you ever fool around with your mother's old-fashioned squeeze-bulb perfume sprayers when you were a kid? Well, they're nothing more than a primitive type of carburetor. Perfume sprayers and carburetors both take advantage of the Bernoulli effect. Daniel Bernoulli was an eighteenth-century Swiss mathematician who was probably goofing around with his own mother's spray bottles when he

came up with his principle. What he found out was this: as the velocity of a liquid or gas increases, its pressure decreases.

That's why air sucked at high speed past a fuel tube inserted into the side of an air horn will draw the fuel out into the rushing air. This effect can be increased dramatically by narrowing the air inlet just at the point where the fuel tube enters it.

That's called the Venturi effect, named after an Italian physicist who first figured out this little trick a couple of hundred years ago. When you narrow the tube, the incoming air must speed up to get through the narrow spot, where it loses more pressure, thus creating an even greater pull on the fuel tube.

There's a lot more to a modern carburetor than just the Venturi effect, but it almost all works on the

Everything you need to install and tailor a Holley comes with the carb.

When it comes to air filters, bigger is better. The ultimate air filter is a K&N. Taller is also good. This one from TD Performance Products will do a great job if the element is changed periodically.

K&N air filters are washable and actually increase performance over what can be had by running with no filter at all.

A single-plane intake manifold gives great performance in the higher-rpm ranges but can be a little soggy on the bottom end.

This is a Performance Products dual-plane manifold. It outperforms many name brands.

same principle. For instance, an accelerator pump shoots extra fuel into the carb when you tromp on the gas suddenly, and a choke increases the air vacuum and draws out a rich fuel mixture for cold starts. Also, jets determine how much fuel is released into the air through the carb.

In addition, float bowls (which operate much like a float in a toilet tank) provide your carb with an adequate fuel supply at all times. A needle valve shuts off the fuel when the float bowl is full. Each of these systems is simple enough in itself, but when you put them all together, the result is several hundred small parts that add up to a complex device.

If you decide you want to rebuild or custom-tailor your own carburetor, even though you'll find some of the basics in this chapter, I strongly recommend that you pick up a book on your particular brand and model of carb and study it before you start tinkering.

If you can afford it and want the ultimate in performance, I recommend sending even a new carb to a place like the Carb Shop in Ontario, California, to have them adapt it and jet it to your engine's needs. You should provide them with all pertinent information, such as engine size, cam duration, and header type, plus what kind of car the engine will be going into and what kind of racing you might want to try.

HOLLEY

Holleys are the easiest carbs to set up. You can buy them in just about any cubic-foot-per-minute (cfm) rating, so you can have exactly what you need for your application. They're inexpensive compared to the new knockoffs of the old Quadra-Jets and Carters sold under other names and provide equal or better performance. And Holley sells literally everything you might need or want to tune your carb yourself.

Because Holleys are modular and have been designed to be easily custom tuned, they're certainly the best choice for the novice street rodder. You can determine the float level in a Holley just by using the sight glass in the side of the float bowl, and you can make any necessary adjustments without even removing the float bowl cover. You can also easily get at the jets and the accelerator pump(s). Every new Holley also comes with the springs and other items you need to fine-tune it.

If you want great out-of-the box street perform-ance with no fuss, I recommend a four-barrel Holley matched to your engine (according to the formula below) and a Holley Weiand dual-plane intake mani-fold to go under it.

ROCHESTER QUADRA-JET

The old Rochester Quadra-Jet was superbly engi-neered and is one of the best small-block carbs ever. It flows 750–800 cfm in stock form and can be set up for just about any street or strip application. The only problem is that it isn't made anymore. New Quadra-Jet knockoffs are available, but they're expensive. You can have the same thing for less by buying a reworked Rochester or, if you already have a Q-Jet on your engine, you can send it out and have it rebuilt and super-tuned to your needs.

Q-Jets will provide race-winning performance with a little tweaking and tuning. The least expensive way to go with a Q-Jet is to rebuild and rejet it yourself, if you have the experience and skill. If not, send it to a shop where it can be custom tailored and rebuilt by experts.

CARTER AFB

These are great carbs too and can be made to run with the best of them. Modern knockoffs of the old Carters are available, but once again, you can save money by having your old one rebuilt and tested. Carters aren't as easy to work on as Holleys, but one point in their favor is that you can change the metering rods in them without removing the float bowl lid. If you have a good Carter already, don't toss it out. Rebuild it and run it. They're hard to beat.

MANIFOLD DESTINY

There are three common types of intake manifolds. The most popular one used for the street on Chevy small-blocks is the dual-plane type. It helps provide better low-end and midrange power but sacrifices a little at the top end.

The second common type of intake manifold is the single-plane configuration. Inline six- and four-cylinder engines generally have single-plane manifolds because they're simple and efficient. V-8 engines suffer to a degree when using single-plane manifolds under certain circumstances because adjacent cylinders (5 and 7) can have open valves at the same time, allowing the fuel mixture to become diluted at low rpm.

Also, because air-fuel velocity is low at low rpm in an open-plenum, single-plane manifold, fuel can condense and puddle out on the manifold floor, espe-cially in cold weather.

On the plus side, single-plane manifolds have shorter, straighter port runners, so at high rpm they really come into their own. They have an edge over dual-plane manifolds up around 7,500 rpm and

Think three carbs are better than one? Not necessarily. The linkage is more complex, and a properly sized four-barrel will work better for most street applications.

beyond. So what it comes down to is this: if you want maximum top-end horsepower and don't mind going from rather sedate acceleration at lower rpm to sudden, tire-smoking torque as the engine comes up on its cam, go for a single-plane manifold. But if you want neck-snapping launches from idle when you hit the gas and steady power up through to the power peak on your street engine, go with a dual-plane manifold.

Cars equipped with a single-plane manifold are harder to drive, though they have an edge in straight-line acceleration at peak power. Cornering can be a real problem if the power comes on abruptly in midcorner, as it can with a single-plane manifold.

On single-plane manifolds, all barrels of the carb dump into a large, common plenum that feeds short, straight runners. The loss of gas velocity at low rpm because of the open plenum is the single-plane manifold's biggest shortcoming, but its straight port runners are its virtue. Air doesn't like to turn corners, especially when it's moving fast.

Most street rodders prefer a good dual-plane manifold because it makes their car more user-friendly. Dual-plane manifolds are set up so that each side of the carb feeds one side of the engine, and it does so through rather curvy runners of different lengths. These are marginally less efficient than straight runners, but they do keep the gas velocity higher at low rpm, giving the carb much clearer signals. The chances of bogging down at low rpm are diminished, unless you install a carb that's too large for the engine.

A tunnel-ram manifold looks dramatic and smoothes airflow while maintaining velocity, but it's definitely not for the street because of its limited power range.

The third type of manifold you sometimes see is the tunnel ram. Some of these use a plenum chamber on top to even out the vacuum pulses, and others use individual port runners right from the carb. Either way, the point of a tunnel ram manifold is to iron out those abrupt turns the air/fuel mixture has to make when it leaves the carburetor and enters the intake manifold. The long port runners help maintain gas velocity into the engine, which helps fill the combustion chambers to the max.

Tunnel ram manifolds have a couple of big disadvantages for street use. The first is hood clearance. The usual solution to hood clearance is a big scoop that blocks your vision to the right of you. The other problem with tunnel ram manifolds is that they provide an advantage only in a limited, high-rpm range. They look impressive but aren't very practical for street use.

AIR FILTERS

This is one situation where bigger is always better. The more filter area you have, the less restrictive the filter will be. Air filters can be especially restrictive if their tops are too close to the carb. The top of the filter should be at least 3 inches above the carb, and 4 to 6 inches is better. The diameter of the filter should be as big as your wallet can accommodate. It has always seemed crazy to me to see street machines with top-quality, Holley double-pumper carbs topped with tiny air filters.

HEADERS & EXHAUST

BY JIM RICHARDSON

Knowing what you want your engine to do, then selecting the right mix of cam, heads, manifold, and carb, along with the right exhaust headers, are all keys to getting more usable horsepower and torque out of your bow tie small-block. Putting together a winning combination requires thought and planning, but the results can be dramatic. On the other hand, carelessly mixing even the best components could easily result in an engine that is less dependable, less enjoyable, and less powerful than the stock one you started with.

Begin by asking yourself how often you will actually be driving around in the 6,000–8,000 rpm range. Are you building a racer that you only want to be able to coax to the strip and don't mind backshifting constantly to get it there? Do you care that the car won't climb hills worth beans and will have a big flat spot in its acceleration just at the rpm range you're used to driving in around town?

Or are you building a hot machine intended for the street that you'd like to run through the traps occasionally, just to see what it will do, but will be driving back and forth to work occasionally? In short, do you prefer a car that has impressive performance but is well behaved, or do you want a wild bronco? Unfortunately, you can't have both in one car.

A radical cam with lots of overlap needs one kind of exhaust headers, and a street rod needs another. If you choose a cam designed to produce midrange grunt, you'll want an exhaust system designed to complement it. The same is true for a cam designed to produce awesome high-end horsepower.

These vintage megaphone headers look good and sound outrageous, but they don't produce the torque or horsepower of later, tuned headers.

A set of old-style ram's horns can be made to work well at lower rpm and are the best choice among stock manifolds.

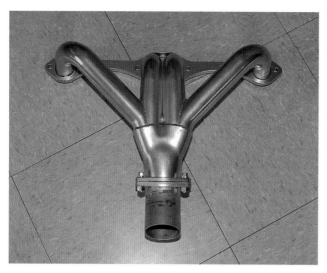

A nice step up from stock ram's-horn manifolds is this set of tight-clearance headers from Doug's Headers.

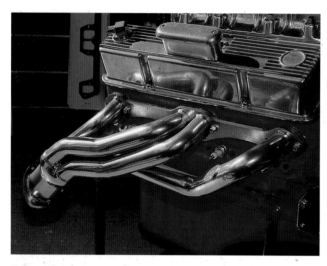

These four-into-one headers produce prodigious amounts of power but within a narrower rpm range than tri-Ys.

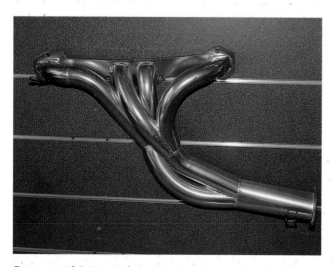

These graceful tri-Y, four-into-two-into-one headers with fairly short primaries would be great for fairly high-revving radical street machines.

At a casual glance, you might think an engine would develop maximum power if it had large-diameter short stacks right off the heads. They certainly looked cool on the old slingshot dragsters. But they don't work so well because the diameter of the header pipes determines the velocity of the exhaust gas and the intensity of the resulting negative pressure wave. If the primary pipes are too short, no beneficial scavenging effect takes place—or if it does, it's at a very high and limited rpm range.

It all has to do with taking maximum advantage of that "fifth cycle"—the overlap between intake and exhaust valve opening and closing—and how much overlap your engine can tolerate. Timing the overlap and exhaust pulses correctly can suck the last of the exhaust gas out of a cylinder and can even help pull in the fresh air-fuel mixture.

STICKING WITH STOCK

The stock exhaust systems on classic Chevy engines were developed to be quiet, durable, and completely adequate for normal driving. They were also designed to fit in crowded engine compartments. In fact, lots of two-barrel–equipped, standard-performance, V-8–powered Chevys come with only one exhaust pipe and muffler, which is all they really need.

Such systems are quieter, less expensive, and don't rust out as quickly as dual systems. Of course, high-performance, four barrel–equipped Chevys came with twin exhaust systems, one pipe for each bank of cylinders. This setup is generally adequate for normal street use, except in rev ranges near the redline of the engine.

Your bow tie mouse motor probably came with cast-iron log manifolds. These are very restrictive in performance situations. The next step up in efficiency would be to find a set of original Corvette ram's-horn cast-iron manifolds with the center exhaust dump going straight down, or canted slightly to the rear of the car. They're less restrictive than log manifolds, less expensive than headers, and still fit nicely in most engine compartments.

The big problem with stock systems at high rpm is that your engine starts developing what is called back pressure. The exhaust gas being pushed out of the system by the pistons is under so much pressure that it can back up into the incoming air-fuel mixture of adjacent cylinders and dilute it, especially when all the exhaust ports dump into a log manifold instead of being separated. The effect is used intentionally to some degree in later, smog-controlled engines to develop a leaner, cleaner-burning mixture, but it cuts performance dramatically.

Stock ram's horns can be opened and port-matched to produce almost as much power as cheap headers. If you use the exhaust gasket as a template and grind the cast headers to the edge of the gasket with your die grinder, you can develop about 65 percent of the performance improvement that a set of conventional headers will make. All it will cost is a little labor, and your exhaust system will be quiet and long-lived.

Stock ram's-horn cast-manifold dual exhaust systems don't develop harmful back pressure in normal service, but they aren't very good for pedal-to-

the-metal performance either because they don't do anything to help the engine perform better. That takes tuning. By tuning, I mean using the high- and low-pressure waves through the exhaust system to increase performance dramatically.

With tuned tubular headers, when the exhaust valve opens, a burst of high-pressure hot gas moves down its individual primary tube at high velocity. This creates a high-pressure wave that sends a low-pressure wave back up the exhaust system. The gas particles don't actually change direction. It works sort of like when you throw a stone into still water. Behind the high-pressure waves are low-pressure troughs pulling the next wave along, though the water keeps moving in the same direction. These low-pressure

Doug's Headers makes tri-Ys for tight spots, too. These will give you great performance and still not get in the way.

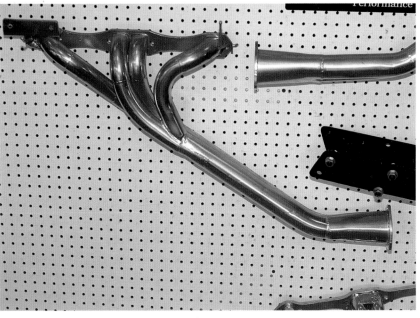

These short, four-into-one primary headers are for racing and produce maximum horsepower at 7,000-8,000 rpm.

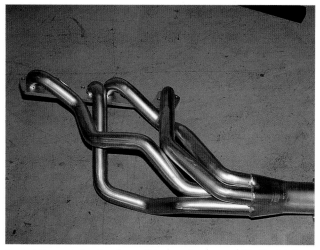
Long primary tubes such as this one keep gas velocity high and produce lots of torque in the low- to mid-rpm range.

Thick, 3/8-inch plates are important to prevent warping because of the high heat at the mating surfaces with the heads. Don't settle for thinner brackets.

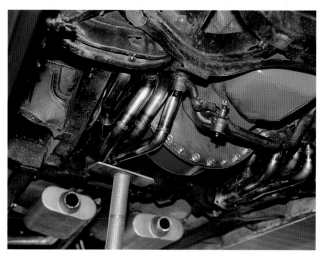
On some later cars with lots of accessories, custom-built headers are necessary to clear everything.

counterwaves can help create more torque at certain rpm ranges, depending on primary pipe length, pipe diameter, and valve overlap.

Incidentally, there used to be a lot of fuss about having equal-length primary tubes, but this hasn't turned out to be as important as once thought, even for constant-throttle racing motors. That's because equal-length pipes, though they might theoretically produce the ultimate torque, can do it only at a very spiky, narrow rpm range. With primary pipes that vary in length by as much as a foot, the benefits are spread over a range of 3,000–4,000 rpm.

WHY TRI-Y?

For street use, tri-Y or four-into-two-into-one headers are superior to four-into-one headers that just dump straight into a collector, or secondary tube. By pairing two primary tubes before having them go into the collectors, you get much more usable midrange torque, and your engine will pull well over a broader range.

These headers don't look quite as cool as the four-into-one headers so popular today, but they don't give you a large flat spot at lower rpm ranges, either. Four-into-one headers are great for racing but not for street use. Tri-Y headers help time the negative pressure waves much better by having that extra step, which makes them work well at more street-usable rpm ranges.

PIPE DIAMETER MATTERS

As a rule of thumb, the inside diameter of a Chevy small-block primary pipe should be about 1.16 times the exhaust valve open area. If you go bigger, you'll slow down the exhaust gas and hurt bottom-end performance. If you go too small, the pipes will be restrictive, and you'll lose velocity because of friction. Also, you'll make the system susceptible to back pressure.

So how does that translate into usable numbers? A Chevy small-block intended to produce 200–400 horsepower will work well with industry standard 1 5/8-inch-inside-diameter primary pipes. From 400–600 horsepower, 1.75-inch-I.D. pipes are what you want. On a Chevy small-block, anything above a 1.75-inch I.D. won't fit without an adapter anyway.

For secondary, or collector tubes, 2.5–3 inches I.D. is about right. Slightly larger collectors may be required for very high performance street engines. Short collector lengths of 18–24 inches are right for a

7,500-rpm radical-cam racing engine, but longer collectors will get you launched faster and are better for street use. The same is true for primary pipes. Longer primaries, in the range of 24–36 inches, help bottom-end power.

MAKING CHOICES

Choose your headers carefully because not every manufacturer makes headers for every application, and quality isn't always consistent. Check any headers you buy for flatness at the mounting flange and for good, clean welds at the joints. When you order a set of headers, make sure to tell the vendor the make and model of your vehicle, the year, and which transmission and accessories your car has. You'll also want to specify whether you want plain pipe, chrome, stainless, or a special coating such as Jet Hot. Plain pipe must be kept painted to prevent rust. I like black barbecue paint for this job.

Chrome looks oh-so-nice until it blues, but it can contribute to hydrogen embrittlement, which weakens the pipe. Jet Hot coats the pipes inside and out to prevent corrosion and is durable. Stainless (if available) is durable but expands and contracts more than mild steel, so it's more prone to leaks and loosening.

INSTALLATION

Installing headers on a fully assembled car isn't as easy as it might seem. Some must come in from the top; others must be installed from the bottom. Talk to the manufacturer, get a guarantee that the headers will fit your application, and read and follow the instructions that come with them. You may have to remove certain accessories to get them in, and you may have to dimple the headers in a few cases to get them to clear everything.

Finally, you'll want to install a crossover pipe or X pipes to help even out the exhaust pulses and quiet the system. A crossover tube will also cut vibration noticeably, and with headers, ringing and vibration can get irritating. To figure out where to place the crossover tube, shoot a little cheap aerosol paint down the exhaust pipes, run the engine for about 20 minutes, then determine just where the paint stopped burning off. That's where to put the crossover, if possible.

MUFFLER MYTHOLOGY

Many old-timers still think that a straight-through glasspack is less restrictive than a reverse flow. Not true. Unless the straight-through muffler has a large inside diameter (which will be much too noisy), it will actually restrict flow. Those cheap glasspacks on my aforementioned Chevy of years ago sounded cool but slowed me down considerably. Some of the new reverse-flow mufflers offer no more restriction than open pipes!

Place your mufflers as far from the engine as possible, and run the exhaust pipes all the way to the rear of the car. Shorter exhaust pipes don't help performance, and you run the risk of dangerous fumes getting into your car. Running the pipes to the rear also helps cut noise in the cockpit. Longer pipes behind the muffler don't make any difference to performance, so there's no advantage to cutting them short.

FINAL THOUGHTS

If you install a set of headers on an engine that has been performing well, it will probably run a bit lean afterward. In that case, you may have to rejet the carb. Retune and retime your engine to make maximum use of your new exhaust system. If you've gone a bit radical, watch those backshifts through tunnels. The local cops may not like your taste in music, either.

CHAPTER

2.6

RECIPE FOR SPEED

BY JIM RICHARDSON

Chili cook-offs (more accurately called chili eat-offs) are like elementary school fights. The first guy to cry loses. Some chili is just too mild to be taken seriously. Extreme chili will make you scream in agony and cry like a baby. The best chili is hot enough for you to prove your manhood yet still enjoy your afternoon.

Good street rod engines are like that too. They're hot, but still fun to drive. They'll leave your opponent crying, but you can still drive home on city streets. They're a careful balance between a well-tuned, basically stock motor and a Funny Car engine that functions well only at the track.

There are as many good recipes for chili as for street rod engines. While I don't have a good recipe for chili, I do have great one for a Chevy small-block

that will leave your opponent cursing (if not weeping) in your dust. I've told you how to go about making it in this book, but here's the abridged ingredient list:

BLOCK

Start with a good 350 carcass. Any of the Chevy small-blocks can be built to the hilt, but piles of good speed equipment are available at reasonable prices to fit the standard 350. Make sure the block is sound and that it's been crack-tested, sonic-tested, and cleaned before you start.

Also make sure its cylinders will clean up at .030 inch over. Yes, most of the small-blocks will go bigger, but you could wind up with structural and heating problems if you punch them out too much.

Here's my recipe: It makes 420-450 horsepower, buckets of torque, and it's built to last. Blend ingredients carefully, then jump in and hang on.

A Scat stroker crank turns a 350 into a bigger engine without making it heavier. It's also the secret behind all that torque.

Holley stamped-aluminum roller rockers lighten the valvetrain and cut friction and wear.

A Hamburger 7-quart pan from TD Performance can add a few horsepower, thanks to its windage tray, and will increase durability in a big way.

This is a Holley 670-cfm Street Avenger four-barrel. It's just right for our torquer motor and looks as good as it performs.

CRANKSHAFT

A stock crankshaft that isn't cracked badly, scored, or bent can be turned down and polished to work for the street. Chevy cranks are tough. But if you want truly awesome torque, go for a Scat stroker crank. They're virtually indestructible and will give you a real edge in competition. You can't wind them up quite as high as an aftermarket forged crank, but they're less likely to crack, and a stroker crank will give you such an off-the-line launch advantage that you'll break your opponent's spirit right out of the hole.

CAM

Camshafts are cheap, so why not buy the best? I like Iskendarian's 270–280 split-duration Megacams or a straight 280 Megacam with hydraulic lifters and stamped, standard-lift rockers—nothing fancy or radical. The 280 will give you lots of midrange kick and sounds wonderful. Isky's 270–280 runs a little smoother and gives you lots of bottom end. I prefer hydraulic lifter cams because they require no routine valve adjustments yet still provide impressive performance.

RODS

If you go with a Scat crank, use the 5.7-inch forged rods with full-floating wrist pins. These rods are a bit longer than stock. This makes the pistons linger a little near the top, so you can take better advantage of maximum cylinder pressure at higher revs. They linger at the bottom too, allowing more exhaust scavenging. Rods longer than 5.7 inches are available, but they push the wrist pins up into the ring package, making such pistons a little frail. Also, unless you're building a high revver, standard H-beam rods are fine. Just make sure you use them with decent big-end bearings, such as Clevite 77s.

PISTONS

Lots of good pistons are available, but I like Keith Black (KB) Signature Series hypereutectic cast-aluminum pistons. They're manufactured using special technology that makes them almost as tough as forged pistons, for a lot less money. You can get KBs in the size you need, and you can get domed, flat, or recessed types. Avoid domed pistons if possible because they mess up the turbulence and flame pattern needed for maximum burn and power. Be sure to use good moly-compression rings and three-piece oil rings: Childs & Albert are my favorites.

HEADS

The 1960s Chevys 68-cc closed-combustion-chamber heads were designed beautifully but are now extremely rare and expensive. They will also push your compression too high, given the rest of this recipe. They're wonderful for racing, but you can't run them on the street on pump gas unless you go to dished pistons, which is just another way to open up the combustion chambers.

A Performance Products dual-plane manifold is an inexpensive alternative that flows better than many of the big-name brands.

An MSD capacitive-discharge ignition system gives you hot spark through 20 degrees of crank rotation at any rpm.

Open-chamber 74–76 cc heads are still common and can be made to perform well with a pocket-porting job. These are also what most of us can afford these days. Don't turn down a set of double-humpers if you can get them for a good price. The later, 1980s-era heads are thin and prone to cracking.

If you can afford it, a set of World Products Sportsman II cast-iron heads will really wake up your small-block. They're a bit more expensive than stock heads, but not that much more after you have your stockers rebuilt. World Products offers 72-cc combustion chambers, so you can run flattop pistons for maximum power without risking detonation. World's castings are much more precise than stock heads and will produce appreciable gains in horsepower right out of the box.

A little careful pocket porting and cleaning up of the port runners will do wonders with Sportsman II heads as well. If you can spring for them, World Products aluminum heads work even better because their superior ability to dissipate heat allows you to run slightly higher compression. Since heads are where most of the horsepower is, it would pay to put as much money as you can into good ones.

OIL PAN

If you have the ground clearance and can spring for one, a Hamburger 7-quart oil pan from TD Performance products is a great way to go. The increased oil volume helps keep your engine's vital moving parts cooler, by keeping the engine's oil cooler. A Hamburger pan will also make sure the

Doug's Headers are tried and true. They're beautifully made and really help pump out the ponies.

A K&N washable air filter is the best there is and makes your carb breathe better because it doesn't restrict flow but makes it more consistent.

engine has a healthy supply of oil in hard cornering and hard acceleration because it has one-way trap doors that keep the oil where it needs to be. Finally, it's surprising how much drag a crankshaft spinning through a sump full of oil creates at high rpm. Hamburger pans have windage trays built in that wipe the crank clean of excess oil and cut down drag.

HEADERS

Four-into-one headers look cool, and if your exhaust system is going to be exposed down the side of a T-bucket, you might want to sacrifice some midrange just to have them. But tri-Y, four-into-two-into-one headers are better for street use because they give you a broader power band. They won't quite give you as much top-end power, but the difference isn't noticeable unless you're building a dragster. Doug's Headers are my choice because I know they're top quality, well designed, and tested. Go with the ceramic-coated types for durability and ease of maintenance.

CARBURETORS

If you're a relative novice, get a Holley. For this recipe, a 670-cfm Street Avenger is ideal and is easy to set up and fine-tune. Parts are readily available to make Holleys do anything you want and to fit any engine you might want to build. Everything you need to tinker with is right out where you can get to it, and Holley carbs are tested at the factory before you ever get them, so they're essentially trouble-free.

A Rochester Quadra-Jet will do a great job, too. In stock form, they flow 750 cfm, which is more than enough for most street small-blocks. If you have a little carb tuning experience or take the time to send your Q-Jet to a place like the Carb Shop in Ontario, California, you can make these carbs perform as well as or better than any of them. They're more complex to work on than the Holleys, and you need to know how to tweak them, but they're great carbs. Although

they're not made them anymore, new knockoffs are available. But it's a lot less costly to redo an original.

INTAKE MANIFOLD

Most street rodders are more comfortable with a dual-plane manifold. A single-plane gives you a rather hard-to-manage and soggy bottom end, though they really come on strong in the higher rpm range. My favorite intake manifold for the street (when using a Holley carb) is the Weiand dual-plane. The manifolds are beautifully made and have been bench proven for flow.

If I had less to spend, I'd go for a Performance Products dual-plane intake manifold. They're less expensive than most performance manifolds and have been shown in tests to flow as well as many of the big-name brands. They're cheap because they're made in China, but the quality is excellent. If you do a little port matching and top one of these with a well-tuned Q-Jet, you'll easily be able to play with the big kids.

IGNITION

The GM HEI system works well and can be used basically as is, but of course, the advance curve on an OEM distributor is set up to meet EPA demands, which is good if your car must meet smog laws. If not, you can play with the advance curve on your stock HEI system or, better yet, buy an after-market HEI unit from MSD. It will come with all the springs and extras to tailor it to your engine and will be beautifully designed.

It's even better to go with an MSD magnetic pickup distributor and add an MSD 6AL spark box and a hot coil. Not only will this configuration give you a hot spark and an advance curve to fit your driving needs, it will give you a multiple spark that will allow a more complete burn, with more power as a result. Once you have such a system dialed in, you can forget regular tune-ups, too.

TURBOS & SUPERCHARGES

BY JIM RICHARDSON

When a normally aspirated internal combustion engine is running, air enters each time a piston is pulled down inside its cylinder on the intake stroke. This occurs because, as the piston recedes, it enlarges the chamber, causing a vacuum. This vacuum is quickly filled by air rushing in through the carburetor, which charges it with atomized fuel on the way. The rising piston compresses the air-fuel mixture. At just the right moment the mixture is ignited, which superheats the air, causing it to expand and push down on the piston. The hot air is then released through the exhaust system. That, in a nutshell, is how a reciprocating engine works.

Atmospheric pressure is about 14 pounds per square inch at sea level, which is what causes the cylinders to fill with air. So it stands to reason that if you increase the air pressure beyond atmospheric by forcing more air into the intake system, you'll have a denser mixture, a bigger explosion in the cylinder, and more power. It's called *supercharging.* In fact, supercharging is another form of upping the compression ratio.

It's not a new idea. The French were supercharging race cars as far back as 1909, with dramatic results. Nothing else you can do to an engine will add as much power. Some people may assume that nitrous oxide injection is a better option, but let me point out that nitrous is just a chemical form of supercharging, albeit a temporary one. Horsepower gains of 30–75 percent are possible just by adding a supercharger. Small-block Chevys can easily crank out 600 horsepower with a blower (i.e., supercharger) attached.

The major catch for most of us is cost. Installing any of the superchargers or turbochargers can set you back $3,000–5,000 at this writing, which is more than most of us will spend on the entire engine. There are a few other drawbacks for the hobbyist working at home, too, such as installation, plumbing, and setting up the ignition. Also, blowers work best with fuel injection, which involves learning more about setting up the system and tuning it. If you're serious about supercharging, several good books are available. I suggest you start with the *Supercharging, Turbocharging, and*

The big Roots-type blower on this Corvette is enough to intimidate the competition but is overkill for street use.

A neatly done turbocharger installation gives this tri-five Chevy classic 900 horsepower to play with.

Pulling the air through the carbs causes its own problems. It would be better if the blower fed the carbs, instead of the other way around.

Nitrous Oxide Performance Handbook, published by Motorbooks International.

Of course, there are limits to how much of an increase in pressure you can put into a Chevy small–block, or any other engine. That's because, as you compress air, it gets hotter. As the air in a supercharger gets hotter it becomes less dense, so the power gains start to diminish. Also, if the air-fuel mixture coming into the engine becomes too lean or too hot, it may explode on its own and cause detonation, which will ruin your engine in short order.

Too much boost, a high compression ratio, or a combination of the two will cause detonation in a supercharged engine. Detonation occurs when the combustion pressure goes so high that the inlet charge explodes before the spark plug fires. When this happens, combustion takes place while the piston is still moving up in the cylinder, which causes a tremendous shock to the pistons, rods, and crankshaft.

Under normal circumstances, the flame speed across a cylinder is 120–200 miles an hour. But when fuel detonates—exploding under pressure before the spark plug even fires—the flame speed goes up as high as 2,000 miles an hour, and the shock destroys your ring lands and pistons. A richer mixture (one with more fuel in suspension) or one that is less compressed is cooler, so it's less likely to detonate. Also, devices called intercoolers can cool the compressed air before it goes into the engine, which helps prevent detonation.

Even when you can get a cool, dense mixture into an engine under high pressure, you need to take into

A blown bow tie certainly wakes up this old Kaiser, but it's strictly a fair-weather show car.

This is what detonation looks like. Explosive shocks to pistons rapidly destroy them.

account whether your engine's bottom end can handle all the extra power. Four to 7 pounds per square inch (psi) increase in boost is maximum for the street, and if you want a reliable car for daily use, keep it down around 4 or 5, max. That's enough to give you good midrange torque yet keep you from running over your own engine parts.

ROOTS-TYPE BLOWERS

Most rodders and engine builders are familiar with the Roots-type blower, which has been around for a long time. Those big, polished blowers you see sitting atop dragster engines are generally the GMC type 6-71. The basic design goes back to the late nineteenth century and was developed to pump air into mines. Inside that big housing on top of the engine are two

sort of figure-eight–shaped metal vanes that rotate in close tolerance with one another to move air.

Because the device can move air much faster than an engine can consume it, the air in the intake manifold becomes compressed. The blowers you see most commonly at the drags were originally developed by GMC for big, two-cycle diesel truck engines. Hot rodders were quick to see their advantages and adapted them to their engines many years ago. These old-style, crankshaft-driven blowers can give you more boost than you'll ever need, look impressive, and make a lot of exciting noise, but they're not the best choice for street use.

Big blowers require a fair amount of power just to turn them over, and they don't fit under the hoods of most street vehicles. They also give you poor mileage if

Late-model injected small-block engines have tremendous potential, thanks to precise fuel metering.

This radical small-block will produce awesome power, but building such an engine is expensive and requires sophisticated tuning skills.

you run them with carburetors instead of fuel injection because the air-fuel mixture must be kept rich to avoid detonation. You can mitigate this by driving conservatively, but then, why would you want a blower? For a dragster, nothing is better than a honking big blower, but on the street, they're sort of like using a sledgehammer when a ball peen hammer would do the job.

A better choice than the Jimmy blower for the street, if you want to use a Roots-type supercharger, might be the B&M two-rotor miniblower. It fits under the hoods of many cars and trucks and works fairly well carbureted while pumping up to 6–8 psi of boost. These are tough, dependable blowers but, as with any Roots-type blower, the vanes are machined to tight tolerances, so good air filtration is a must.

My favorite Roots-type blower for the street is the Weiand Pro-Street 142, offered by Holley Weiand. They're small and fit nicely under most hoods. They also work well with Holley carbs or injection set up expressly for them. Holley can help you custom order your supercharger for your particular application. These blowers are well made, durable, and produce awesome low-end torque as well as high-end horsepower.

SCREW-TYPE SUPERCHARGERS

Whipple offers some nice screw-type blowers that are a variation on the Roots supercharger. They use two rotors that are like interlocking coarse-thread screws. The original design comes from Sweden, and the advantage of it is that the air is compressed before it enters the intake manifold, so there is less heat. Whipple superchargers have an excellent reputation.

TURBOCHARGERS

Turbochargers use the pressure of the escaping exhaust in an engine to spin a turbine. This drives an impeller, forcing air into the intake manifold. Turbochargers can provide truly impressive horsepower gains, but they also have a few drawbacks, including throttle lag. Anyone who has followed Indy car racing for a long time will remember when Kevin Cogan looped his car at the start of the 1982 race and took out Mario Andretti and A. J. Foyt. It was embarrassing for Cogan, but it was an easy mistake to make.

Turbochargers don't provide boost at low rpm, and their bearings and turbines can suffer from the extreme heat generated by the exhaust system if not properly cooled. They also require more extensive plumbing than other types of superchargers. On the other hand, if used with an intercooler and with their oil properly cooled, they're incredible.

Garrett is my choice for turbochargers. They've been racing for years, and their turbochargers are on most of the Indy cars. They're also the turbo of choice in other venues where supercharging is allowed. Many major manufacturers have installed Garrett turbochargers on their offerings in the past 20 years, and these units have proven themselves reliable. Around town in low rpm ranges, your car toddles along like any other car, but then when you put your foot in it out on the highway and the turbocharger spools up, you get a real kick in the pants.

Turbos are great for higher altitudes, too. If you're building a street rod in the Colorado Rockies, you might as well consider adding one to your small-block. Many diesel truck manufacturers run Garrett turbochargers and have found them reliable and indispensable in the mountains.

CENTRIFUGAL SUPERCHARGERS

These have been around for a long time (Graham used them in the 1930s), but they've become popular again with manufacturers such as Buick, Pontiac, and Ford. It's probably easiest to think of them as crankshaft-driven turbochargers. They give you boost at lower rpm and back off when you do, so there's no throttle lag. They're also easy to install, and they fit under the hoods of most vehicles.

Eaton makes bolt-on units for new cars which, combined with modern fuel injection and ignition management systems, are quite impressive. They're also quiet, reliable, and street legal in all 50 states. The only problem is that Eaton doesn't provide kits for the street rod builder, so a lot of fabrication would be required if you want to adapt one of their centrifugal superchargers to an older engine.

Powerdyne also sells centrifugal superchargers that are easily bolted on to newer (1993 and later) small-block engines, but they're not designed to fit older engines, and no kits are available.

For most street uses, your Chevy small-block can generate ample power without going to the expense of a supercharger. Many well-engineered aftermarket components are available for far less money and will really wake up your engine. Unless you have the time, expertise, and money, superchargers aren't worth the trouble. They're marvelous devices that provide awesome power, but if you don't know what you're doing, they can make awesome trouble for you as well.

FRONT SUSPENSION

BY TIM REMUS

When building a rod from scratch, the front suspension is a crucial consideration. If you're modifying a stock machine, your concerns are simply tuning. If you're rolling your own, the overall style of the car will be the biggest factor dictating which front suspension is right for you. There's no point in spending the extra money for a polished independent suspension if the car is a resto-rod or traditional ride.

As Pete Chapouris, a custom design expert, likes to say, "If it's an open-wheeled car, then it needs a dropped axle. If it's a fat car, then we might want to put an independent front suspension under it."

In addition to the car's style, its use and your personal opinion are important when trying to decide which of the many available front suspensions to install. If you want to go around corners like a Ferrari, a dropped axle won't do the job. Ask yourself, "How do I like to drive? What do I expect from this car in terms of handling and cornering?"

The front suspension is important for at least three reasons: it's generally more visible, it carries more weight, and it steers the car. Choosing the front suspension is one of the more complex decisions you'll need to make while planning and building the car. This is a situation where each menu choice leads to another menu. Choose a dropped axle, for example, and the next menu asks whether you want to use four-bar linkage or split wishbones to hold it in place. Click on the four-bar option, and the next drop-down window asks whether you want to use a tubular or I-beam axle.

A beautifully finished front suspension is a functional work of art.

This 4-inch dropped tube axle is available in various widths, with either a 2 or 2 1/4-inch perch boss. Chrome plating is available as well.

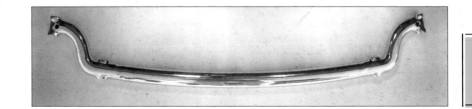

One of the simplest front
suspension systems uses a leaf
spring for a clean, low look.

Kingpin kits include the pins themselves,
the bushings that need to be pressed
into the spindle and then reamed to fit,
the bearings that support the spindle, and
assorted hardware.

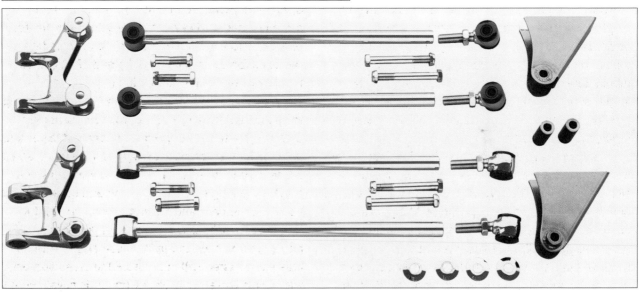

Four-bars became popular with the advent of the dropped tube axle, though some people like them simply for their visual
appeal. This kit uses all stainless components and urethane bushings.

WHICH SUSPENSION IS RIGHT?

In theory, an independent front suspension handles and rides better than a dropped axle. With a twin A-arm suspension system installed under your car, a bump encountered by one wheel has less impact on the other wheel and the car's occupants. As the name implies, by acting independently, each wheel is better able to rise over bumps and steer around corners while keeping a good grip on the road.

However, nothing is cooler than a nice dropped axle mounted with a buggy spring up front and a pair of split radius rods to hold it all in place. So, as Pete Chapouris, a custom design expert, points out, the choice of a front axle (especially on an open-wheeled car) is largely an aesthetic decision.

Having made that decision, the next choice is the type of linkage you're going to use to hold the axle in place. The nostalgia craze seems to get stronger and stronger, which means that more and more hot rodders are choosing the traditional split wishbones or hairpin radius rods. The other option is a four-bar linkage—what might be called the choice of a modern traditionalist.

Purists will point out that hairpin radius rods (or split wishbones) put a slight twist on the axle when only one wheel goes over a bump. The twist occurs because each axle end has its own pivot point. Essentially, the wheel that hits the bump swings upward on the arc of the radius rod, so it experiences a caster change while the other does not. Replacing radius rods with a four-bar linkage solves that problem. Because the four-bar linkage acts as a parallelogram, one or both ends of the axle can go up or down with no caster change and no twist on the axle.

The twist that an early Ford axle experiences while going over a bump is the reason you can't use a tubular dropped axle with split wishbones. Modern tubular axles consist of a center tube with cast or forged ends welded to it. Tubular structures resist twisting, so the twist will cause the welds to fail—if not today, then next week.

Many of these decisions and their implications are made easier by manufacturers who offer their suspension systems as a kit. Buy the axle, and the linkage comes along as part of the package. Many go so far as to make the spring, spring perches, spindles, and brakes all part of the assembly you buy.

If you prefer to buy components individually, you need to be sure all the pieces will work together on your particular frame. Already mentioned is the need to avoid using split wishbones with a tube axle.

Another common mistake is using Heim joints or spherical rod ends at the end of a four-bar link. As Eric Aurand from Chassis Engineering explains, "You only want four-bars to move in one plane vertically, but spherical rod ends allow lateral movement. That lateral movement gives the car what I call a 'beer truck' kind of ride." What should be used instead are the simple urethane bushings that come with most four-bar kits.

Most dropped axles are available in two or three widths. Unlike a rear-axle assembly, which is measured flange to flange, front-axle widths are measured between kingpin centerlines. The drilled and dropped axle in the SO-CAL catalog comes in a 47 1/2-inch width. The common 46- and 48-inch width became standardized in typical hot rod fashion. Jim Petrykoski from Metal Fab explains: "The original Ford axles were something like 50 or 52 inches wide, but when people started to drop the axle, they just reshaped it, which meant it got narrower. When Jim Ewing started Super Bell Axle Company, he offered a dropped axle in a 48-inch width. Then, when the first disc brakes were offered, they moved the wheel out about an inch on either side, so pretty soon Jim offered a 46-inch axle for cars with disc brakes. In the end, what you're trying to do is put a 5 1/2- or 6-inch wheel, 14 or 15 inches in diameter, on a stock car with fenders and still be able to use the full turn radius."

When working with dropped axles, also consider the distance between the bosses for the spring perches. That measurement must match the length of the spring you intend to use. The front crossmember used on early Ford frames is another piece that must be chosen to match all the others. Early hot rodders discovered years ago that using a Model A front crossmember in a Deuce frame would lower the front of the car. Today, SO-CAL makes a crossmember designed for use in both Model A and 1932 frames that lowers the front end by 1 inch.

A discussion of the front crossmember brings up the subject of caster. Most hot rodders want their cars to have some rake, with the front end lower than the rear. It gives the car that aggressive stance and a sense of motion—almost like they're moving when they're standing still. That's all fine and good, but as you raise the back and lower the front, you tip the front axle forward and lose some of your caster angle. So you need to buy a crossmember with a little extra caster built in or install the crossmember with a little extra angle. Pete Chapouris says, "People forget that when you rake the car, the caster goes negative. You might need 9 degrees of caster to net

A couple of different approaches to front suspension.

out at 6. Our crossmember allows you to run more positive caster without putting a bind in the spring or the spring shackle."

Some controversy surrounds the use of a Panhard rod with a buggy-spring dropped-axle front suspension. A Panhard rod attaches to the axle on one side of the car and to the frame on the other, minimizing side-to-side motion between the axle and frame. Though plenty of hot rods out there have straight axles and no Panhard rod, Pete Chapouris feels the Panhard rod is a necessary part of a straight axle installation: "Basically, if you use a buggy spring and a cross-steer setup, then you need a Panhard rod. Without a Panhard rod, with a Vega cross-steer, you cause the axle to swing on the shackles, creating 'bump steer.' We also like to install a steering damper; it ensures there is no side-to-side shimmy. Our straight-axle installations always include a Panhard rod and damper."

PREVENTING BUMP STEER

We've all heard the term "bump steer," meaning that a bump will cause the car to move from the steering line chosen by the driver. These little problems crop up when the axle and steering linkage move through different arcs as the car goes over a bump.

Though problems can occur with any type of steering, bump steer is best illustrated by looking at drag-link steering. Bump steer in this system occurs when the bump causes the axle to move forward or back more than the drag link as they swing through their arcs. The effect is a little different depending on the style of axle mounting, but the end result is the same. Basically, the axle and the end of the drag link that attaches to the axle must move through the same arcs when the suspension moves up and down over bumps.

In a cross-steer application, such as with a Vega or Saginaw steering box, bump steer is caused by side-to-side axle movement rather than front-to-rear. Any axle movement to the side during suspension travel will push or pull on the drag link, causing the dreaded bump steer. As Pete Chapouris points out, street rods with a transverse leaf spring mounted with a shackle at either end can allow lateral axle movement on the shackles. To avoid this problem, most street rod equipment manufacturers recommend a Panhard rod. The Panhard rod prevents side-to-side axle movement, but it must be designed and mounted carefully, so as not to create more problems than it solves.

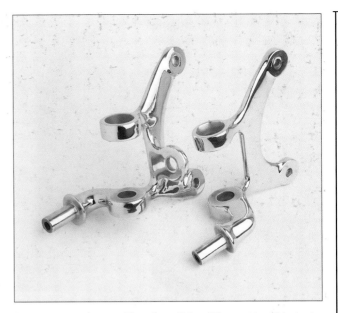

For traditional cars, there's nothing like a pair of hairpin radius rods with stainless steel batwings. These batwings come with a provision for mounting the Panhard rod.

General installation guidelines include the need to keep the Panhard rod parallel to, and the same length as, the drag link. More specific recommendations can be had by consulting with the manufacturer of the front suspension and linkage. With these cross-steer applications, the steering gear and linkage should be mounted so the pitman arm is pointing straight ahead when the gear is in the center of its movement. The gear should also be mounted so the drag link is parallel to the tie rod.

Another cause of front-end shimmy is worn kingpins or axle ends. With loose or worn kingpins and bushings, a bump in the road can induce the dreaded "straight-axle shimmy." When installing a dropped axle, you have to be sure the pins fit tightly in the ends of the axle (sometimes a problem with used axles) and that the bushings in the spindle are correctly reamed for a good fit between the bushing and the pin.

Many hot rod suppliers will ream the bushings before the axle or spindles are shipped. It's one of those jobs that requires precision and should be done by an experienced shop. If you buy spindles and need to have the bushings installed and/or reamed, any good shop that services trucks or truck chassis should be able to help you out.

The other thing to keep in mind after the dropped axle is installed is the need for frequent applications of lubricant. Though we've all become accustomed to no-lube tie rod ends and ball joints, kingpin bushings still require frequent attention from that old-fashioned grease gun hanging on the wall.

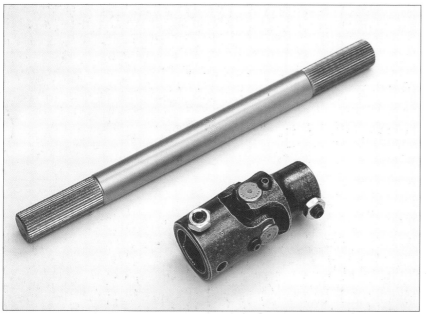

Steering shafts and the necessary
U-joints are available as a kit
like this one, which utses
Borgeson U-joints.

Another well-finished front end.

Camber is simply the tilt of the tire in or out as seen from the front. True vertical is zero camber. A tilt to the outside at the top is positive, and a tilt to the inside is negative.

INDEPENDENT FRONT SUSPENSION DESIGNS

Independent front suspension systems come in a wide variety of styles and prices. For the budget-minded rodder, a number of companies offer a Mustang II–type front suspension crossmember. You install the crossmember in your new or old frame and then add the suspension components, either stock Mustang or aftermarket. These can be scrounged at the local used parts emporium or purchased new. Most street rod companies in this market offer various upgrades over the stock Ford pieces.

The first upgrade usually replaces the narrow lower arm and its support strut with a much wider lower arm that doesn't need the strut. This makes for a cleaner installation and eliminates the strut support. Most companies also offer tubular upper and lower arms to replace the original stamped-steel arms. Of course, you can go one step further and order the arms in chrome or polished stainless for extra glitter.

If you're looking for more than a simple Mustang II suspension, a number of companies build complete stand-alone front suspension systems that come with the crossmember, arms, spindles, and all necessary hardware. Some of these assemblies have been designed from scratch for the street rod market and feature billet aluminum or tubular steel arms and polished coil-over shocks.

Heidt's, for example, offers their Superide, with upper and lower arms on each side supported by a nice coil-over shock assembly. This package comes with a crossmember that ties everything together. By using the coil-over shock-spring, the design eliminates the huge spring pocket seen on Mustang systems.

Kugel Komponents offers their Phase II independent front suspension. This system uses upper and lower arms, a coil-over on each side for support, and a crossmember designed to fit various hot rod frames. They also make independent suspension for cars with "pinched" frames and a high-tech pushrod

Having the correct caster for your car means it will go down the highway in a straight line, without the need for constant minor steering corrections. Caster also helps the steering wheel return to the straight-ahead position after a turn. Caster recommendations are different for straight axles and independent suspension, with most straight axles needing considerably more positive caster.

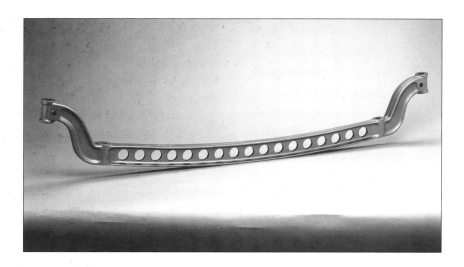

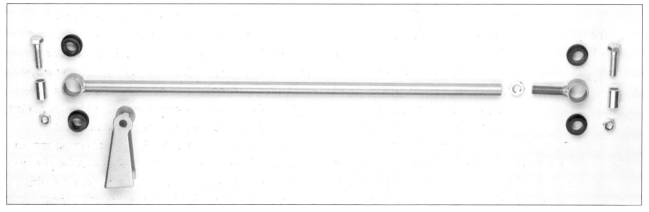

Toe-in is important to the way your car goes down the road. Too little or too much can make a car prone to wander, almost like insufficient positive caster.

type of suspension that moves the coil-overs inboard in Formula One fashion.

Corvette components, both the latest C5 pieces and those from earlier models, are used in systems offered by Fat Man, Chassis Engineering, Mike Adams, and others. This makes it easy to use the latest Corvette suspension and brakes on both ends if you desire. Gibbon Fiberglass and Chassis Engineering also offer torsion-bar front suspensions for 1935 to 1940 Ford cars.

POTENTIAL PROBLEMS

When buying a front suspension, whether it's a simple Mustang II unit or something more exotic, there are a few things to watch for.

First, a Mustang II system should use stock Ford geometry and the stock mounting position for the steering rack. Changing the position of the upper control arm or the length of the tie rods used with the Ford rack-and-pinion gear can lead to unpleasant consequences.

Second, a lot of unseen engineering goes into any good front suspension. While you don't have to

understand all the engineering, it makes good sense to buy from well-known companies. Ask the manufacturer or the dealer plenty of questions, and don't sign the check until you're satisfied with their answers.

Third, when in doubt about what to buy, find someone at the next show with a suspension like the one you lust for and ask him how it works in the real world. Did the manufacturer provide good instructions? How hard was the system to install, and was the manufacturer there to help with any questions that arose during the installation? Most rodders will be more than happy to discuss their experiences.

RIDING ON AIR

This independent-suspension section wouldn't be complete without an examination of the somewhat new air-ride systems. Most of these replace the spring(s) with an air bag from Goodyear or Firestone. The bags themselves are manufactured from the same two-ply material used to make the air bags seen on 18-wheel tractors and trailers. This whole technology is really a carryover from commercial trucks.

That's not to say all these air-suspension systems are the same. Some are designed from scratch to take advantage of the air bags, while others simply replace the spring in a Mustang II front suspension with an air bag. In all cases, the bags are connected to an air compressor controlled by a panel within the car.

Most independent-suspension systems experience camber change as the suspension moves up and down. Many designs do this intentionally, so that the outside tire tilts in and gets a better grip on the road as you roar around a curve. Yet that camber change might not be such a good idea when you're dealing with suspension systems designed to operate over a wide range of ride heights.

When considering one of these air-bag designs, decide how much you're really going to use the height adjustment. Do you want to simply find a good ride height, close to a standard street-rod ride height, then lower the car when you park? Or do you want to be able to vary the usable ride height by 3 or 4 inches?

Systems designed from scratch around the air bags tend to offer the greatest height adjustment with the least amount of camber and toe-in change. Some offer a conventional bump stop, so that if you pinch a line or let all the air out of the system, the suspension can't settle so far that any components are damaged. Others use bags designed with internal cushions that provide a final compression or rest stop.

The air-bag systems come to the table with a number of advantages and disadvantages. On the positive side, this technology allows the builder to set the car in the weeds for that really hot profile yet drive it home like any other car, crossing speed bumps with impunity. If you load the car with four friends and a small trailer out back, all you need to do to compensate is dial up a little more pressure and head out the driveway. Finally, air suspension is progressive: the more the suspension is compressed at a given pressure setting, the more it will resist further compression.

The cost of this new technology includes the cost of the pump and control unit and any cost to retrofit one of these systems to an existing car. Cars with air bags are more complex and have more things to go wrong, but that may not be a consideration for many hot rodders. Ultimately, these systems are best suited to fat-fendered cars and trucks, for one simple reason: the bags are ugly. There's no way to build an air bag that isn't black or one with the aesthetic appeal of a polished coil-over.

STEERING LINKAGE
Between the steering wheel and the two front tires is the steering linkage. Once again, a few options here should be mentioned in the interest of good decisions.

CROSS-STEERING FOR DROPPED AXLES
By far the most common style of steering linkage currently used with a dropped axle is the cross-steer system. This style of steering mounts the steering gear to the left frame rail. The drag link runs from the pitman arm, which is connected to the steering gear, across to the right-side steering arm.

What we call "bump steer" can occur with any type of steering linkage, usually because someone didn't take the time to think through the various components being used and how they interact as the suspension moves up and down. If, as the suspension compresses or extends, the steering linkage moves through a different arc than the axle itself, you have essentially "steered" the vehicle. Axle movement, front to rear or side to side, can cause this problem.

In a car with cross-steer linkage, it's important to keep the tie rod and drag link parallel and the pitman arm pointing straight ahead when the gear is in the straight-ahead position (in the center of its movement). Worm-gear types of steering gears have a built-in "high point" at the very center of the movement. This is built in to compensate for any wear that might occur. The shaft of a properly adjusted steering gear will actually require slightly more torque to turn as it goes through this high point. In general, the Vega steering box (or newly manufactured copies of it) is suitable for lighter-weight hot rods, such as Ford up to 1934. Larger cars, such as fat-fendered Fords and GM cars, should use the slightly larger Saginaw 605 box, Saginaw 525 box, or equivalent.

Most street rod builders recommend the use of a Panhard rod with a dropped axle to avoid side-to-side movement of the axle as the car goes over bumps and around corners. Installation of the Panhard rod must be considered carefully, however, so the axle and the drag link move through the same arcs. If in doubt, the builder can always call the company that manufactured the suspension parts for help with placement and installation of the Panhard rod.

DRAG-LINK LINKAGE
When it comes to the steering linkage used with straight axles, there is a plan B. Early hot rods and a few bucket Ts use what's known as a drag-link style of linkage. This system positions the drag link on the left

side of the car, connected between the steering gear and a left-side steering arm. Despite the fact that many old Indy roadsters ran exactly this type of linkage, it can be troublesome to install correctly. Unless the style of the car dictates a drag-link type of system, most builders are better off with a cross-steer linkage. Those who go ahead with linkage running on the car's left side need to take care that the axle doesn't experience any fore and aft movement as it moves up and down over a bump and that the steering linkage is carefully laid out.

When it comes to deciding which type of steering to install in a solid-axle car, Pete Chapouris is a big believer in cross-steer linkage: "To use the drag-link type of steering correctly it has to be laid out right," he explains. "With the Model A, the pivot points were in the general area of each other, but when people build cars like that now, there's just so many things that can go wrong. A lot of guys do it because of the nostalgia thing. But look at the old cars. The Pierson Brothers coupe is a cross-steer car, and that was built in 1949.

When Henry started using cross-steer, the hot rodders of the day followed suit. The cars we build now, they all use cross-steer linkage. It's just so much better."

RACK AND PINION GEAR

If this were a class or seminar, someone would be sure to raise a hand at this point and ask, "What about using a rack and pinion gear with a dropped axle?"

The answer is no. You can't. Well, you shouldn't use a rack and pinion with a dropped axle. Sure, we've all seen it done, with varying degrees of success. That doesn't mean it's a good or a safe idea. First, the rack has to be mounted to the axle, then some kind of flexible link must be fashioned between the steering shaft and the gear that moves up and down with the axle. Not a good plan.

Where a rack does work extremely well is when it's used with an independent front suspension and is designed to work with that suspension system. As mentioned before (but we'll mention it again), the rack and the suspension must be matched. To avoid bump

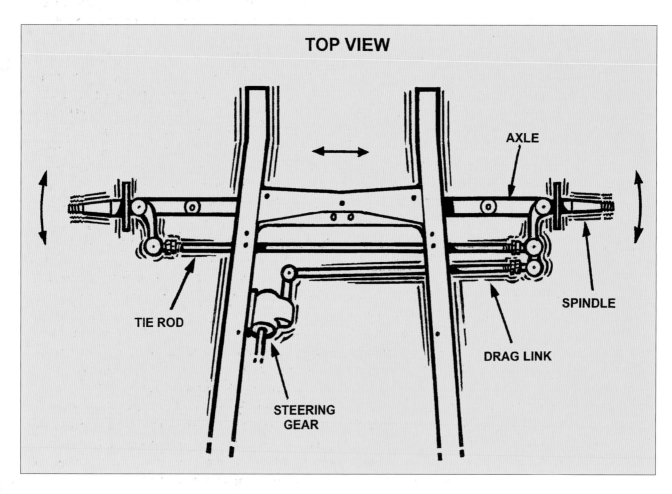

TOP VIEW

AXLE

TIE ROD

SPINDLE

DRAG LINK

STEERING GEAR

A straight axle with a buggy spring or transverse springs can move relative to the frame unless a Panhard rod is used. For this reason SO-CAL recommends the use of a Panhard rod and has designed a bracket for the Panhard rod into the right-side batwing. Unless a Panhard rod is properly laid out and installed, it can cause as many problems as it solves.

steer, the ends of the tie rods must move through the same arcs as the control arms. This happens only when the two systems are designed from the start to work together—or someone has carefully matched an independent suspension package to a particular steering rack assembly.

POWER STEERING

As the street rod industry matures and many of us drive bigger, heavier cars, the need arises for power steering. Not a problem, you say—I'll just use the power version of that Ford rack-and-pinion and hook it up to the handy-dandy GM power steering pump. The problem this time isn't geometry but pressure—namely, that the GM pump puts out way too much pressure for the stock Ford rack. Correctly solving the mismatch involves using a shim kit in the flow control valve or an adjustable power steering valve from a company like Heidt's.

POPULAR STEERING GEARS

Conventional steering gears are often called worm gears because of the shape of the internal gear. A good example and longtime favorite with street rodders is the Vega gear—now being remanufactured, so you can purchase one brand-new. Another popular GM gear is the 525, a late-model manual gear that's just a bit bigger than the tried-and-true Vega. GM power steering gears can often be used in many typical cross-steer applications. Most of the steering gear mounting plates will accept either a manual or a power gear. The problem with power steering in cross-steer situations is the tight fit on the left side of most V-8s when installed in most street rod chassis.

GEOMETRY AND ERGONOMICS

This brings us to the topic of mockups, a concept that definitely applies to the steering column and place-ment of the steering gear. In the case of a worm-style gear, the exhaust headers or manifold are often pretty close to the gear, whether it's power steering or not. You probably want to clamp or tack-weld the mounting plate for the steering gear to the frame, in what seems like the most logical location. Then install the engine and check the clearance between the shaft and gear and the engine, mount, and exhaust.

In addition to good geometry, you need to consider the ergonomics. That is, the column should be mounted where it feels most comfortable for the driver. With the column temporarily mounted, make sure the lower part is high enough that you can move your foot from one pedal to the other without running into it.

Next, locate the steering gear on the frame rail so that the shaft connecting the column to the gear is as straight as possible. With the wheels pointed straight ahead, the steering gear must be in the center of its movement. Although many hot rod builders and shops position the gear so the pitman arm is parallel to the ground, that isn't necessary for good geometry and may make for a more complex linkage between the column and the steering gear.

Remember that it's easier to modify a header tube or change to a different style of exhaust manifold than to design a shaft with multiple U-joints and a support bearing. Also, a number of pitman arms are available for the most popular gears. These can be an aid in finding the ideal position for the gear and will affect the gear's effective ratio and leverage. For instance, installing a longer pitman arm will make the steering quicker. Though U-joint manufacturers say the joints will work at angles up to 25 or 30 degrees, a smaller angle is always better.

For the steering shaft, use high-quality, needle-bearing U-joints. Less expensive U-joints do not use needle bearings to support the cross-shaft but are generally meant for industrial applications and have no place in your steering shaft assembly. Borgeson and various dealers sell complete kits with U-joints and a shaft, as well as vibration dampers and collapsible shafts for safety. Support bearings and brackets for three-joint shafts are available as well.

The mounting plate used for the steering gear must be well mounted, preferably welded, to the frame rail. Even a minuscule amount of flex between the bracket and the frame or the gear and its bracket will be magnified, resulting in loose and vague steering.

Among the parts you have to keep matched are the tapered ends of the tie-rod ends and the holes in the steering arm or pitman arm. Even similar-appearing ends use tapered studs with different diameters or different degrees of taper. Because all the components that make up the steering linkage are critical to your safety, be sure the taper and diameter of the tie-rod end matches perfectly the hole it fits into . . . and don't forget the cotter key.

REAR SUSPENSION

BY TIM REMUS

The previous chapter emphasized the importance of the front suspension. That doesn't mean the rear suspension is unimportant or that you shouldn't give careful consideration to the type of rear suspension that best suits your new rod. Many roadsters leave the rear suspension open to view, which means it can be an important part of the car's visual package. Even if yours is a fat-fendered car with a mostly invisible rear axle, the linkage, springs, and rear-end assembly certainly contribute to the ride, handling, and ride height.

A discussion of independent versus solid rear axles runs parallel to the discussion of front axles. An independent rear suspension provides better handling and ride (in most situations). The downside is cost and mechanical complexity.

While the high zoot cars in the magazines might have a fully independent and polished rear suspension from Kugel or a converted Corvette or Jaguar system, that doesn't mean you can't install a solid Ford 9-inch rear end with coil or leaf springs. Millions of cars and thousands of hot rods are motoring around today on nothing more sophisticated than a solid rear axle, two springs, and the linkage necessary to keep it all in place.

SOLID-AXLE OPTIONS

A solid rear axle can be supported in a variety of ways: two parallel leaf springs, a single transverse buggy spring, a pair of coils, or a pair of air bags. Henry Ford liked the buggy spring, used on most of his cars up to 1948. Today, that option is less popular, though the kits and components available from SO-CAL (and a few others) are making the buggy spring a more viable rear suspension choice than ever before.

Before deciding which is the best suspension option for your solid rear axle, consider the options.

LEAF SPRINGS

Though they are not flashy, there's nothing wrong with leaf springs. They're durable and readily available and make a good suspension, especially under heavier, fatter cars. Spring assemblies such as those from Posies come with slippery, synthetic buttons under the end of each leaf to minimize internal "stiction," one of the inherent disadvantages of leaf springs.

Another way to eliminate friction from within the spring pack is to eliminate the pack and use a single leaf. However, these products seem to have some problems, and many have been withdrawn from the market.

Height adjustment is difficult at best with leaf springs. Sure, you can always use lowering blocks, like the kids did on their 1952 Fords, but wouldn't it be better to buy the right spring the first time? To lower the rear of the car, some rodders pull one or more leaves from the spring pack. Before following suit, however, consider that all those leaves in the pack were designed to work together. The best solution is to ask the person who manufactured the spring or rear suspension kit whether the springs have been de-arched and what the ride height will be when the springs are used with a car like yours. If you already have the spring and the rear of the car sits too high, a good spring shop can de-arch a leaf spring assembly or reverse the eyes to lower the car.

For the ultimate in sex appeal, it's hard to beat a polished independent rear suspension.

Ladder bars make a nice, simple, functional rear suspension that works with either a buggy spring or a pair of coil-overs.

COIL SPRINGS

Often the suspension of choice for early cars, coil-spring rear suspensions come in at least four different styles, each with certain advantages and disadvantages.

The straight and simple parallel four-bar might be the best-known; four-bar kits are available from every

A simple rear suspension system using a single leaf spring. This is great for cars intended to look good, but performance will be as basic as the system.

You can simplify frame construction with this rectangular rear crossmember. It's made from .120-inch-wall-thickness mild steel tubing, and the mounting bungs for coil-over shocks are already installed.

major street rod manufacturer and catalog company. Just weld the brackets to the rear end, another set of brackets to the frame, connect with the four links, and add coils or coil-overs. Like all rear suspension kits, installing the four-bar suspension requires that you carefully set up the rear end at ride height before welding on the four-bar brackets. One big advantage of a four-bar is that the pinion angle doesn't change as the suspension moves through its travel (just as a four-bar front end has no caster change).

One disadvantage is that welding on the rear-end housing generally warps the housing, which must be checked and repaired by a qualified shop after the brackets are installed. Another is that unlike some other coil-spring rear suspension systems, the parallel four-bar system needs a Panhard rod to eliminate side-to-side axle movement. This means one more bracket to bolt or weld to the axle housing and the need for a matching bracket on the frame.

Some builders use a triangulated four-bar system. This positions two of the bars parallel to the car's axis, like a standard four-bar system. The other two bars are mounted at an angle, so they can absorb side loads and eliminate the need for a Panhard rod. The problem is the way the angled bars sometimes get in the way of the exhaust system as it snakes its way to the rear of the car. And though thousands of these are in use, some builders don't like the way the lower and upper links move in different planes, which puts the upper bars in a bind when the suspension moves up and down.

Ladder bars, another option in the coil-spring world, are about as simple as a suspension system gets. Welded to the axle housing, each "ladder" runs well forward and connects to brackets and a

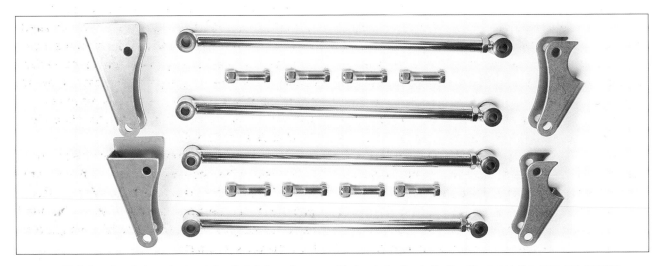

This parallel four-bar kit is designed for Model As and comes with brackets for both the frame and the rear end housing. It's available in standard steel or stainless.

crossmember near the middle of the chassis. Roy Brizio states that he often uses ladder bars on the cars built in his shop, and for good reason. "With ladder bars, you bring all the torque to the center of the car, and the torque acts on the center of mass, the way Henry liked it."

A ladder-bar system requires a Panhard rod when coil springs are used, and the bars can get in the way of a dual exhaust system. The rear end supported by ladder bars also experiences pinion-angle change as the suspension moves up and down, in much the same way a split-wishbone front suspension experiences caster change as the wheel goes over a bump.

The final installment in this coil-spring suspension treatise is a seldom-used suspension called a three-bar. Think of a parallel four-bar system without the top bars. Now add one shorter, upper link and a Panhard rod. Simpler than a four-bar, the three-bar provides good traction and a good launch and is often seen on true drag-race cars.

ACT INDEPENDENTLY

The street rod and hot rod industry has grown tremendously in the past 10 or 15 years. Nowhere is that growth more apparent than in the wide range of independent rear suspensions available for the typical hot rod.

Not long ago the options included mostly the converted Corvette or Jaguar rear suspension systems. A few of the catalogs offered kits that made it possible to convert one of the systems to street rod use. Boyd Coddington's shop took the Corvette independent system to a new plateau and made it their own. Today, independent rear suspensions come in as many flavors as ice cream. Kugel, Heidt's, and Dutchman are just three of the companies that manufacture complete standalone independent suspension systems based on the Ford 9-inch rear end.

These rear suspension systems were designed from the start to be installed in your hot rod. If you're afraid that the torque of a street Hemi or 502-cid Chevy will spit those Jaguar spider gears out onto the pavement, try a bulletproof Ford 9-inch as the foundation for a very trick independent rear suspension system. Now add axles available in various lengths, connected to heavy-duty U-joints, supported by trick cast or billet aluminum supports.

This is ingenuity at its best. Extremely durable, these independent rear suspensions come as a

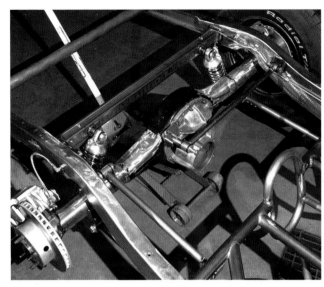

The air bags used for rear suspension are slightly different from those used on the front. The system shown here from Art Morrison is intended to be used with its own frame.

complete assembly with their own subframe, ready for installation in the chassis of your choice.

If the standalone assemblies seem a bit expensive or you like to get your hands really dirty and do everything yourself, a number of companies offer kits that allow Corvette rear suspensions to be adapted to street rod use. Chassis Engineering offers trailing arms and crossmembers to install pre-C5 Corvette suspension components in a variety of hot rods. Fat Man makes complete rear subframes to convert C5 (late-model) Corvette components to nearly any hot rod application. Art Morrison, too, has Corvette suspension kits meant for hot rods.

No matter which style of rear suspension you install, independent or solid-axle, you should consider the position of the wheel in the rear fender opening (assuming there are rear fenders). Some fat-fendered cars use an axle centerline from the factory that positions the rear wheel slightly to the front of the fender opening, which means you probably want to move the centerline back slightly. This is another reason to spend time with the car mocked up in the shop with the chassis at ride height.

If you buy a rear suspension kit, ask the manufacturer where in the fenderwell their kit positions the rear wheel. Or follow the example of builder Steve Moal, who likes to roll the mockup outside, so he can stand back and really assess how the car "sits" and how all the parts work together.

SHOCKS & SPRINGS

BY TIM REMUS

Though shocks and springs might seem simple, they're in fact complex and certainly important enough to warrant a separate chapter.

First, let's start with a spring that supports a weight. If you compress the spring and let go, it doesn't just bounce back to the starting point. No, it goes well past that point before reversing direction and going through a series of diminishing oscillations that eventually bring it back to the starting point.

If we're describing the spring that supports one corner of your hot rod, the up-and-down motion makes it difficult to keep the car under control. To dampen those oscillations, a shock absorber is used.

WHAT'S A SPRING?

Springs are classified by their rate—how far they move when supporting a certain weight. The spring that's part of a hot rod coil-over might be rated at 200 pounds per inch, meaning that 200 pounds will compress the spring 1 inch. Most coil springs are linear in their rate: if 200 pounds compresses the spring 1 inch, 400 will displace it 2 inches (obviously this will change as a coil spring approaches coil bind).

A variable-rate spring provides a progressive rate. By winding the coils more tightly at one end (or by decreasing the diameter of the wire), the engineer is able to create a spring with a soft rate for the first inch or two of travel and a stiffer rate for the final two inches. Some manufacturers offer a dual-rate spring, made up of two different springs stacked on top of each other. Small bumps compress both springs, which provides a softer effective rate. When the softer spring coil binds, the rate of the stiffer spring kicks in.

If you think about it, a typical leaf spring with five or more leaves is a variable-rate spring. A soft bump will cause only the long main leaf to deflect slightly, while a big pothole might deflect all the leaves in the pack.

What we call leaf springs are technically semi-elliptic leaf springs. Full-elliptic springs are seen on some early cars and consist of two sets of leaves acting against each other. The two sets form a full ellipse. Most of these consist of a pack of flattened "leaves." The main leaf has an eye at either end; these eyes attach to the frame, with a bushing at one end and a shackle at the other.

Leaf springs have been popular from the earliest days of the automobile and were used to soften the ride on great-granddad's buggy. Part of the allure of leaf springs, especially in the early days of automobiles, is the relative ease with which they can be built.

Even the local blacksmith can hammer one out from a piece of heated steel and then give it temper with a dip in the vat of cooling water. Leaf springs have a second advantage: they locate the axles or suspension members, thereby simplifying the construction of early automobiles.

The downside to a leaf spring includes a certain minimal sex appeal. Besides that, leaf springs are heavier for a given capacity than a coil spring. However, they compensate for some of that weight gain by eliminating one or more suspension arms.

When I spoke with Ken Fenical, owner of Posies and perhaps the best-known manufacturer of hot rod springs, he was excited about quarter-elliptic springs. Essentially, these applications take what we call a leaf spring and cut it in half. Seen recently on the front of

Polished shock bodies and chrome-plated springs make for a good-looking coil-over, especially important when the suspension is highly visible. Like most high-quality shocks, these are available with a variety of springs and offer a six-position adjustment for rebound damping.

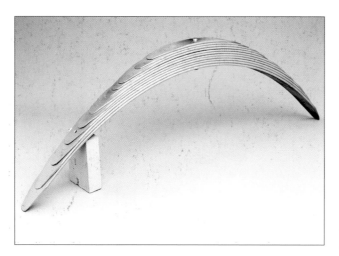

This spring pack is specifically manufactured to work with the 1940-Ford-style rear main leaf and provide a good ride and the correct ride height on a 1932 Ford.

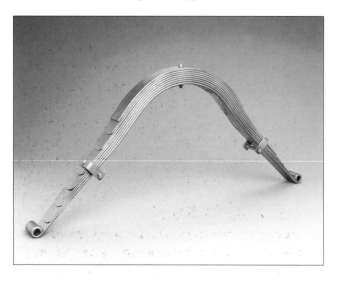

This narrowed Model A rear spring is intended to be used with the Model A-style quick-change crossmember.

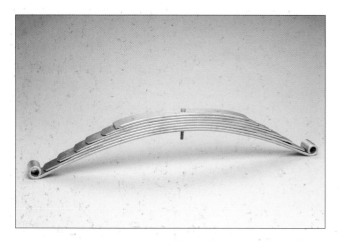

The front spring needs to be matched to both the weight of the car and the front axle. This example from SO-CAL, designed to work with 1932 Fords, is available in three versions.

some nifty track-roadster-type hot rods, the quarter-elliptic bolts the thickest part of the spring pack to the frame and then attaches the end of the main leaf to the axle.

BUYING SPRINGS

Buying leaf springs is pretty much a matter of matching your needs to the growing number of spring options in the catalog. These springs are typically listed by application, not by their rate.

In terms of strength and how high from the ground a particular spring will put your car, the best advice comes from the manufacturer. Many of the springs are available in standard form or de-arched to help get the car low and minimize the need for lowering blocks.

De-arching is an option for any leaf spring (and a better idea than removing individual leaves). You need to decide how much lower you want the car and give that specification to the boys at the spring shop. Before proceeding, consider that de-arching effectively makes the spring longer and can create an unusual shackle angle. In some cases, the upper shackle pivot may have to be moved back an inch or two.

If your street rod runs coil springs at one or both ends, then the options for spring choice are a little different. In the case of a Mustang-type suspension, the springs are usually ordered at the time you buy the suspension kit. If the springs come from the junkyard or swap meet, remember that not all Mustang IIs or Pintos came with the same springs. Later cars and cars with air conditioning or the V-6 engine used heavier springs. The best recommendation for spring strength in these cases can probably be had from the manufacturer of the suspension kit.

When you go looking for coil springs in the junk-yard, note that small increases in the diameter of the spring wire make large changes in spring stiffness. Second, by cutting the number of coils, you make a coil spring stiffer, not softer. Third, small decreases in the diameter of the spring itself result in relatively large increases in stiffness. As the spring gets bigger in diameter, it also gets softer.

At this point, we have to insert a warning concerning coil springs: a compressed coil spring stores an enormous amount of energy. Coil springs have the capacity to kill and maim. If you aren't familiar with the removal and installation of coil springs, ask for help or truck the whole thing down to the local suspension or front-end shop.

Experienced builders advise owners that it's better to go too soft than too hard when choosing springs. Most manufacturers offer technical assistance in the choice of both springs and shocks for your car. A constant-rate coil spring should never bottom out, or "coil bind." When you bottom out the coil, it stresses the metal and causes fatigue. Be sure the coil springs aren't too long for the job and that the axle hits the snubber before either the shock or coil spring reaches the end of its travel.

Before buying coil-overs for your car, consider the mounting angle of the shock and spring assembly. As the coil-over moves from vertical to horizontal, the spring's effective strength is reduced. At a 20-degree lean, for example, the effective spring rate is only 88 percent of the original rating. So if your coil-overs are mounted at a 20-degree angle from vertical, you need to use a 227 lb/in. spring to get a true 200 lb/in. spring rate.

The manufacturer of the springs for your coil-over may offer to exchange them if they turn out to be too stiff or too soft—it's worth considering when looking at two competing brands.

New to hot rods is the air spring, a concept that OEM auto and truck manufacturers have used for some time. Air springs come to the party with a number of inherent advantages. One is light weight; another is the air spring's progressive nature.

The formula for an air spring is $F = pa$, where F is the force applied to the spring strut, p is the air pressure in pounds per square inch, and a is the area of the piston. Assuming no temperature change in the air

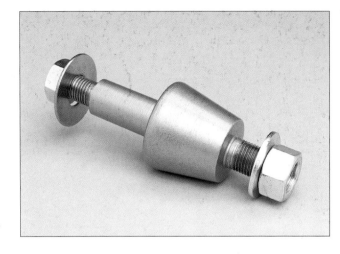

This lower rear coil-over stud is intended to space the shock far enough away from the housing that the spring won't rub on the rear end.

and that the bag or air spring does not deflect (which would change the volume), when you cut the area in half, you double the pressure. In the real world, there probably is some bag deflection and some temperature change, yet for all intents and purposes the air spring offers the hot rodder a spring with a progressive rate without the need for sophisticated linkages or specially wound coils.

SHOCK ABSORBERS

Damper is the correct term to use when describing the hydraulic device that damps a spring's oscillations. Like leaf springs, shock absorbers have been used since the earliest days of the automobile. The first

This set of shocks comes with a set of struts to replace the shocks during the mockup and installation of the suspension system.

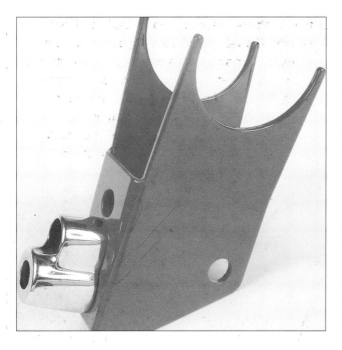

This lower coil-over bracket comes with three mounting holes for height adjustment. The spacer moves the coil-over away from the rear end and also spreads the load to two mounting holes instead of just one.

Built from billet aluminum, this Viper coil-over is meant for street rod applications. Available for front or rear, the Viper has adjustable valving for rebound damping.

shocks were friction shocks. As the name suggests, these early shocks worked by rubbing a series of discs together to dampen the up-and-down movement of the springs. The problem was their tendency to exert their greatest resistance at the beginning of movement. Once the initial "stiction" is overcome, a friction shock offers reduced resistance to movement. This is pretty much the opposite of what an engineer looks for in a shock absorber. Ever the innovator, Henry Ford was one of the first to understand the importance of shock absorbers, even on an inexpensive car, when he specified hydraulic lever shocks for the new Model A.

Today, tubular hydraulic shocks are virtually the only type used, and many of these use gas charging to improve the characteristics of a standard hydraulic shock absorber.

UNSPRUNG WEIGHT AND SHOCK ABSORBERS

At this point, we need to digress and discuss sprung and unsprung weight, terms you're likely to see if you pick up a book or article about suspension design for cars. It's also a factor you should consider when trying to decide which shocks, brakes, and wheels to buy. Most of the car (the frame, engine, and body) is considered sprung weight—weight supported by and acting on the springs. The wheels, tires, and brake components, on the other hand, are considered unsprung weight.

Consider your car as it goes down the road and hits a sharp bump. The bump forces the wheel up, compressing the spring. One of the goals of any good suspension system is to keep the tires on the pavement. When the bump in question drops away quickly, you want the wheel to change direction rapidly and stay in contact with the asphalt.

The problem at this point is the momentum of the wheel and tire, which makes them want to continue moving upward even after the pavement falls away. The compressed spring is trying to force the wheel and frame apart. How much of the spring's energy raises the car and how much of it forces the tire down depends on the ratio of sprung to unsprung weight.

A lighter wheel/tire/brake assembly will react more quickly to irregularities in the road while at the same time feeding less energy into the rest of the chassis. The compression damping of the shock absorber controls the sprung weight of the car, or how fast the spring is compressed as you hit a certain bump at a certain speed. The rebound damping, however, controls the movement of the unsprung weight—the wheel, tire, and hub assembly—as they change direction and move away from the car.

Early shocks were lever-action hydraulic shocks, though today most cars are equipped with tubular shocks. Simply put, tubular shocks have a piston inside that pushes oil through internal valves and passages as the shock is compressed and extended. By changing the internal valving and oil viscosity in a shock, manufacturers can alter the rate of compression and rebound to suit a particular vehicle. A Detroit sedan might come with shocks that are much softer on compression than they are on rebound—done as a means of achieving a good compromise between ride and suspension control. Hot rod shock absorbers tend to be valved closer to 50/50 (the same on compression and rebound).

The more sophisticated shocks use valves that respond to speed and inertia. A sharp bump encountered at relatively high speed compresses the shock quickly. A high-quality shock senses this speed of movement and unseats a large orifice, so the shock is effectively softer in this situation. The same shock will open a smaller orifice for a smaller bump. Essentially, the shock automatically changes its rate from soft to firm.

BUY THE GOOD STUFF

Fluid friction provides the damping in a modern shock absorber. A shock that works too hard, however, will heat up as the result of that friction. Cheap shocks allow air to mix with the oil, and the oil itself to change viscosity due to the heat. Either situation results in poor and inconsistent damping as the piston moves through an aerated froth of hot oil.

Inconsistent damping control and aerated oil are problems overcome by high-quality shock absorbers. In a quality shock absorber, all the components, from

pistons to shafts, are larger and are built to higher standards. The valves that control the damping are much more sophisticated, to better handle a variety of road conditions and driving styles. To better handle the heat, the amount of oil is increased. For better cooling, the body of the shock can be made of aluminum. To prevent aeration of the oil, the shock is gas-charged or filled with a premium oil that won't change viscosity.

MOUNTING TIPS

Though it sounds too obvious to mention, experienced builders say they often see cars where the upper and lower shock mounting pins (on a double-eye design) aren't parallel. Though most of these eyes are lined with rubber, the rubber bushings will compensate only for minor misalignment. Serious misalignment can cause the shock to wear out prematurely, bind, or even break the mount.

Shocks aren't meant to take the place of the rubber suspension snubbers. Though it's generally all right for the shock to limit the suspension travel in extension, you don't want the shock to be the limiting factor on compression. And, like all rules, this one has an exception. That exception is the shocks, mainly coil-overs, that come with a small synthetic doughnut located on the shaft, just under the head. These cushions are made from some high-tech material developed by firms like Koni to take the place of the external rubber and synthetic snubbers seen on most OEM applications. In some cases, the size and design of the built-in snubber can be changed.

Speaking of snubbers, Jim Sleeper from SO-CAL points out that in cars with limited suspension travel, the snubber effectively acts as another spring. If your car routinely hits the suspension stops and they're hard enough to "bounce the car up into the air," you're going to have a car that's hard to handle.

BRAKES

BY TIM REMUS

People are always talking about the "good old days." Well, things weren't always better back then—at least not for hot rodders. First, there weren't nearly as many components and kits available for the first-time builder. Second, some of the kits and components that were available left a lot to be desired.

Case in point is the early Mustang II front suspension often used by street rodders looking for independent suspension. While the suspension itself usually worked fine, many of those kits and clips came with the factory Mustang II brakes. The result was a hot rod with 9-inch rotors and a single-piston factory caliper.

If the car in question was a nice light coupe, everything worked just fine. On the other hand, if it was a fat-fendered sedan with a big-block, air conditioning, and a small trailer out behind—well, that's another story.

You'll notice that all the current ads for brakes in the hot rod and street rod press talk about how their system uses some derivative of the Mustang II suspension, but one that's upgraded with "vented 11-inch rotors and a midsize GM (or something similar) caliper." Nearly everyone has learned their basic physics: brakes that work on a 2,000-pound highboy can't stop a car that's nearly twice as heavy, especially at high speed.

The textbooks talk about kinetic (moving) energy and explain the basic relationship between kinetic energy, mass, and speed. Your car's kinetic energy equals half its weight multiplied by the speed squared. When you double the weight, you double the kinetic energy. Increasing the speed makes a nonlinear change in energy, however. Doubling the speed produces four times the kinetic energy (all other factors being equal). Of course, energy can't be created or destroyed, only converted to another form—in this case, heat. Thus, when you stomp on the brake pedal at 80 miles per hour, you're converting four times the kinetic energy into heat than you are at 40 miles per hour.

What all this really means is that the little nonvented, wimpy rotors from an American econobox just aren't going to do the job for your 1940 Ford sedan. You need bigger rotors and bigger calipers that can dissipate the heat. After all, these are hot rods.

The bigger rotors that now come standard with many brake kits work to your advantage in at least three ways. First, the larger diameter gives the caliper more leverage. Second, larger rotors allow you to use larger calipers. These come with bigger pads that are better able to grab hold of the spinning rotors. Finally, the larger components, both rotors and calipers, are better able to absorb the heat, simply because of their increased surface area (especially with vented rotors) and mass. The other bit of physics we should slip in here is the fact, probably well known, that the front brakes do at least 70 percent of the stopping on a hard brake application.

So, unless there are overriding aesthetic considerations, the front brakes should be discs. They're self-cleaning, they cool faster than drum brakes, and they also provide more total braking power for a given amount of weight than drum brakes.

Stopping a custom requires brakes that have both the right look and the proper amount of performance. This machine features gorgeous vented drum brakes.

The Lincoln Versailles rear end with disc brakes makes for a neat assembly that requires no adaptations, special brackets, or second caliper for the emergency brake.

As many Detroit manufacturers do, you may want to use discs in front and drums in the rear. In that case, what you want is more than just raw stopping power. You want balance in the total system. Whether it's a disc/drum system or pure discs, you need brakes big enough to handle the weight of your car, front and rear components that are compatible, and a master cylinder with a bore diameter of the right size to apply both the front and rear brakes.

The discussion of disc versus drum brakes brings up the new disc brake system designed by Paul Carrol and sold by the SO-CAL Speed Shop. A perfect combination of form and function, the SO-CAL "finned Buick brakes" use a Wilwood two-piston aluminum caliper and 11-inch vented rotor to provide good, modern stopping power. With a backing plate styled after an early Ford and a cover that looks exactly like a Buick brake drum, the whole

affair comes off looking like a very traditional set of drum brakes.

To match the Buick "drums" used on the front, SO-CAL has recently announced a new Buick drum for the rear. This new rear brake drum is actually a cover that slides over the rear drums used on a typical Ford 9-inch rear end. When viewed from the back, these new covers look exactly like a finned Buick brake drum.

HOW YOUR BRAKES WORK

When you step on the brake pedal, you displace hydraulic fluid from the master cylinder and create hydraulic pressure in the system. Because the brake fluid is a noncompressible liquid, the pressure created at the outlet to the master cylinder is applied fully to the pistons in the calipers or wheel cylinders. None of this pressure is "used up" compressing the fluid link between the master cylinder and calipers. When you're buying or installing the brakes on your hot rod, it's a good idea to keep in mind the two laws that govern hydraulic behavior: pressure in the brake system is equal over all surfaces of the system, and a fluid cannot be compressed to a smaller volume.

The problem with all this hydraulic business that we need more than pressure—we also need volume. This brings up the fascinating subject of hydraulic ratios.

A demonstration might help explain the need to match the master cylinder with the calipers or wheel cylinders. The pressure of the hydraulic fluid at the master cylinder outlet is determined by that old formula from high school: Pressure = force/area. If you put 10 pounds of force on the master cylinder piston with 1 square inch of area, you've created a pressure of 10 psi. If you apply 10 pounds of force to a master cylinder with only 1/2 square inch of piston area, you've created twice the pressure: 20 psi.

Remember that the full pressure created at the master cylinder outlet is available to apply to either calipers or wheel-cylinder pistons. So if we apply that 10 psi of pressure to the caliper with 1 square inch of piston area, the force on the brake pad will be 10 pounds (Force = pressure x area). If you double the piston area, you also double the force on the brake pad. Thus, the way to achieve maximum force on the brake pads is with a small master cylinder piston connected to calipers with large or multiple pistons and a large total area.

Now you get smart and decide to eliminate any need for a power booster by using a master cylinder with a small-diameter piston. There is, as always, a tradeoff here. The smaller piston doesn't move as much fluid as a larger one, and the pedal may be right on the floor when you've finally moved it far enough to displace enough fluid to push the pads against the rotor.

This brings you to the realization that what's needed here is a good balance between the master cylinder and the calipers or wheel cylinders. You can't just go to smaller-and-smaller-diameter master cylinder pistons or bigger-and-bigger-caliper pistons. In the real world, you probably want more pressure but still need a master-cylinder piston big enough to displace a certain volume of fluid.

Most experienced hot rod builders suggest you build the right system the first time, without relying on a power booster to overcome deficiencies in the design of the overall brake system.

You need to design the system around a good manual master cylinder and then consider the ideal balance between front and rear brakes (whether it's four-wheel discs or not) and how that balance is achieved. Detroit uses a combination valve between the front and rear brakes to help balance out a disc/drum brake system. That combination valve does more than "balance" the brakes—in most cases, it helps the system overcome two little problems with a disc/drum brake system.

The first little fly in the ointment when building a combination system is that drum brakes require more pressure for their initial application than disc brakes. Drum brakes, with their big shoes, return springs, and relatively large distance between the shoes and the drum, require approximately 125 psi to push the shoes against the drums with enough force to slow down the car. Disc brakes need only about one-tenth as much pressure to push the pads against the rotor with enough force to affect the car's speed.

The first job, then, of the factory combination valve is to "hold off" the front brakes until the system reaches approximately 125 psi. In this way, the car uses both the front and rear brakes to do the stopping, even on a light pedal application.

Job two for the combination valve is to slow the pressure rise to the rear brakes on a hard brake application. An easy stop from slow speed produces little weight transfer, and the rear tires maintain good traction. Consider the same car stopping hard from high speed. In this case, a great deal of weight is transferred onto the front tires. This leaves the rear tires with little bite and in danger of locking up. In this situation, the proportioning function in the combination valve limits the rate at which the line pressure is applied to the rear brakes, to prevent the rear tires from locking up.

Many professional builders don't use a combination valve, simply because it's hard to find one designed for a hot rod. Instead, they rely on the often-seen adjustable proportioning valve to limit the pressure delivered to the rear brakes.

USING RESIDUAL PRESSURE VALVES

A fair amount of confusion surrounds the use of residual pressure valves in a brake system. Drum and disc brakes have different needs here, and even all the disc systems don't have the same requirements.

A drum brake system, any drum brake system, needs a 10- to 12-pound residual-pressure check valve in the hydraulic system. On OEM applications, this valve is usually built into the master cylinder. As the name suggests, these valves maintain a small amount of pressure on the drum brakes at all times. This keeps the lips of the wheel-cylinder cups expanded out against the bore, preventing air ingestion past the cups when you release the brake pedal. This means that when you buy a master cylinder, you need to buy one with the correct bore diameter and match it to the type of brakes, disc or drum, used on either end of your new car.

The use of that same 10-pound residual check valve on a disc brake system will create brake drag, quickly ruining the pads and rotors. You need a check valve on a disc brake system only when the master cylinder is mounted lower than the calipers. In such cases, a 2-pound check valve prevents the fluid in the caliper from siphoning back to the master cylinder.

BRAKE FLUID

You might think brake fluid is just that, brake fluid. However, the shelves at the auto parts store carry at least three separate grades of brake fluid, which is essentially a specialized hydraulic fluid designed to operate in a potentially dirty environment under a wide range of temperatures. Obviously, the fluid must stay viscous at below-zero temperatures yet resist boiling at the high temperatures brake components are often subjected to. If the brake fluid boils, it becomes a gas and thus a compressible material, resulting in a spongy brake pedal.

The three grades of brake fluid commonly available are DOT 3, DOT 4, and DOT 5. DOT 3 and 4 are glycol-based fluids with dry boiling points of 401 and 446 degrees Fahrenheit, respectively. Either fluid is suitable for use in disc brake systems. There are two basic problems with DOT 3 and DOT 4 brake fluids: they tend to absorb water from the environment (they are hygroscopic), and they attack most painted surfaces.

Glycol-based brake fluid containers must be kept closed, so the fluid won't pick up moisture from the air. Because the DOT 3 or 4 brake fluid in your car will pick up some water, no matter how careful you are, it's a good idea to flush the system with fresh fluid every couple of years. Remember that brake fluid contaminated with water boils at a much lower temperature and can be corrosive to components.

DOT 5 fluid is silicone based and has a higher boiling point of 500 degrees Fahrenheit, dry. This more expensive fluid doesn't absorb water and doesn't react with paint (though silicone fluid can stain paint if not washed off quickly).

Like every other advance, silicone brake fluid has its tradeoffs. It costs more, it's slightly compressible, it aerates more easily than glycol-based fluid, and it's said to cause swelling of the brake cups and seals after long-term exposure. Some brake-component manufacturers don't recommend the use of silicone fluid, so be sure to check before filling the master cylinder. And once you've filled the master cylinder, don't switch from one type of brake fluid to another—they're not compatible.

THE PURCHASING DECISION

Before buying, consider that job number one is stopping and slowing the car during street driving (remember, these are street rods). They may be hot rods, but they're not race cars. Though the race car stuff may look impressive, it doesn't always work better than—or even as well as—components and systems designed for street use, including good old OEM stuff from Detroit.

What you buy will depend on your budget and intended use as well as the car's weight, bolt pattern, spindle, and style. In general, you want to buy as much brake as you can for a given amount of cash. An engineer once told me, "When you're considering brakes, more is usually better. More surface area, more pistons, and larger calipers."

Given the fact that the front brakes do 70 percent (or more) of the stopping in a hard stop, it makes sense to put your best foot forward. Always put the best brakes on the front.

The high-performance brake assemblies with polished aluminum calipers may look really trick—and most of that equipment works as good as it looks—but that doesn't mean you can't adapt OEM components from Detroit for the front or rear of the new hot rod. You simply have to be sure the parts you use are in good condition (if in doubt buy new or rebuilt components), that they are large enough to deal with your car's weight, and that they are matched to the other components in the brake system.

When considering the rear brakes, it helps to remember that you need more than brakes—you also need a good emergency brake. If you're using stock drum-brake assemblies in the rear, you simply need to buy cables and hardware and hook up the stock emergency brakes. If, on the other hand, you're using four-wheel disc brakes, the choice of rear calipers becomes more important because it also determines your emergency brake options.

Rear disc-brake calipers fall into two categories: those with and those without an integral emergency brake. Most of the calipers with an integral emergency brake are from Detroit, though Wilwood now makes a rear brake caliper with an integral emergency brake.

Corvette brake components are turning up on hot rods in increasing numbers, and there's certainly nothing wrong with using them, as long as you keep the system balanced and remember that not all Corvettes used the same brakes.

The calipers used on pre-1984 'Vettes have a host of problems all their own and should probably be avoided entirely. In 1984 the Corvette got a major redesign, including new brakes. The new single-piston calipers include a saddle assembly that reinforces the caliper. Some clever hot rodders have removed these saddles as a way to make the calipers work with small-diameter wheels. There is such a thing as being too clever, though: these saddles are part of the caliper assembly and should not be removed.

From 1984 to 1988, Corvette rear calipers used a separate emergency brake made up of small shoes that expanded against the inside of the rotor. A better choice for the street rodder might be the 1989 and later Corvette rear calipers, which feature a cable-operated emergency brake built into the caliper.

Other cars that use four-wheel discs with an integral rear emergency brake include some Camaros, Toronados, and Eldorados. In the Ford line, certain Lincoln Versailles and even some Granadas used the 9-inch rear end with factory rear disc brakes, and these calipers include integral emergency brakes. However, the latest rear calipers from Ford, used on many Explorers and T-Birds, use a very small-diameter piston and should be avoided.

Aftermarket calipers with no integral emergency brake on the rear axle will force you to come up with your own emergency brake. Some people choose to install an additional rotor mounted at the rear U-joint, clamped by its own mechanical caliper. The potential downside to this is that with a nonlimited-slip rear end, if you jack up one wheel, the car can roll off the jack. You can also mount additional, mechanical calipers on the rear rotors, but be sure these are substantial enough to handle emergency and parking duties on a 3,000-pound automobile. In other words, don't use little mechanical calipers meant for a 300-pound go-cart on your Chevy sedan.

BRAKE SERVICE

Hot rods tend to be the recipients of maximum care during any kind of installation or repair. Yet when working on the brakes, it's essential to go that extra mile to ensure that the brake installation is absolutely bulletproof.

When working on the brakes, it's important to follow the same procedures used by certified mechanics when they do brake work. Start with good attention to detail and follow that up with extreme cleanliness when dealing with the hydraulic system. To bleed brakes, most mechanics start at the bleeder farthest from the master cylinder (or that half of the master cylinder in a dual-reservoir system). If you've never bled the brakes before, you can get help from a good manual, such as Motors, or from the company that sold you the brakes. Another good source of brake service information is the Internet, where many Web sites include some good troubleshooting information.

Inactivity is hard on brake parts. Overhaul or replace wheel cylinders and calipers that come along with the rear end or front calipers you drag out of the junkyard. Discard any old factory rubber hoses and replace them with new components. Master cylinders, too, should be overhauled or simply replaced with new components. Be sure any master cylinder you use is a two-chamber design. Solvents will attack the rubber used as seals in brake systems, so all cleaning of hydraulic parts must be done with clean brake fluid.

Whether the old brakes you're repairing are disc or drum, many of those old pads and shoes contained asbestos. Wear a good respirator or air mask during the disassembly of used brake components, avoid the use of air tools, and don't clean everything up by blowing the "dust" off those old assemblies.

If you've never packed and installed a set of front wheel bearings before, swallow your pride and read a service manual. Plenty of bearings have been ruined because someone was overzealous in tightening the spindle nut or didn't get enough grease packed between the rollers, where it's needed.

When it comes to flexible hoses, braided lines look great and may be stronger than stock flexible hoses. Most, however, are not DOT approved and could cause your car to fail a state inspection (depending on which state you live in).

As for hard lines, a panic stop can generate as much as 1,600 psi in the hydraulic system—too much pressure for anything but an approved steel brake line,

Designed for disc brake applications, these chrome-plated, ribbed backing plates mount inside the rotor and add extra sparkle to the front end.

with double-flare fittings or systems specifically designed for automotive brakes.

Perhaps the most important step you perform is the examination of the car's brakes when the work is finished. Pressurize the system with a size 12 sneaker on the brake pedal, then crawl around under the car to check for leakage or seepage from every fitting, caliper, and wheel cylinder.

Before you're finished with the brakes, do a careful road test. Remember that new brake shoes haven't seated against the drums yet, and the hydraulic system might still contain a bit of residual air. In either case, the result can be a soft pedal and reduced braking on the first few applications. Take it easy on the first few stops. Don't be afraid to come back in and rebleed all or part of the system. Disc brakes don't need adjustment, but drum brakes, whether self-adjusting or not, need to be adjusted per the recommendations in the service manual.

DISC BRAKES

While not rocket science, caliper overhaul requires a certain finesse. If you've never done it before, take them to the shop down the street or just buy rebuilt assemblies. If you ignore this advice and force the caliper piston from the bore with compressed air, be sure the piston doesn't become an air-powered projectile. Stuff the caliper cavity full of rags first, and

be sure to keep your fingers out of the way when applying air to the caliper. Once apart, pitted caliper pistons need to be replaced, the caliper bore should be thoroughly cleaned with the correct brake hone, and the groove for the main piston seal must be cleaned thoroughly. The new seal and the piston should be lubricated with brake fluid or brake-assembly fluid before being installed.

Most of the calipers from Detroit are single-piston designs that float, so the force of a single piston is divided equally between two pads. If the pins or the sliding surfaces are dirty and rusty, the caliper can't float. You must be sure to clean all sliding surfaces, and replace the pins on GM calipers if they're rusty.

Many of the popular front brake kits mentioned earlier for the Mustang II and some early Ford axles combine an 11-inch ventilated rotor with the intermediate or larger GM caliper. The rotor used in some of these kits is thinner (.810 inch) than the stock GM rotor (.960 inch); that's why some of these kits also supply a spacer to be used behind the inner brake pad. If you leave out the spacer, the piston comes out farther than the GM engineers intended. This might be all right until the pads become worn, the end of the piston is pushed past the inner seal, and you lose the front brakes.

Nonfloating aftermarket calipers come with a series of small spacers. You'll need to use these to center each caliper as it mounts over the rotor. That way, each piston moves out of the bore the same distance on a brake application.

Caliper brackets should be original or come from a good aftermarket supplier. The full force of a panic stop is transmitted to the chassis through that caliper bracket, so don't skimp. Use a good bracket and bolt it to the spindle assembly with the hardware supplied with the kit or grade-8 bolts.

When you mount your new or rebuilt caliper to the caliper bracket, be sure that the bleeder screw ends up at the top. If not, you'll have to bleed the brakes with the calipers off the bracket. Next, hook up the hoses. Hoses should be new and carefully chosen to ensure they're the correct length. It's easy to install a hose that's too short or too long—a hose that will tear on a bump or rub on a tire. During the chassis mockup, be sure to run the suspension up and down and turn the wheels back and forth, to check for any potential clearance problems.

When ordering aluminum calipers, it's a good idea to specify stainless steel pistons.

Vented rotors handle the heat of stopping better because the vents help them cool and they have more total mass. A number of aftermarket vented rotors are designed to replace the solid rotors that came with many Mustang IIs and Pintos. They use stock bearings and come in a variety of five-bolt patterns.

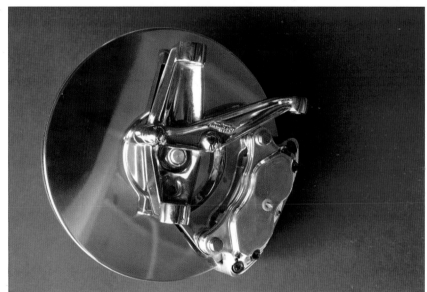

DRUM BRAKES

When rebuilding the old drum brakes, the hardware and springs that hold and retract the shoes should be replaced at the same time you're doing all the other work. Many good automotive parts stores and some street rod vendors sell brake hardware kits for most drum-brake applications.

On a drum brake system, adjust the brake shoes correctly before adjusting the cables for the emergency brake. Too much tension on the emergency-brake cables or linkage won't allow the shoes to come back against the stop at the top of the backing plate, which makes it impossible to adjust the shoes correctly. So be sure to adjust the brake shoes correctly before you worry about adjusting the cables and linkage for the emergency brake.

A few more tips for drum brake assembly: Don't get greasy fingerprints on the new brake shoes. If you do, carefully sand off the greasy spot with some 80-grit sandpaper before slipping on the drum. When installing used components, be sure to have the old drums turned before installation. Have the shop check the drum's finished diameter against the maximum given by the manufacturer, to ensure they aren't cut too far. The same applies to disc rotors, which can't be cut past a certain minimal point.

HARDWARE

BY TIM REMUS

The subject of nuts and bolts, something that seems at first so simple, could easily be the topic of two or three separate books. The fastener specifications used by NASA and the military do indeed fill volumes.

The trick is to remember that we're not building space shuttles, only hot rods. This doesn't mean that we don't need good bolts, lines, and hardware because we do. Where the space shuttle might be assembled with titanium fasteners, grade-8 steel is good enough for nearly anything we can bolt together on our hot rods.

SO WHAT'S A BOLT?

Simply put, a bolt is nothing more than a threaded fastener designed to screw into a hole or nut with matching female threads. But let's get a little nomenclature out of the way first. Technically, a *bolt* is a fastener without a washer face under the head, while a *cap screw* has a washer face under the head. For the purposes of this chapter, male threaded fasteners will be called bolts. Other bolt definitions include:

Minor diameter: the diameter measured at the smallest point, the bottom of the thread troughs on either side.

Major diameter: the diameter measured at the largest point, the tops of the threads on either side

Shank: the unthreaded part of the bolt's shaft.

Bearing surface: the raised and polished portion just under the head of a quality bolt or cap screw.

Length: measurement from the lower edge of the bearing surface, or the bottom of the head, to the end of the bolt.

Grip length: length of the unthreaded portion.

Thread length: length of the threaded portion.

LOAD, STRESS, AND STRAIN

Before looking too closely at exactly how good a grade-8 bolt is, we need to look at the types of loads bolts are subjected to and how those loads are measured.

Technically, the *load,* measured in pounds, is the force placed on a bolt or the force to which the bolt is subjected as it resists an external force.

Bolt descriptions are often followed by a psi figure. A good steel bolt might be rated at 150,000 psi. The pounds-per-square-inch figure is derived by dividing the load in pounds by the cross-sectional area of the bolt. This is known as the *stress* within the bolt.

If you put enough load on a bolt, it will change dimension, if only slightly. That change in dimension is known as the *strain.* As you continue to increase the stress on a bolt, it will continue to change dimension, but not linearly. At lower levels of stress, the bolt will "snap" back to its original dimension when the stress is removed. Beyond a certain point, however, the metal will have been stretched so far that it is unable to snap back. It's that point we've all experienced— the point where you feel the bolt "give."

Quality fasteners pull double duty when finishing a custom vehicle. They look good, of course. More important, they hold the machine together.

A quality cap screw has a raised surface under the head that bears on the surface it is tightened against. A good bolt or cap screw also has the head affixed at exactly 90 degrees to the centerline of the shank.

Allen bolts come in a variety of head styles, including the popular button head. Buttons must be used with discretion because the shallow socket head won't allow as much tightening.

Nuts with the integral synthetic collar make good locknuts and are available stainless or chrome plated. The only downside is the fact that the collar eventually wears out.

The give that's communicated through the wrench to your hand is known as the *yield point*. The bolt has stretched so far that it can't snap back to its original dimension. In most cases, if a bolt reaches its yield point and you don't tighten it further, it can be screwed out of the hole or out of the nut and may look just fine. But a close inspection will reveal that it's now longer than it was originally. Even if you can't detect the change with the naked eye, the bolt should be tossed in the trash.

If you continue to increase the stress past the yield point, the bolt will continue to stretch until it can stretch no further. The *ultimate tensile strength (UTS)* is the point at which the bolt breaks.

All of this makes a bit more sense when you consider it graphically. At lower stress levels, the graph of bolt stress versus strain is a nice straight line. Increases in stress create proportional increases in strain. Everything is nice and predictable until the line going uphill across the graph takes a sharp turn to the right.

The point at which the stress-and-strain graph hits its peak is the yield point. The metal has deformed at the molecular level and will continue to deform further with greater and greater amounts of stress until it ruptures.

Though most of us don't think about it (at least I never did), we want to tighten the bolt, or bolt and nut combination, until we've created a strain on the bolt, but not so far that we've exceeded the yield point.

TYPES OF STRESS

Bolts, or bolts and nuts, are asked to handle two types of loads. In the case of a cylinder head bolt, tightening the bolt to 100 foot-pounds puts enormous tension on the bolt. There is no side-to-side movement of the head. The bolt's job is to clamp the head in place and hold it there against the enormous pressure of compression and combustion.

If the bolt is holding an upper suspension arm or shock absorber in place, there is little tension on it—the load in this case is trying to shear the bolt into pieces.

Most of the bolts used on hot rods are loaded in tension—we are clamping something together with little or no side load. Most bolts are only about 60 percent as strong in shear as they are in tension.

We should also consider that shear can be further subdivided into single and double. A double-shear joint is much, much stronger than a single-shear joint.

BOLTS THAT GET TIRED

The subject of stress leads to the related concept of fatigue—the idea that even if the bolt doesn't break when you torque it down, it might break six months later, after a couple of million "on and off" cycles. High-quality bolts are designed to resist fatigue through the use of good alloys, high-quality manufacture and heat treatment, and good design. A good bolt has carefully manufactured threads and the correct heat treatment at the right point in the bolt's genesis. The head must be exactly perpendicular to the bolt's axis (even an error of just a few degrees increases stress within the bolt enormously), and the threads must blend smoothly into the unthreaded shank of the bolt.

HOW BOLTS ARE MADE

Most quality bolts are made in a rolling or forming operation. The raw stock, or "wire," is rolled through special dies that form the threads without any cutting. Though the method may seem odd, the reasons bolts are made this way are numerous and hard to refute.

First, cutting threads is time-consuming. Second, cutting leaves rough edges behind, while a quality rolling operation leaves a smooth, polished surface. Third, cutting threads means cutting across the grain of the bolt, making it much weaker. Rolling threads, on the other hand, encourages the grain to flow with the threads. Also, the rolling operation compresses or forges the surface of the threads, making them much stronger.

Less expensive bolts are made from mild steel, steel with a low percentage of carbon (ignoring stainless and exotic bolts for now). Bolts of this nature are weak and malleable. By adding a higher percentage of carbon, the strength of the material goes up, but so does the brittleness. This is a costly tradeoff when it comes to bolts loaded in tension, which need to retain some of their springiness to be effective.

Good bolts are commonly made from medium carbon steel, with other additives that provide strength without making the material too brittle or glasslike. One such additive is manganese; another popular combination is chromium and molybdenum (chromemoly). Good raw material, in combination with careful heat treating, can create bolts that are both strong and forgiving.

It's important not only that the bolt be heat treated but that it be heat treated before the thread rolling is done. Heat treating done after the threads are formed tends to anneal or normalize the compressed surface of the threads created by the dies, essentially undoing the "forging" done during the thread forming process.

THREAD SPECIFICATIONS

What we often call NC and NF (national coarse and national fine) are actually UNC and UNF (unified national coarse and unified national fine). This system came out of the confusion that arose during World War II when English mechanics tried to repair American airplanes with Whitworth (a British thread standard) nuts and bolts. The ensuing troubles convinced the Allies that they needed some type of unified thread form. The "unified" system they settled on retained most of the existing American standards and specifications. For those of us who still work within this American or unified system (as opposed to the metric system), those standards developed 50 years ago are still valid.

HOW STRONG IS STRONG?

Bolts are measured in pounds per square inch of tension or stress. The ultimate tensile strength is the point at which the bolt breaks. The other specification given for quality bolts is the yield point, at which the bolt will no longer bounce back to its original dimension once the stress is removed.

A grade-2 bolt, sometimes called a hardware-store bolt, is rated at 74,000-psi UTS up to a size of 3/4 inch. This same bolt has a yield strength of 57,000 psi.

Moving up the scale, a grade-5 bolt, the point where good bolts start, is rated at 120,000-psi UTS and has a published yield point of 92,000 psi. Grade-5 bolts are considered good enough for most general-purpose automotive use, engine covers, and light

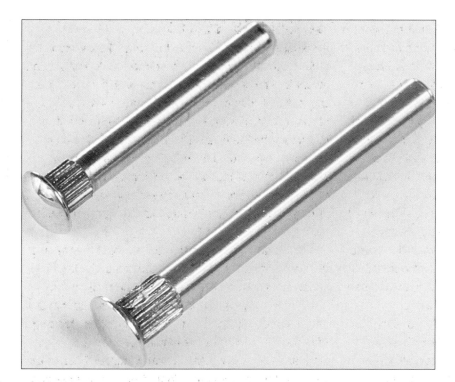

A good use of stainless steel door hinge pins for 1932 Fords and other vehicles.

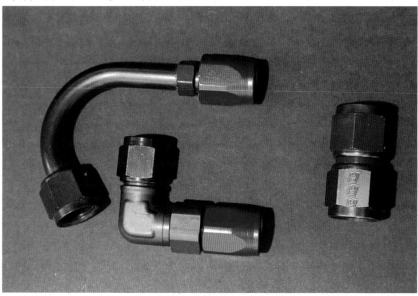

AN-style fittings for fuel, oil, and coolant lines come in various shapes and configurations, some designed for a crimped collar, some for a hose clamp, and some for a do-it-yourself compression-type connection.

double-shear duty. These bolts can be identified by the three radial dashes found on the head.

What many of us consider the ultimate bolt, the grade-8 bolt, is rated at 150,000 psi UTS and 130,000 psi yield strength. These can be used in heavy-duty double-shear applications, assuming the shank is the correct size for the hole it's being inserted into. A grade-8 bolt is generally considered an upgrade for engine assembly situations. Some builders get to a certain point where they simply don't want to use anything of lesser quality. Grade-8 bolts have six radial dashes on their head.

A variety of fasteners have UTS ratings of well over 200,000 psi. Aircraft and aerospace often require bolts with these higher ratings. In automotive use, the most common application for these high-strength fasteners is connecting-rod bolts, which may have a rating of 260,000 psi or more, especially for competition applications.

ALLEN BOLTS

Universally known as "Allen" bolts (Allen is actually a trade name), socket-head cap screws (SHCS) are loved by many hot rodders and most motorcycle nuts. The small head can be an advantage in many situations, but most of us use them for their apparent precision and the feel of "machinery" they lend to anything they touch.

Though many books state that all SHCS bolts are at least 170,000 psi for UTS, or better than a grade-8 bolt, this is no longer true. As with all the other hardware you buy, you now have to be careful where, and from whom, you buy your SHCS bolts. In particular, the chrome-plated variety are often only about a grade 5, but you don't know unless you ask. You also have to realize that these bolts often come with relatively long threads, which may have to be shortened with a die grinder or hacksaw.

The other little problem with these bolts is the small size of the head, meaning it's hard to use the full strength of the bolt to clamp things together. And if you use a standard washer under the head it will deform later, leaving you with a loose bolt. The answer is to use a hardened and ground washer under the head.

The only thing cooler than an SHCS is one with a button head. These little rounded heads look like rivets. The problem is that the button head allows for only a very shallow socket that won't let you get a good grip with the wrench. So don't use the button heads if you need serious clamping pressure.

The only people who like these socket-head cap screws more than hot rodders are custom Harley-Davidson builders; it follows that any good Harley-Davidson dealership or aftermarket shop will have a great selection of these bolts.

Chrome plating a bolt weakens it slightly. Compensation is provided by the fact that these are generally strong bolts to start with. Anyone who has used these bolts soon discovers that rust often develops down inside the head because the chrome-plating process just can't get plating down into those crevices. To make it worse, if the heads point up, they hold water! The answer is to use the little chrome caps that snap into the socket or put a dab of clear silicone on the end of the wrench the first time the bolt is used.

You can have your own bolts chrome plated, but considering the availability of chromed bolts, it's not a good tradeoff. While the nickel and chrome plating aren't very thick, the process does add to the dimensions of the threads, and that shiny bolt you just had plated might stick when it goes into the hole (or more likely when you try to screw it out). If you do have a bolt chrome-plated, be sure to mask off the threads, so they don't grow in size.

If in doubt about any bolt or nut, it's a good idea to chase the threads with a tap or die. If the die is doing much cutting, it indicates a problem with the bolt, and the best approach is to look for a replacement.

STAINLESS BOLTS

A discussion of stainless bolts is one of those topics sure to start an argument at the rod run. Many builders swear by stainless fasteners. They love the look and the fact that they never rust. You might say that chrome bolts never rust, but there's always the issue of flaking chrome or the way the inside of the Allen heads always seems to rust. Rust isn't a problem in the head of a stainless Allen because no coating is used. If you suggest that stainless bolts aren't as strong, their proponents respond, "I use grade-8 stainless, and they're great!"

If you add chromium to steel, you get the material we commonly refer to as stainless steel. The 300 series stainless steels are some of the most common; a typical example might contain 18 percent chromium and 9 percent nickel, in addition to a small percentage of carbon. While 300 series stainless bolts are resistant to corrosion (they're often called *CRES* in the industry, for *corrosion resistant*), they're not as strong as a grade-5 bolt. Most fastener-industry charts place them somewhere between a grade 2 and a grade 5, with a UTS of roughly 85,000 psi and a yield strength of only about 35,000 psi.

Some stainless bolts are rated to more than 200,000 psi UTS, but most of these are 400 series and are not commonly encountered in shops where we buy our bolts. The other problem with these 400 series stainless bolts is that they rust!

Stainless bolts also work-harden in service. What all this means is that stainless bolts are best used for light-load situations. Because they stretch easily and work-harden in service, some builders insist on using them only once (more controversy). Stainless threads also tend to gall, so it's a good idea to use Loctite or anti-seize compound to minimize metal-to-metal contact at the surface of the threads.

WHAT KEEPS IT TIGHT

You might think that the lockwasher is what keeps the nut on the bolt or the bolt in the hole. Actually, what keeps the bolt from unscrewing itself is friction between the male and female threads. By tightening the bolt to somewhere near the yield point, we have in effect stretched the threads. This stretch keeps the tension on the bolt and the friction intact between the male and female threads. Most locking washers and nuts work not so much by "locking" the nut as by maintaining this tension between the threads.

Because stronger bolts have a higher yield point, we can tighten the grade-8 bolt tighter than the grade-5 bolt (assuming the female half of this relationship is up to the task) and create more friction and more tension in the bolt.

The tension that keeps the bolt tight can also be the bolt's undoing. Consider the threads as a ramp wound around an axis. When you tighten the bolt, you're using mechanical force to move a load "uphill." No matter how tight the bolt is, anything on that ramp will always have a tendency to slide downhill.

It takes only a few degrees of rotation to eliminate the stress within a tightened bolt. What this means is that the cotter key that "keeps" the nut on the ball joint, or the safety wire used in competition, is meant primarily to keep the bolt and nut from falling off altogether once they become loose. The cotter key won't keep the bolt tight. What will help keep the bolt tight is a Nylok-type locknut, an all-metal locknut, a good split-ring lockwasher, one nut "jammed" up against the other, or a drop of Loctite properly applied.

Loctite comes in a confusing array of grades, some meant for light-duty work, others meant for parts that will never be unscrewed again. Most of us think of Loctite as "blue or red." Red is meant for heavy-duty applications, while blue is for smaller and presumably less important applications. The blue Loctite most commonly encountered in an automotive shop is either number 242 or 243. Both are considered "a medium strength threadlocker for fasteners up to 3/4 inch." Number 243 has a slight advantage, in that it's slightly stronger than 242, is quicker to set, and is more tolerant of a little oil on the threads. The common red 262 Loctite is a "high-strength threadlocker" and will require "extra effort and possibly heat for removal."

No matter which one you use, they work best on clean threads and require free metal ions and an oxygen-free atmosphere to work. What this means is that oily threads should be cleaned with Loctite's own Clean 'n Prime or something that leaves no residue behind, such as Brake Klean.

NUTS AND OTHER FEMALE THREADS

A bolt or cap screw isn't worth much without a matching set of female threads. Those threads might come in the form of threads cut in a casting or a nut with female threads designed to match those on the bolt.

Most of us have been taught that "a fine-thread bolt is stronger than a coarse-threaded bolt of the same size and rating." That statement is true when you have a bolt and nut combination clamping some-thing together. The fine-thread bolt and nut are stronger because the minor diameter of the bolt is larger than it would be for a coarse-threaded bolt, and because there is more net contact between the threads on the bolt and the nut.

The fly in the ointment comes when a high-quality 170,000-psi bolt is screwed into a casting made from iron or aluminum. Now we have a mismatch between the strength of the material the bolt is made from and the material the casting is made from. To compensate for the fact that the steel is much stronger than the cast iron or aluminum, the threads in the casting are often cut in a coarse thread. The larger, coarse threads in the casting increase the shear strength of those threads, making for a stronger assembly. Coarse threads are also better suited to the coarser texture of many of these cast materials.

FINAL WORDS OF WISDOM

After some years of turning wrenches, both as an amateur and a professional, it's embarrassing to realize that I've been doing many of the wrong things to bolts for much of that time. What follows are a few of those mistakes.

Don't cut "just one more thread" on that bolt. We've examined the care that goes into the manufacture of a good bolt—don't undo all that craft by cutting more threads. If it's the only bolt you have for the job and it's too long, put a washer or two under the head until you can get out and buy the correct bolt.

Don't torque a stud down into the casting. The threads at the bottom of the tapped hole are rounded slightly, due to the shape of the tap (even if they're cut with a bottoming tap). When you torque the stud into the hole, you put all the force on those few bottom threads. Studs should be screwed in finger tight. Use Loctite if necessary to keep the stud in place. Some mechanics go so far as to drop a small ball bearing down into the hole and then screw the stud down finger tight, until it contacts the bearing.

Don't use bolts with long, threaded shanks in shear applications. Buy one of the better cap screws, maybe even an AN (Air Corps/Navy), MS (military specification), or NAS (National Aircraft Standard) bolt from the airport, with the proper nonthreaded shank of the right length and the right diameter.

A bolt should be long enough, whether used in shear or tension, that when the nut is fully tightened, at least one full thread protrudes from the end.

Anytime you're in doubt, take the time to use a torque wrench. When you're torquing a bolt, much of the torque is used to overcome friction between the male and female threads and not to put the correct amount of stress on the bolt. Any dirt on the threads increases the friction, so be sure the threads are clean.

The other point worth repeating is to always use anti-seize on the threads of chrome and stainless bolts.

PLUMBING

When it comes to moving the common liquids around under the hood, the aftermarket now provides a vast number of choices. Yes, you can still use the good old OEM stuff or the materials available at the local automotive store. There's nothing wrong with that, as long as you use quality materials and install them with care.

When it comes to plumbing, however, more and more builders of hot rods are looking for an upgrade. Driven by a desire for quality and certain aesthetic considerations, many builders want braided hose with anodized aluminum ends. Companies like Earl's, Aeroquip, and others provide high-quality hoses with or without braided stainless covers, with matching ends. Both the hose and the hose ends are available as extremely high-quality components suitable for competition, or in three or four less stringent grades more suitable for street use.

First, we have to back up and explain that much of this high-end hose market started as surplus from the military and thus uses the AN measuring system. AN fittings all have 37-degree flares instead of the more common 45-degree flares used in most American OEM lines and fittings. Hose sizes are often indicated by one or two digits, all of which makes sense when you realize there is a method to the madness.

Common AN line sizes are "dash three," "dash four," and so forth. Dash three is generally written "-03". What does that mean in the real world? The 3 is the numerator of a fraction with 16 as the denominator. So -03 equals 3/16 inch. It gets a little confusing because the 3/16 doesn't indicate the exact inside diameter or even the outside diameter of the line. When the system was first implemented, each size was designed to replace an existing hard-metal line with a flexible line of about the same inside diameter. Thus, -03 has about the same I.D. as a standard 3/16-inch brake line. Get it? A dash four (-04) has the same internal diameter as a 4/16 or 1/4-inch steel line.

GETTING THE HOSE

The hose you use depends primarily on the fluid being moved, the pressure of the liquid, and exactly how

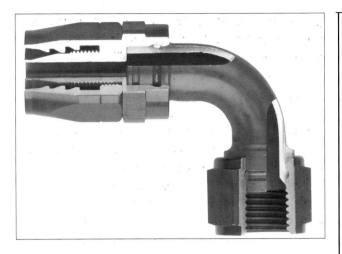

This cutout shows one type of reusable compression-style hose end. Specific hoses require specific hose ends, all designed as part of the same system.

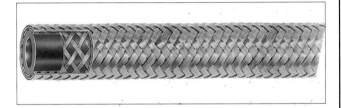

Designed to work with the reusable hose ends, this AQP Racing hose can be used with fuel, oil, or coolant, in temperatures from -55 to 300 degrees Fahrenheit. Available sizes run from -04 to -32.

trick you want the finished product to be.

In the case of water hoses, nothing is wrong with using molded hoses from the local auto parts store. If you know the size of the inlet and outlet and the approximate shape (you can even bend up a template with a piece of wire or coat hanger), most counter workers will help you find the right molded hose from among their substantial stock. The key is to use brand-name hoses and avoid the tendency to force the hose into something other than the preformed shape because most hoses will collapse at that point.

The stainless outer braid most of us are so enamored of is available raw, as are the colored hose "ends" (which are actually covers for the stainless hose clamps) that go along with the braided stainless look. This way, you can buy molded hoses and then cover them with braided stainless. The braid does more than provide that nice race-car look—it protects the hose from abrasion.

What you want to avoid are the corrugated radiator hoses—for aesthetic reasons, if no other. If you have to run the water a long distance, straight pipe

Stainless steel through-frame fittings like these make the job of plumbing the frame with brake lines much neater.

These neat, high-quality fuel manifolds are available pre-assembled for most popular carburetors.

can be used, with rubber "connectors" at either end. Any hard line like this must have beaded ends, so the clamped ends can't slip off. Any good radiator shop can make up a straight section of tubing and also do a nice job of beading the ends.

Like water hoses, flexible gas lines can be made up of the black neoprene hose available at the local auto parts store. Because current fuels have so many new additives, use only current, brand-name fuel lines. In most cases, a fuel line like this will slip over a

simple barbed fitting, where it's secured with a hose clamp. Remember, EFI systems run far more fuel pressure in the lines than was experienced in any part of a carbureted a fuel system, so pick your fuel lines and clamps accordingly. Upgrades in fuel lines include a variety of reinforced and braided hoses available from the aftermarket, most of which use brand-specific anodized ends.

These ends could be a chapter in themselves. A little time spent with an Aeroquip or Earl's catalog will open your eyes to the huge selection of hoses and ends available. The very best are good enough for competition use. At the other end of this aftermarket hose-end selection are the simple barbed fittings. But unlike the stuff from the auto parts store, these fittings are anodized in red or blue and look great when used with a stainless overbraid and clamp cover of the same color.

For many carburetor applications, fuel manifolds are available pre-assembled from a variety of sources. Fuel lines for Holley carburetors or a standard three-deuces are among those that are easy to find.

As always, you need to make sure the hose you use is intended to handle the application, be it gas, oil, or the high-pressure line to the power steering gear. The lines used between the automatic transmission and the cooler, for example, are designed specifically for transmission fluid. If you use something besides a barbed hose end, be sure it's matched to the hose brand and size. High-quality hose ends come in various configurations, so be sure the one you buy is the one you want, and follow the manufacturer's directions for assembly and testing.

BRAKE HOSES

If you assemble a radiator hose from aftermarket parts and it blows while you're cruising down the highway, you've created a mess and an inconvenience. In the worst case, you could damage the engine if the temperature is allowed to go too high before you shut it down. If the same thing happens with a brake hose, you've created more than an inconvenience.

The only truly approved hard line for brakes is the OEM-style steel hose with double-flared 45-degree fittings. Hot rodders often lean toward the stainless steel hose with 37-degree single-flare AN fittings. Though aesthetics drive much of these decisions, there's also the "I want this car to have the best of everything" mentality at work here, along with the related refrain, "I want this car to last forever."

Yes, a stainless line will last "forever," but in reality, a standard steel line will last nearly that long. From personal experience, it's obvious that steel lines commonly last a minimum of 15 to 20 years, even when the car is used daily in Minnesota's salt-infested winter driving environment.

When it comes to flexible brake hoses, a similar dilemma arises. DOT-approved hoses are the big, ugly black ones. The hoses everyone wants to use are the braided stainless hoses with anodized or polished ends. These braided hoses are made up of a Teflon liner inside a stainless braided cover. The hose can be purchased raw from companies like Earl's and Aeroquip, or pre-assembled hoses can be purchased with a variety of ends factory-installed. Most of these are rated at a minimum of 2,000 psi operating pressure and a burst pressure of more than 10,000 psi.

For most brake applications, an AN -03 hose is the right size. Clutch hydraulic systems probably require a -04 because they move a larger volume of brake fluid. Call me conservative, but I recommend buying the hoses factory assembled with the ends already installed. They can be ordered in nearly any length; if you can't get exactly the right fitting on the end, a whole raft of adapters is available to convert the pipe fitting thread in the caliper to the AN fitting on the brake line (for example).

A few final notes on brake lines and fittings. Pay attention to the flare—don't try to mate a 37-degree hose with a 45-degree fitting on the caliper or chassis. Yes, the materials are soft and will probably "give" enough to mate the two, but seepage and failure are likely results. If you have to mate the typical American 45-degree system with the AN 37-degree system, conversion fittings are available to do just that.

Be sure all the hoses you mount, especially the flexible ones, can't come in contact with a suspension member or the edge of the tire as the suspension goes from full extension to full compression or as the tires go from lock to lock. If you run the lines inside the frame, don't put any connectors where you can't see them, and be sure to test for leaks. Leak testing is part of the installation process. When everything is finished and the system is bled, get someone to literally stand on the brake pedal while you carefully crawl around underneath with a light, inspecting every fitting for any sign of leakage.

Whether you run the lines inside the frame or outside, they must be clamped in place. A variety of aluminum and stainless clamps are available from the aftermarket, to make your installation as neat as possible.

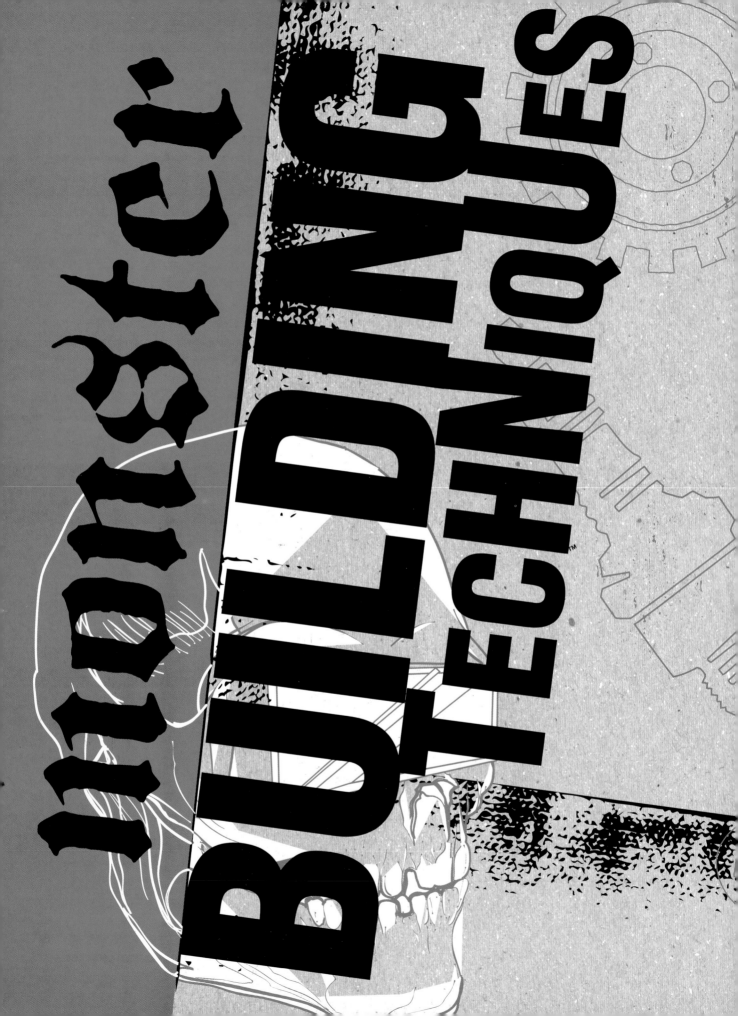

PART 3

MONSTER MANTRA #2:

INGENUITY CONQUERS ALL

"Sometimes you have to do what's right, even if it doesn't make you look good."

—Jim Day, metal fabricator/sculptor, episode 8 team member

In episode 8, the Monster team faced a challenge that got tougher as the build went on. How do you make a 1989 20-passenger bus float? When the winch-system test went awry, the group was faced with a burnt motor and a flawed system. With hard work, cooperation, and a little testy interaction, the bus was finished—and floated just as intended. The lesson? Use your head and you can overcome the toughest customization challenges.

COMPARING
WELDING
PROCESSES

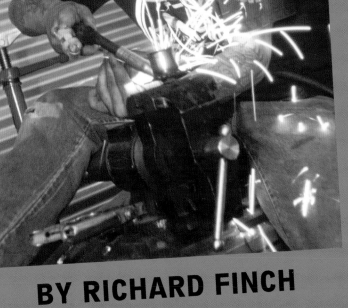

BY RICHARD FINCH

The first welding process used in building airplanes was oxyacetylene gas. A 1932 airplane builder's handbook specifies gas welding SAE 1025 thin-wall steel tubing to build airplane fuselages. Most of the mild steel tubing specified for building airplanes was 3/4-inch and 1/2-inch diameter by .035-inch wall thickness. Chrome-moly 4130 steel tubing did not become generally available to homebuilders until several years after WWII was over.

Heliarc welding came next, generally in the mid- to late 1950s. But heliarc welding equipment was relatively expensive and bulky at first.

Wire-feed welding, now called MIG welding, first became popular for heavy-duty welding in the auto industry when manufacturers used this process to mass-produce car and truck frames. In this chapter we will look at these welding processes, to help you decide which one best suits your finances and your intended use.

TUNGSTEN INERT GAS (TIG) WELDING

In this process, a high temperature but confined arc is formed that heats the base metal to the melting point for fusion welding.

TIG uses less heat to join metal than either MIG or gas welding. TIG welding is by far the most controllable of all manual (not automatic) welding processes. It is so accurate that you could weld a thin piece of .010-inch steel sheet to a thick piece of 6.000-inch steel billet and not burn through the thin sheet, yet get good penetration into the thick billet.

In fact, TIG welding allows for fusion welding without the addition of filler rod, making it possible to produce welds without extra weld seam buildup. With a foot pedal amp control or a thumb amp control on the TIG torch, you can strike an arc, start a tiny weld puddle, and without moving the puddle or adding welding rod, you can maintain the same weld molten puddle for minutes or even hours at a time. That is how controllable TIG welding is.

The advantage to this precise control is that it provides adequate time to properly add filler rod to the puddle. You can strike an arc, form a puddle, then carefully and accurately add just the right amount of filler rod at exactly the right place in the molten weld puddle.

RACE CARS

TIG welding is almost the universal choice in the construction of Formula One, Indy cars, Indy Lights,

Shown above is stick welding, which creates excessive smoke, bright light, and sparks.

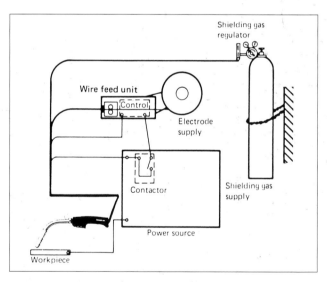

Typical MIG or wire-feed welding setups require these basic elements for operation.

and the smaller formula cars such as Formula Ford and Super Vee classes. The reason for this is the relatively small number of cars built in each of these classes. TIG welding is the most accurate of all welding processes, and with fewer cars to build, it doesn't matter so much that it takes a little longer to fabricate suspension and systems parts.

Look at Michael Andretti's backup Indy race car front suspension. It's made from 4130 steel tubing that has threaded inserts TIG welded in each end. MIG

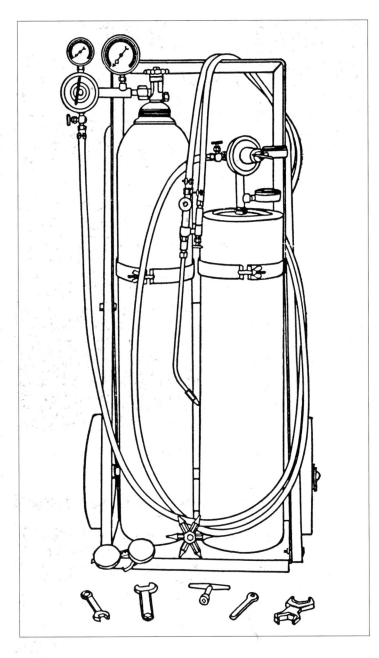

Gas welding setups haven't changed much since the early years. This drawing shows a typical commercial oxyacetylene welding rig used in the 1930s.

welding would not be adequate for those spindly-looking suspension tubes because MIG welding cannot be controlled accurately enough to make 100 percent sound welds. In the Jim Russell Formula Ford race car, note the smooth, accurate TIG welds in the frame and suspension. Again, MIG would have been less effective here because of the need for 100 percent accurate welds. And in the Buick V-6 Indy Lights radiator installation, it's easy to see that gas welding or MIG welding those parts would not have been easy or sound, if possible at all.

METAL INERT GAS (MIG) WELDING

This emerging process is commonly called wire-feed welding because a thin wire is fed into the weld puddle by an electric-motor drive system. It is quickly gaining popularity because it is easy to operate and is relatively fast. A TIG welder can weld about 6 inches of .050-inch steel sheet in one minute, whereas a MIG welder can weld up to 24 inches of the same material in one minute.

There are pros and cons to MIG welding the more exotic thin-wall 4130 steel tubes and thin sheets of 4130 steel used in aircraft construction. Here are some of the considerations:

PROS

It's easy to turn on the power switch, turn on the gas, and merely point the gun and pull the trigger to wire-feed-weld race car frames and aircraft fuselage structures. It's possible to weld a lot more inches per hour with MIG welding than with any other process because the welding filler metal is on a spool of wire that can be fed into the weld continuously, for as long as the welder holds the trigger down on the welding gun.

Usually, the MIG bead is a sound weld, almost as sound as a perfectly done TIG weld. Once the amps, volts, and wire-feed speed are properly adjusted, MIG welding is a high-quality process.

CONS

Probably the primary difficulty is that once you squeeze the trigger on the MIG gun, you're committed to move right along making a weld bead, ready or not. If you make a bad start, sometimes you have to stop, grind or cut out the bead weld, and start over.

Another problem is the normal tendency of an electrode-fed arc weld to start off cold. That means that each start of the arc is not fully penetrated for the first fractions of an inch of weld bead. Once the MIG weld bead is established, the heat and penetration are normal, but it always starts off cold.

Another disadvantage to MIG welding is that the process is highly intolerant of any gaps in the fit-up of the parts. Usually, the MIG wire is .025–.030 inch in

TIG welding is the easiest, cleanest, and most precise of all manual welding methods. The author is TIG tack welding a towbar bracket for one of his airplane projects using a modular MIG-TIG welder.

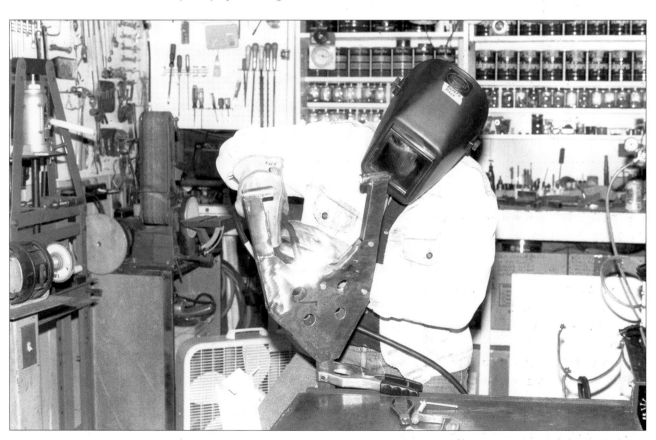

MIG welding with a 75/25 percent CO2/argon gas outer shield is the fastest but least accurate of all manual welding processes. The author MIG welds a towbar here.

Gas welding (oxyacetylene gas), as the author demonstrates here, is a relatively clean and dependable metal joining process, although less accurate than TIG welding. However, it's far less expensive than most other welding processes.

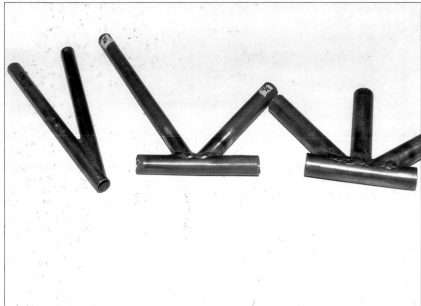

These aircraft-grade 4130 tube assemblies were welded by (left to right) TIG, MIG, and gas. TIG is cleaner and more accurate. MIG is fast and less accurate. Gas is slow and somewhat less accurate but reasonably priced.

Race car driver Michael Andretti's backup Indy race car makes use of TIG welding in the delicate but strong front suspension. Most of the welding on his car is TIG.

Most of the frame and lightweight fabricated front suspension on this Jim Russell Driving School Formula Ford car is TIG welded for strength and neatness.

You can see the TIG-welded aluminum radiator filler tank (at left) on this Buick V-6 Indy Lights race car. The TIG-welded exhaust system is complicated but actually easy to fabricate by proper fitting and TIG welding.

The author TIG welded both engine mounts, all the turbocharger brackets, the stainless steel exhaust wastegates, the aluminum air boxes, and the gas heater exhaust on this Aerostar. He also MIG welded all six seat frames. Silver solder was used to make strong electrical connections at the rear-mounted dual 12-volt batteries.

From the mid-1970s on, Bellanca Viking airplanes featured a MIG-welded fuselage, tail structure, and landing gear assemblies. Before about 1975, they were welded by TIG and gas.

Bellanca Citabria aerobatic airplanes feature MIG-welded 4130 steel-tube fuselage and tail structures. A completed Citabria is in the background.

This closeup of the Bellanca Citabria door frame shows the detail of the MIG-welded tubular structure, door hinge plates, and finger doublers that make this a strong fuselage.

This Glastar experimental airplane employs riveted aluminum wings and tail and a MIG- and TIG-welded 4130 steel-tube structural frame under the fiberglass skin of the fuselage.

This VW Scirocco-class SSB race car complied with SCCA racing rules, with the addition of a TIG-welded roll cage, TIG-welded window net brackets, and TIG-welded 5-point seatbelt restraint brackets.

Most of the frame welding on this ARS race car is by MIG.

diameter, and if there is a gap of more than the diameter of the electrode, the wire can slip into the crack and not make a weld bead. Another disadvantage of welding small-diameter thin-wall tubing with MIG is that once you accidentally burn a hole in the tubing, it's hard to fill the hole without stopping to make a patch for it, or you may have to use gas welding to patch holes.

RACE CARS

A number of classes of racing depend on a few constructors to build relatively large numbers of race car rolling chassis. The requirements to provide dozens of tube frame race car chassis dictates using the fastest fabrication methods. MIG welding fills that need.

AIRCRAFT

Many aircraft fuselages have been MIG welded in the past 25 or 30 years. Obviously this welding process works, and airplanes or components welded by this process have had few or no problems as a result of it. Although it may seem that the inherent need to start welding cold and to weld a steady, straight bead would be a problem in small-diameter thin-wall tubing, there are several solutions. Often, the demands of quantity require the faster construction methods possible with MIG welding.

GAS WELDING

The oldest aircraft welding process is still a good, dependable process. Oxyacetylene welding is very much the same as it was in 1920. The two gases,

Stick (arc) welding was used to attach the brake-drum backing-plate adapter ring to the axle on this 1938 Army Air Force training airplane wheel assembly. Arc welding is obsolete for aircraft assembly since TIG and MIG processes were invented in 1945 and 1955, respectively.

This World War II observation airplane axle assembly was fabricated by gas welding. This process is still viable and structurally adequate for similar aircraft.

oxygen and the fuel gas acetylene, are the same as they have been for 100 years or more. The gas welding torches have slowly evolved, but a torch made 50 years ago would still be a dependable aircraft welding torch. And gas welding rigs are still the least expensive of all welding setups.

The neutral flame (equal pressure of oxygen and acetylene) combines to produce a flame temperature at the inner core of about 5,000 degrees Fahrenheit, a temperature also used in TIG welding. The difference is that the oxyacetylene flame produces fewer BTUs (units of heat) and produces much more heat of a lower temperature at its outer flame.

What this means is that in the process of welding a butt joint of thin-wall tubing, the heat-affected area of the tube will be several times larger with gas welding than with TIG or MIG. But that's seldom a problem. The flame does heat the assembly up more, but in steel and aluminum thicknessses of less than .100 inch, the gas welding torch is adequate.

Gas welding has a few difficulties. When you attempting to weld inside corners, the flame is blown back toward you, making the heat on your hands uncomfortable. Another difficulty is welding next to an edge of tubing or plate. The heat of the torch is considerably broader than with TIG or MIG, which causes sharp edges to want to melt away. The solution is to add extra length to the joint to be welded and then trim it to the correct size after the weld is completed.

SHOPPING
FOR
EQUIPMENT

BY RICHARD FINCH

You can calculate your budget and go shopping for your welding equipment. In this chapter, we'll look at your choices and make suggestions about where to look for equipment.

Up front, you should know that some stores sell cheap welders and can't even tell you how to use the machine. You can buy arc welders for less than a hundred dollars and MIG welders for less than two hundred. I've seen several of these machines and tried them out. These welders could turn you against welding pretty fast! They'll make you think welding is an art you can't master.

Leave them at the store where you found them. If you did accidentally buy one, it's unlikely you could ever find repair parts for it and highly unlikely you could even get it to work the way it's advertised.

WHERE TO GO

RETAIL STORES
Much like car dealerships, service after the welding supply sale is as important as the initial purchase. Shop at least three or four local dealers before you decide where to do business. Retail welding stores vary widely in service. Don't fence yourself into doing business with a bad dealer.

TENT SALES
Tent sales, usually held in parking lots of established welding-supply businesses, are great places to see new technology and get bargains on name-brand equipment. At one tent sale, I discovered a new, light-weight, square-wave TIG and stick welder that would be perfect for small shops, home shops, and as a portable welder in a big shop. It was so new that the few brochures about it were photocopies that had

pencil-marked changes. About six months later, I saw the first full-page color ad in a monthly magazine.

MAIL ORDER
Two of my gas welding outfits came from mail-order dealers, and they both work okay. One gas welder was advertised to work *almost* as well as a TIG welder,

You can buy a good, dependable, TIG stick welder like this Lincoln Idealarc at company closings and school closeout sales. This is a good TIG welder but lacks the newer square-wave features.

Tent sales like this one at welding supply outlets are good places to find sale prices on welding equipment and to try out the newest welding equipment.

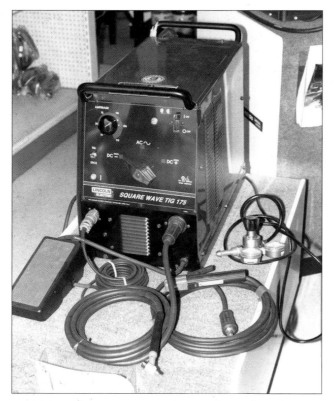

One of the newer square-wave AC/DC TIG and SAW (stick) welding machines is this 175-pound, 175-amp Lincoln square-wave welder, complete with all accessories except a cart and argon bottle.

The next step up in a TIG welder is this electronic control panel Lincoln square-wave TIG 255-amp welding machine.

but it doesn't. I didn't expect it to, so I'm not disappointed. But if I had expected it to be as advertised, I would have returned it for a refund. The lesson here is to make sure you can return *any* piece of welding equipment if it doesn't perform as advertised. But don't wait too long to request a return. Companies frown on people who buy equipment, use it for a project, then ask for refunds.

USED WELDERS

One local college recently shut down its entire machine shop program and sold all the machinery at 10 percent of acquisition cost. A large aviation corporation in this same area recently went out of business and sold everything, including several high-quality TIG welders, at an auction. These units sold for 10 to 20 percent of original acquisition cost. Good-quality, name-brand welding equipment should last for 50 years or more if properly maintained. Consider buying used equipment if your budget is low.

NAME BRANDS

In the last 10 years, many welding companies have been sold or merged with other companies, often forming new companies with new names. The same phenomenon is still happening. Two longtime, well-known welding equipment manufacturers, Miller Electric and Hobart Brothers, merged under the management of Illinois Tool Works. Also under the same management are PowCon, Oxo, Tri Mark, Corex and McKay, other longtime companies in the business. Therefore, it's wise for anyone who plans to stay current in the welding field to visit American Welding Society meetings, visit your local welding trade schools, and attend at least two or three welding trade shows every year.

GAS WELDERS

Don't buy the cheapest discount-store or mail-order torch you can find. Stick with brand names such as Victor (now Thermadyne), Harris (now Lincoln), and Smiths (still Smiths) You might also want to investigate the pistol-grip Dillon/Henrob as a second torch. One loss-leader at those tent sales is the small, portable gas welding and cutting rig. But make sure you can buy extra tips and extra rosebud tips for any torch you decide to buy. No spare parts should mean *no sale*!

TIG TORCHES

TIG torches come in many sizes and qualities. For most aircraft welding, a small water-cooled torch is the best, such as a torch that can be adapted to gas lens operation. The best way to shop for a TIG torch is to ask to see a selection of collets, chucks, and cups for that torch. If you can buy a full range of collets, from .020 up to 5/32 inch, you can expect good service from the torch. If parts aren't available, don't even think about buying it.

SQUARE-WAVE TECHNOLOGY

Just as in the computer industry, electronics have progressed in welding equipment to provide a smooth-output arc for AC aluminum and magnesium welding using square-wave technology. This technology also smoothes out DC output when welding steel, stainless steel, and titanium. My advice is not to buy any new TIG or MIG welding machine until you've compared square-wave technology with the original AC/DC equipment. My guess is that you'll go with a square-wave welder. All the name-brand welder companies now manufacture these machines.

PORTABLE RIGS

Trailer- or truck-mounted portable welding rigs are a thing of the past. New inverter technology makes it possible to have a pipe-welding-capacity welding power supply not much larger than your arc welding helmet that you can carry in the trunk of your car. Currently, none of them will weld aluminum or magnesium, but you can expect that to change.

MODULAR ADD-ONS

For about half the price of the lowest-cost TIG welder,

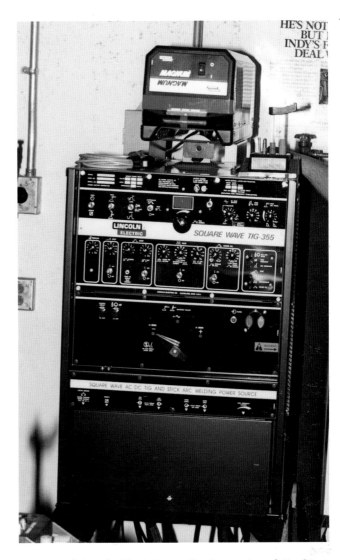

Tim Marr of Lincoln Electric proudly shows a top-of-the-line square-wave 355-amp TIG and stick welder that has numerous extra features.

The dream of many home shop welders as well as those with portable weld rigs is this 190-amp TIG welder that runs off 110-volt house current or 220-volt shop current. It's a DC-only welder that weighs only 19 pounds!

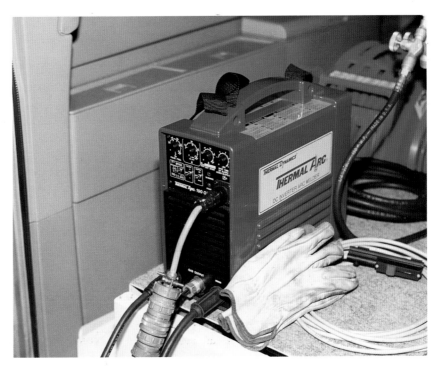

ESAB Corporation makes the original Heliarc welders. These 252-amp and 352-amp TIG and stick welders also feature square-wave technology.

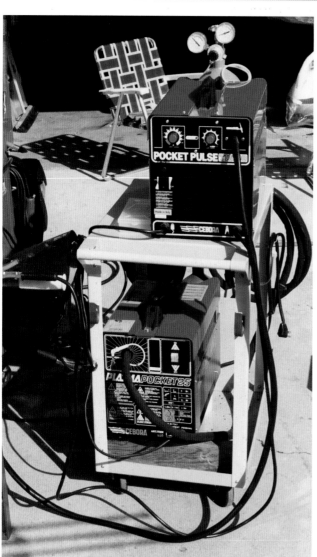

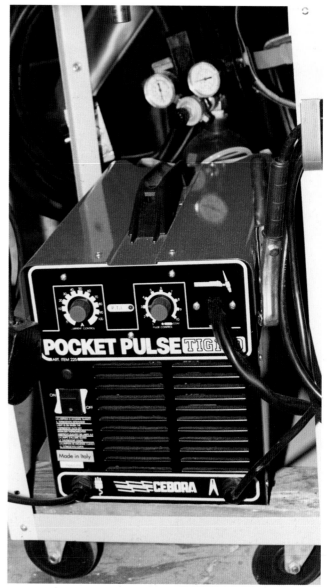

Daytona MIG Company specializes in mail-order sales of this Pocket Pulse TIG DC-only welder and the 110-volt Pocket Plasma Cutter that are nice for small shop use or as backup machines in larger fabrication shops.

This 220-volt Pocket Pulse TIG machine is made in Italy and sold by Daytona MIG Company through ads in car magazines.

Modular TIG adapters such as this MTA160 sold by Daytona MIG make it possible to use the transformer from a MIG welder or a DC-only stick welder to have TIG capabilities.

Electronic welding helmets let the welder see the TIG, MIG, or stick at a sunglasses #3 shade before striking the arc, then change to #10, 11, or 12 lens shade virtually instantaneously after the arc is started.

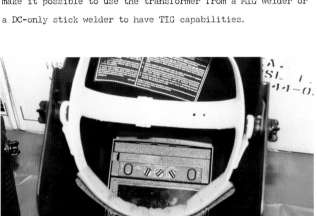

The back side of the Jackson electronic welding helmet shows the five buttons that adjust the shades at which this helmet will operate.

The author's favorite-size TIG torch is this Weldcraft WP-10 with a short back cap. This water-cooled torch will weld up to 1/4-inch-thick aluminum and steel.

Tim Marr demonstrates the TIG torch thumb control that starts and stops this large water-cooled torch without the need for a foot control. You can't operate a TIG foot control when you're on your knees trying to weld something a foot off the floor.

Every TIG welder needs to ask Santa Claus to bring him one of these TIG cradles made by Raterman Manufacturing of Santa Clara, California. It conveniently holds all the TIG parts a welder needs.

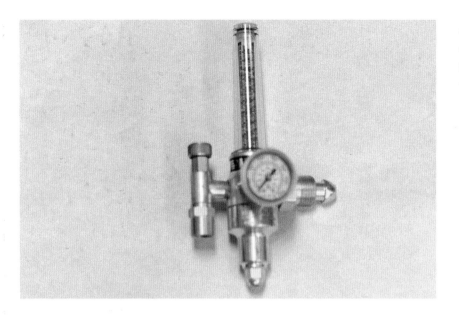

An often-forgotten accessory for a TIG welder is a second argon flowmeter for back-gas-purging stainless steel and titanium welds.

This heavy-duty TIG or MIG torch water pump pays for itself in recirculating cooling water rather than letting the water go down the drain.

Miller Electric of Appleton, Wisconsin, makes this closed-circuit coolant radiator for TIG and MIG water-cooled torches.

Miller Electric sells this 150-pound Econotig welder that does AC/DC TIG welds as well as stick welds.

you can purchase a modular TIG add-on that features capacitor start or, in some products, high-frequency (the best) start. This means that if you have a "good old" stick welder or a "good old" wire-feed welder, you can use its transformer to power a TIG torch, even with a foot pedal control and argon gas timing.

ELECTRONIC HELMETS

For many years, welders who did stick, TIG, and MIG welding were forced to aim the torch, stick, or gun at the weld with their helmet up, then shake their head to lower the helmet and hope their aim at the weld joint hadn't moved. This problem was the biggest obstacle to learning to weld quickly. Even us oldtimers never really mastered the "flip the helmet down" trick. And we always had to stop welding, raise the helmet, and look to see if we'd made a good weld.

Some savvy engineer figured out an electronic welding lens that's a shade 3 (sunglasses shade) when no welding arc is present and a shade 10, 11, or 12 as soon as an arc is struck. The change isn't instantaneous. You do see the arc, but only for about 1/500th to 1/125,000 of a second. What this means is that at the end of a long day of arc welding, your eyes will itch about the same as if you'd spent the day at the beach without sunglasses. These helmets start at $100 and cost up to $275 or more. They really do contribute to much more accurate arc starts in stick, TIG, and MIG welding as well as plasma arc cutting.

THUMB CONTROLS

You won't always be able to TIG weld at tabletop level. A day will come when you must weld standing

These modular units, which allow fabrication shops to tailor their welding equipment to the needs of the shop, are becoming more popular.

on a ladder or the weld is 6 inches off the floor. For many years, the solution to those hard-to-reach TIG welds was to lay a brick on the foot pedal and hope for the right amount of heat from the torch or go find a helper to push the pedal for you when you said to. Welds made this way were never as good as they could be.

The solution to that TIG welding problem is to buy a thumb- or forefinger-operated TIG amp control switch that you tape to your TIG torch with Velcro. You won't use the switch much, but when you do need it, you'll be happy you have it.

For repeatable, high-quality TIG, MIG, and stick welding, Miller provides a full control panel on this Syncrowave 250 arc-welding power source.

A higher-powered Miller Syncrowave 500 constant-current AC/DC arc welding power source is suitable for large shops with lots of big welding jobs.

EXTRA FLOWMETER

For less than $90, you can buy a spare flowmeter for use in making back-gas purges of stainless steel and titanium welds. The price of the extra flowmeter is so low that just one critical weld project will pay for it. This is not a starting kit item because you might weld for many hours before you ever need to back-gas-purge something, but when a stainless steel or titanium weld project comes up, by all means invest in a spare flowmeter.

PLASMA CUTTER

Plasma cutting has many advantages, especially when you compare cutting chores to hand hacksaw cutting, oxyacetylene torch cutting, and the high cost of making dies for stamping out small parts. These machines cut pencil-thin kerfs in any metal and leave little dross or slag on the back side of the cut.

The big advantage to plasma cutting is that it cuts all metals with equal ease. Plasma will cut a stainless steel plate into exhaust pipe flanges just as easily as it will cut the same thickness mild steel plate. And without changing at settings, you can immediately cut out 6061-T6 aluminum plate for welding special intake manifolds.

Stainless steel is one of the hardest of all the common shop metals to cut. It is so resistant to cutting that it will dull an expensive, high-speed bi-metal hacksaw blade in just a few seconds. Then the new blade is just scrap. The only efficient way to cut stainless steel of any thickness from .020 up to 3/8 inch is with a shop-air-operated plasma cutter. Cutting stainless steel plate or sheet, aluminum plate or sheet,

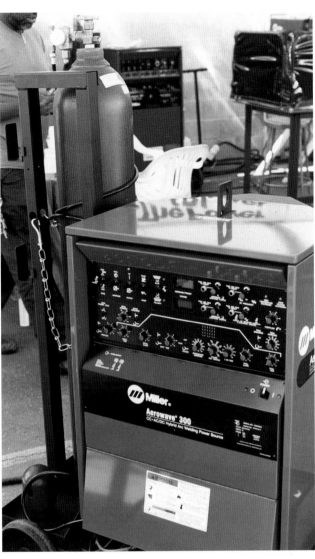

This is a high-tech TIG welder purported to be able to weld aluminum race-car blocks back together with ease.

Every welding shop, regardless of size or types of welding, should have one of these portable gas welding/cutting/heating rigs.

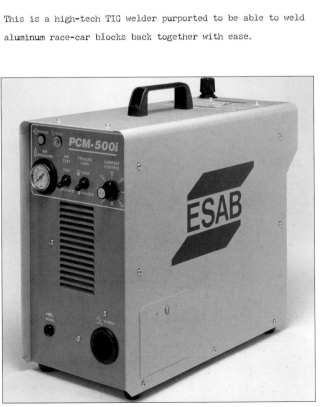

Portable plasma cutters are a time- and money-saving investment if your shop spends two hours a day in metal fabrication.

The author paid $15.00 for this new, air-operated die grinder and cutoff wheel. Any shop should have one or more of these.

Defective welds are easily cut out with an air-operated die grinder, as the welder is doing here on a Lycoming engine mount.

Buy several of these magentic angle jigs. Once you use one, you're addicted.

4130 steel plate or sheet, and even brass and copper with plasma is almost as easy as drawing a line on the metal with a marking pen. But free-hand plasma cutting leaves an often shaky cut line, so you should try to provide a guide for your cuts with a plasma cutter.

Any welding shop that uses a TIG or MIG welder for even two hours a day would benefit from a plasma cutter. Any shop that fabricates mild steel or stainless steel exhaust systems absolutely must own a plasma cutter, especially for cutting out 3/16-inch and 1/4-inch flanges for the pipes.

Plasma cutters are available for 110-, 220-, or 440-volt operation. Mail-order welding supply companies all feature 110-volt plasma cutters, but some bottom-of-the-line cutters must be push-started, which is not very useful. Remember the motto: "Try it before you buy it" or make sure you get a satisfaction guarantee.

SHOP TOOLS

Every weld shop must have one or more air-operated cutoff tools and a small angle sander. Tubing benders are a necessity, and several new models exist today. Many new benders feature hand-operated hydraulic jacks to make smooth, wrinkle-free bends in thin-wall tubing. Most of these tubing benders will be mail-order purchased. You can find addresses and phone numbers in race car magazines and aircraft builders' magazines.

PART 4

BEAUTY IS SKIN
DEEP

"The irony of this project is
that I was just watching a show
on how to survive in a car when
it's underwater."

–Jesse James

In episode 3, a Volkswagen Beetle is
transformed into a working swamp
boat. Making a car float and driving it
with a prop and second motor was
a challenge the team met with aplomb.
One of the remarkable results was how
good the Beetle looked afterward.
The key to that was a gorgeous custom
paint job with three different orange-
pearl base coats, one hot pink base
coat, two coats of gold-ice pearl, and
a clear coat on top. The lesson?
A killer paint job makes the machine.

CHAPTER
4.1

PAINT YOUR
MONSTER

BY DENNIS PARKS

With the automotive paint products now available, you have perhaps the best opportunity ever to achieve a perfect paint job. What you must realize before you start is that there's much more to painting a car than squeezing the trigger on a spray gun.

Get the body as straight and as smooth as possible. Painting over imperfections is only going to highlight them. Follow the guidelines in this chapter for

> "Paint time depends on color scheme and design. Basic colors are usually only a couple of days. Pearls, candies, metal flakes, and other exotic colors take about an extra two days. The Impala/Ice-Resurfacer was a two-day project, but in an upcoming episode you'll see a project that took 126 man-hours to complete."
>
> —Tom Prewitt, Custom Painter,
> Damon's Custom Creations

making the surface perfectly paint-ready. You must also mix primers, hardeners, topcoats, and catalysts as directed. The directions are included with the product . . . you just have to read them. The chemistry of automotive paint has already been determined for you. There's no reason to try to "improve" the characteristics of any paint product. Mix the components as directed, apply them as directed, allow them to dry as directed before applying successive coats, and you can create a professional paint job on your car.

You must also have the right tools, and as with most jobs, that also requires the correct safety equipment. Today's paint products are safe to use, but only when used properly. Correct safety equipment, such as respirators, rubber gloves, and painter's coveralls, is essential. Learn what safety equipment is required for each type of paint product.

AUTOMOTIVE PAINTING DEFINED

Depending on the job at hand, paint can be applied to automobile bodies in more than one way. Initially, our cars or trucks roll off the assembly line with a fresh coat of paint. Eventually, they begin to need slight touchups to keep nicks or scratches from blemishing their fresh appearance. This is usually done with a small brush attached to the cap of a bottle of touchup paint. If wear and tear necessitates the painting of small body items or trim, you might use a spray can to bring that finish up to snuff. If your automobile has sustained collision damage, repair will usually involve repainting the affected panel(s) or sections with conventional paint spray guns.

The techniques used to apply automotive paint are determined by the type (and amount) of coverage needed and the condition of the existing surface material. You wouldn't use a full-size spray gun to touch up a small scratch; nor would you expect to use a touchup brush to refinish an entire panel. Likewise, paint from a spray can might be "close enough" in color match and texture to refinish or modify a trim panel, such as a grille or body molding. If the entire vehicle is going to be repainted, however, paint specifically meant for automotive refinishing should be used.

To achieve a visually acceptable, compatible, and durable paint job, use products designed to suit the existing paint finishes or undercoat preparations. The finest paint job in the world will not last if the various layers of body filler, primer, sealers, and final topcoat are not compatible. Simply put, don't try to be a chemist when it comes to repainting your car.

DETERMINING THE TYPE OF PAINT ON YOUR CAR

Before the advent of high-tech polyurethane paint products, cars were painted with either enamel or lacquer products. Each had its own distinct character-

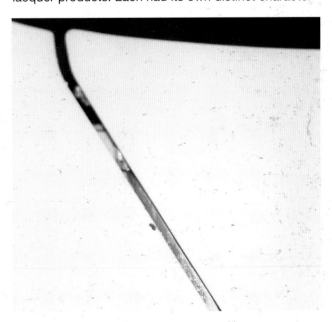

Difficult to see in the photo but readily apparent to the owner of this Oldsmobile is a small scratch on the top edge of the right front fender. About 1/8 inch wide and 3/8 inch long, it's typical of the kind of blemish that can easily be remedied with some touchup paint.

A small scratch on the sheet metal or the edges of this nameplate is the type of damage touchup paint is designed for. The small brush in the cap of a typical touchup bottle would work well to refinish this emblem, whether you remove the emblem or not. If you had some bulk paint designed to be sprayed, you could pour some into a small container and use a fine artist's paintbrush to touch up the emblem.

On the other hand, this rearview mirror is better suited to a spray can of touchup paint. It would be better to remove the mirror to avoid a substantial masking job. Sanding the surface with 400-grit sandpaper, cleaning it with wax and grease remover, then spraying on a couple of thin coats of touchup would work wonders.

istics. Enamels were quick and easy, generally covering in one or two coats and not requiring any clearcoats or rubbing out. Lacquer, on the other hand, required multiple coats but allowed imperfections to be easily rubbed out and quickly repainted. Its fast drying time afforded painters the opportunity to fix blemishes almost immediately.

Although both paint products offer benefits, they cannot be used together on car bodies because they're not compatible. It would be all right, under proper conditions, to spray enamel over lacquer when surfaces are properly prepared, but lacquer applied over enamel will almost always result in wrinkling or other severe finish damage. This is because the

solvent base for lacquer paint (lacquer thinner) is much too potent for the rather soft materials used in enamel products.

Product compatibility factors are also extremely important today. This is not confined to just enamel, lacquer, or urethane bases. Every product in an entire paint system must be compatible with the surface material to which it will be applied as well as with every other product in the system. For example, using a PPG reducer with a BASF hardener in a DuPont paint product is asking for trouble. The individual products were not designed as parts of a single, compatible paint system, and as a result, the color, adhesion, and surface flow of that combination could be adversely affected.

Before arbitrarily purchasing paint for your car, you need to determine what type of material currently exists on the vehicle's surface: enamel, lacquer, or urethane. On newer vehicles, factory paint jobs are all going to be urethane based, as enamels and lacquers are quickly becoming history. For your vehicle, it's worth asking your local paint supply jobber for information on what kind of paint was applied at the factory. For cars still clad in factory paint jobs, paint codes are listed on their identification tags. In addition, auto body paint and supply store jobbers can determine the type of paint and color from the vehicle identification number (VIN) on older vehicles or from a separate paint and options tag on newer vehicles. This makes material identification easy when you plan to match existing paint.

If your car or truck has been repainted with a type of paint or color different from its original factory job, you'll have to obtain paint code numbers from a paint can used during the repaint or from some other source, such as the painter who completed the job. With luck, that person kept track of this information and will make it available to you.

Should you not be able to determine paint codes or information relating to the type of paint used on your car, you'll have to test an inconspicuous spot on the vehicle body with lacquer thinner. You could also test a spot on an area already slated for repaint. Dab a clean, white cloth with lacquer thinner and rub a spot of paint. If color comes off immediately or the spot begins to wrinkle, the paint type is enamel. Should color wipe off onto the cloth after vigorous rubbing, lacquer paint is present. If nothing wipes off, the paint is probably a type of urethane.

To determine if finishes include coats of clear paint over their base color, sand an inconspicuous spot with 600-grit or finer sandpaper. White sanding residue indicates a clearcoat finish, whereas a color residue demonstrates that the body was painted with a color material only.

I can't place too much emphasis on the importance of determining the type of paint currently covering the surface of your car before you apply new coats of fresh paint. About the only exceptions would be vehicle bodies that have been stripped to bare metal in preparation for complete new paint system applications. If you're still unsure about the type of paint on your car after this test, or if you have any other related questions or problems, consult a professional auto body paint and supply store jobber. Be up front and attentive with that person to receive definitive answers and patient assistance. Remember, applying mismatched coatings to an existing finish can ruin the whole paint job.

NICK AND SCRATCH REPAIR

No matter how hard you try to guard against them, small nicks or paint chips find their way onto new paint finishes much sooner than expected. For vehicles driven on a daily basis, this dilemma is simply unavoidable. Along with rock chips that occur in traffic, parking lot door-slammers are merciless. Add to that a long list of other accidental and careless mishaps and, sooner or later, your new paint job will suffer some degree of minor damage. Fortunately, you

Whenever you use spray paint, touchup or otherwise, the spray can should be warm for best results. This will help thoroughly mix the ingredients of the paint and will give the propellant its maximum power. If you need to warm the spray paint, allow it to sit in a sink of warm water before use. Just make sure you don't heat spray cans over their recommended safety temperature, which is clearly indicated on the label. Never hold the can over a flame!

This late-model Ford pickup truck is in for a total repaint. All trim, lights, door handles, bumpers, and virtually anything else that can be removed will be, rather than masked. Something to remember with pickup trucks is that for a complete paint job, the bed needs to be removed. This one will be before all of the prep work is completed.

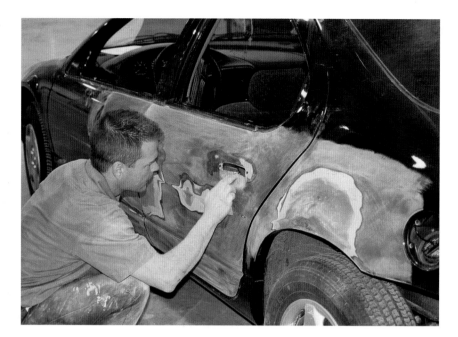

This Dodge sedan suffered some minor damage to the driver's-side doors and rear quarter panel. None of the damage was severe, and almost all of it could be repaired by the hobbyist. Careful attention to detail during the body repair and prep work will go a long way toward making this sedan look like new, once the repairs are completed.

The VIN tag on this pickup truck gives a code that can be deciphered by an auto paint jobber to provide the correct color of paint. Before mixing the paint, it would be a good idea to confirm that the new paint is going to be blue (in this case), just to verify that the vehicle hasn't been repainted or mistagged.

can repair small nicks with minimal work, provided they're small and the affected paint job is not exotic. You'll need some touchup paint, a small artist's or lettering paintbrush, and masking tape.

Small bottles of stock factory colors of touchup paint are commonly available at auto body paint and supply stores and a number of auto parts houses. Mostly supplied for newer cars, these touchup paints match the paint code on your vehicle's ID tag. They're applied using a small brush attached to the bottle's cap or with an artist's fine paintbrush. For years, auto enthusiasts have successfully used the clean end of paper matchsticks to apply touchup paint.

Clean the damaged area with wax and grease remover and then closely mask off the nick or nicks. Stir or shake the touchup paint as needed. Now, simply dab your paintbrush into the paint and retrieve a small amount of paint on the tip of the bristles. Apply that drop of paint to the nick. Don't attempt to fill in the entire nick depth with the first paint dab. Wait for a while to let the first dab set up, then apply a second small dab.

Continue the dabbing and setting up until paint has filled the nick to just over the surface. It should be obvious before you quit that you've applied touchup paint above the height of the main finish—in other words, it should look as if you put on too much paint. Then let the new paint cure. Don't touch it for a week to 10 days.

After this drying period, mask the nick again. This time, mask a wider area. Then use 1200-grit sandpaper with water to gently smooth the nick area and bring the surface of the new paint down to the surrounding finish. The masking tape will prevent unnecessary sanding on the surface surrounding the repair area.

When you've smoothed the newly applied dabs of paint to the same level as the rest of the finish, remove the masking tape. Then use polish to further blend the repair into its surroundings. If polishing scratches appear, graduate to a finer polish. Let the repair cure for a few weeks before waxing.

Minor nicks and scratches can sometimes be polished or buffed out. They must be shallow and expose only paint at their deepest point. If primer or bare metal is visible, apply new paint.

It's imperative to cover nicks as soon as possible, especially when bare metal is exposed. Oxidation quickly attacks bare metal, beginning a rust and corrosion process. Like a cancer, oxidation spreads undetected beneath paint, until damage is so extensive that flakes of paint peel off at random. Prior to the advent of convenient touchup paint bottles, auto enthusiasts applied dabs of clear fingernail polish to nicks in efforts to protect bare metal and deter the progress of oxidation, rust, and corrosion.

Compared to tiny nicks, long, deep scratches may pose more serious problems. Although minor scratches may be touched up in basically the same fashion as nicks, long strokes with a touchup paintbrush may be too rough or noticeable. Depending on the color and type of paint finish, you may be better off carefully sanding scratches smooth and then feathering in new layers of fresh paint with an aerosol touchup can (available at some auto parts stores and auto body paint and supply outlets) or a regular spray-paint device.

PANEL PAINTING

With the possible exception of a few special automobiles, most vehicles are composed of a number of separate sections welded or bolted together. Professional auto body people generally refer to these sections as panels—for example, quarter panels and rear body panels.

In a lot of body collision or simple repaint situations, painters have to spray complete panels in lieu of spraying specific spots. Spot painting a number of minor ding repairs scattered over an entire hood panel, for example, would probably turn out looking

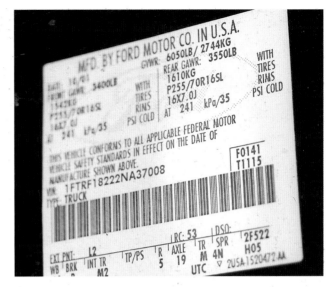

Newer vehicles use paint and options tags to provide the paint code. On some vehicles, the VIN is included on this tag, while on others, it's located elsewhere. If you're having difficulty finding the paint and options tag, your auto paint and supply store should be able to offer assistance in determining where it's located on your vehicle.

something like a leopard. This work would be much easier and the finished look much more uniform and professional if the entire hood were completely prepared and painted all at one time. The determination of whether to spot paint or cover entire panels depends on the type and style of the existing paint finish, size of the repair area, and ability to blend new paint into the surrounding body paint area.

Some situations allow for painting just parts of panels, as opposed to entire units. These might include lower panel sections up to featured grooves, ridges, or trim lines on doors, fenders, or quarter

This Dodge sedan is almost masked sufficiently for the application of primer sufacer, which will extend beyond the repair area yet not completely to the masked edge. The color coat will cover the entire left rear quarter panel, and both doors will be painted. To match the rest of the car, the painter may need to blend clear onto the trunk, roof, and front fender.

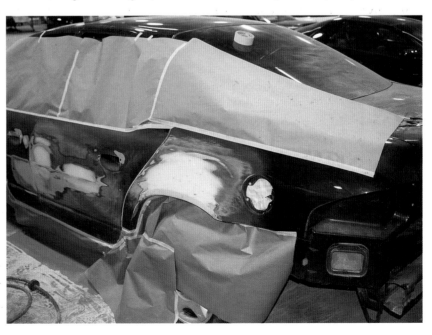

This is your typical fender bender that could be repaired by a novice bodyman. The fender is slightly wrinkled, but the sheet metal has no major creases. In days gone by, it would be necessary to remove the inner fender panel (and whatever accessories were in the way) and hammer the dent out from behind. Stud guns available now would allow you to weld small studs onto the outside of the fender, then use a slide hammer to pull the dent out. Either method would require at least a skim coat of body filler to finish the repair.

panels. Special graphics or vinyl stripes might also serve as perimeters to cordon off particular areas, allowing for partial panel repaints. A ridge or trim line draws the eye away from the paint itself, making minor color variations unnoticeable.

With the advent of basecoat/clearcoat paint systems, color blending has all but eliminated panel painting. Even though the correct paint code may be known, the surface prepped properly, and the paint applied flawlessly, any panels painted separately from others will most likely not match the rest of the vehicle. Your ultimate goal is to apply paint in such a way that no definitive edges are visible, making that area appear as if it had never been repaired or repainted. Some single-panel repaint jobs require that adjacent panels on either side be lightly sprayed with feather coats of paint. This is done to help a primary painted panel's new finish blend in with surrounding panels.

Color blending can be done with single-stage paint products, but basecoat/clearcoat is recommended for the novice. Although the actual color of the repaired area may not match the adjacent panels exactly, the blend will create the illusion that the affected area was never damaged. On the other hand, two adjacent panels painted separately are quite noticeable when reinstalled on the vehicle.

COMPLETE PAINT JOB

On a partial repaint job, approximately 70 percent of the work involved is surface preparation, and only 30 percent is related to paint application. For a complete paint job, approximately 95 percent of the work is surface preparation, while only 5 percent is spent applying paint.

Many people do not understand that the condition of body surfaces prior to paint application directly affects the outcome of a paint job. Every speck of dirt, sanding scratch, pinhole, or other tiny blemish is magnified to a great extent after paint has been applied over it. The flawless, even quality of the surrounding paint draws the viewer's eye directly to the imperfection. Automotive paint, even in multiple layers, is still a very thin coating and simply will not

On this Dodge truck, a small portion of the passenger door required attention, and the roof had to be replaced because a tree fell across it. The small area of the door requiring bodywork was masked off from the rest of the door, although the entire door will receive paint before the repair is completed. When masking for actual paint application, the door or any other panel would never be masked with a square like this, unless the desired paint scheme called for a checkerboard pattern.

Before painting and even before most of the surface preparation, the bumpers, grille, door handles, mirrors, and everything else that could be removed were removed from this Ford pickup truck. The headlights will be left on in this case because masking paper will eventually cover the entire front of the vehicle.

cover up even minor flaws the way, say, house paint might. If it isn't smooth, don't spray it!

Complete paint jobs call for all exterior body trim to be removed. You should take off door handles, trim pieces, mirrors, emblems, badges, key locks, radio antennas, and anything else attached to your car's body. This reduces the need for intricate masking and prevents accidental overspray onto these pieces as a result of inadequate masking. Likewise, it allows paint to cover all vehicle body parts evenly and greatly reduces the chance of paint buildup or thin coat coverage on areas obstructed with handles, adornments, and add-ons.

Removing body trim and accessories requires hand tools to loosen nuts, bolts, and screws. Other pieces held in place by adhesives or double-backed tape may require an adhesive remover product. Take your time and remove items so that none of them are broken or damaged.

Once you start taking parts off your car, you'll probably be surprised at the number collected. In addition to door handles, key locks, and trim, you'll be removing light assemblies, reflectors, grille pieces, bumpers, license plates, mudguards, and a lot more. Therefore, develop a systematic storage plan, so nothing gets lost or broken.

Have plenty of sturdy boxes on hand to store related parts as you take them off body areas. Keep fender parts together in one box, door items in another, and so forth. This way, when you start replacing them after paint work is completed, you'll be able to quickly and easily locate all necessary body and trim pieces as well as their fastening nuts, bolts, screws, clips, and so on. In addition to boxes,

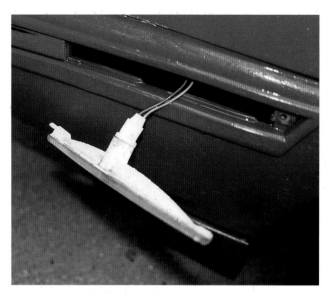

Most side marker lights are held into place by one or two small screws. Where Phillips screws were once common for this application, Torx head screws are typically found now. Make sure you use the proper type of screwdriver or tool. This particular light uses only one screw. The tab on one end is positioned into the opening, then the single screw holds the assembly in place. To completely remove the lens assembly, twist the bulb's socket while holding the lens assembly. The wires and the bulb can then be stuffed down into the opening in the fender to keep them out of the way.

Although much of the sheet metal in the engine compartment is blocked from plain view by the engine, accessories, and trim panels, it would be noticeable if it were a different color from the rest of the car. For that reason, think twice before attempting a color change paint job on a vehicle that isn't going to be completely disassembled. To paint the engine compartment correctly, you would remove the engine and accessories, steam clean the compartment, then perform the standard sheet-metal prep work. On a vintage restoration or hot rod project, that would be standard procedure, while on a daily driver, it most likely wouldn't be practical.

resealable freezer bags work well for temporary storage of small pieces and parts. Use a magic marker to note the contents on the storage label.

Expect to spend plenty of time sanding every square inch of your car or truck's body surface before picking up a spray gun. All imperfections must be smoothed or repaired to give paint a blemish-free bonding base. By itself, paint is not thick enough to hide sand scratch swelling or pinholes. For those problems, products such as primer sufacer are used, which also have to be sanded and smoothed to perfection if paint is expected to coat evenly and be visually attractive.

COLOR CHANGE PAINT JOB

Changing the color of a vehicle involves additional considerations. This is more difficult on some vehicles than others. For a complete color change, it will be necessary to paint the engine compartment, doorjambs, and interior. Unless you're extremely good with a detail gun and masking procedures, it will be necessary to remove the engine to repaint the engine compartment. If you're repainting a vehicle that already has the engine out, this is of little consequence, other than the additional sanding and surface preparation. This also holds true for the interior, although much of the interior will be covered by upholstery.

COLOR SELECTION

An important part of any paint job is picking the right color. If you're simply repairing and refinishing a dented fender on a late-model vehicle, this is not a big deal. However, if you're building that long-awaited hot rod or custom, the choice of a color may be more diffi-cult than you would think. No matter what you're painting or how you go about choosing the color, look at your anticipated color under as many different lighting conditions as possible to make sure it's the right color for your vehicle.

Because so many different automotive paint colors are available to choose from, it may become confusing or downright frustrating trying to pick just one dynamic color for your car. Have patience. Look at issues of car and truck magazines to get ideas of the colors other enthusiasts are using. Attend car shows and talk to fellow car buffs about how they arrived at certain paint schemes. These conversations may lead you to good suppliers and products and also help you avoid mistakes your fellow enthusiasts already have made.

Whether your vehicle is a bone stocker or highly modified, with a minimal amount of searching, you're bound to find at least one magazine that caters to your automotive interests. These magazines can be a great source of ideas for paint schemes and colors.

Contrary to popular belief, you don't always need flashy colors to stand out in a crowd. Longtime custom car painter Roger Ward painted his 1932 Ford roadster Nissan taupe (light tan) at a time when every one else was painting their hot rods Porsche Red. His roadster stood out from the sea of red and still seems timeless when all those other cars have been repainted a time or two already.

Many times, especially for older classic and vintage automobiles, certain color schemes prove more appealing than others. While a pink 1957 Thunderbird may be a head turner, an equally pink 1956 Oldsmobile may look out of place. Experienced car painters have a knack for envisioning the outcome of cars painted specific colors. From their experience around body shops and car shows and through reading thousands of auto magazines, they know which colors look best and are in style for most types of vehicles, from sports cars to pickups and late-model sedans to classic coupes.

If yours is an older project car that's finally ready for paint and you find yourself in a quandary as to what color to paint it, locate a local club whose members share an interest in the same make, model, or general vintage. A few casual conversations with them should help you to at least narrow your color choices to a select few. If there's any chance you may someday sell the vehicle, picking a color

that's in keeping with its style and vintage may make it a hotter prospect.

MATCHING THE OLD

A word of caution about color codes printed on VIN or color and options tags is in order. Believe it or not, occasionally the codes do not match the color that was really sprayed on the vehicle. With the vast number of automobiles manufactured each year, the percentage that have incorrect codes is small but alarming. When you take the color code from your vehicle to the local automotive paint retailer to purchase paint, tell them the basic color of the vehicle. If the color code you supply yields yellow paint but your car is black, the paint jobber will want to know before mixing a gallon or two of paint that you won't be able to use.

If this happens, you can choose a color from a large selection of paint selection charts. Automotive paint shops have volumes of OEM paint chips

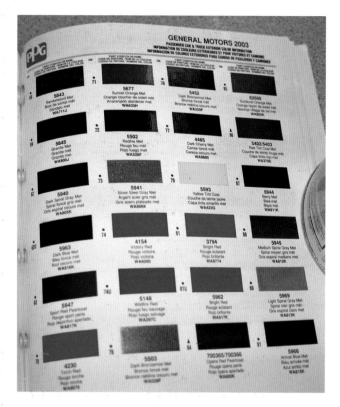

This photo of a 2003 General Motors color chart shows five similar shades of red, and other colors also have similar shades. The "plain" red for a Chevrolet may be different from the red on a Buick or a Pontiac. Although they may look the same in a paint chip book, they can be noticeably different when sprayed side by side. Some colors shown in the sample book are for underhood or interior use and will not have as much gloss. Before you select a color, view it in sunlight, not just the store's fluorescent lighting.

categorized by year and vehicle manufacturer. If you're looking for paint to match a 2003 Chevrolet Monte Carlo for example, you could go to the 2003 General Motors portion of the paint selection chart and probably find what you're looking for.

Similar colors from different years or manufacturers may be close yet somewhat different. When you find a color that looks close, ask the painter if the color you selected is actually for a Monte Carlo. The color you selected may be for a Camaro or a Corvette but not the correct color for your Monte Carlo. When there were fewer colors for cars, finding an exact match was much easier.

Another reality is that for each color code, multiple formulas will provide paint acceptable by the vehicle manufacturer. The reason is the robotic paint process used by vehicle manufacturers. As an example, the first 10 vehicles going down the paint line are supposed to be black, followed by 10 that are supposed to be white, 10 red, 10 yellow, and 10 blue.

By computer control, the paint spraying system is purged at each color change. In our example, 9 of the first 10 vehicles will be black, but the tenth will be slightly lighter than the 9 before it. The first two or three white vehicles will be slightly grayer than the middleones, while those at the end of the white session will be slightly pink, due to the red in the system.

Of the red vehicles, the first few won't be as vibrant as the heart of the run, while the end of the run will have more of a yellow cast or orange appearance to them. Of course, the yellow vehicles are affected also. The first few may yield a "dirty" yellow compared to the middle of the batch or the slightly green-appearing vehicles that would result from the end of the yellow run.

This characteristic is not limited to any one manufacturer or color, although certain colors of certain vehicles are more commonplace. For any color code entered in the paint formula database, a prime formula is displayed. Formulas for all known variants of this same color code are also displayed. Each variant has a code that indicates such properties as "less red, more yellow" or "less white, more red." Some color codes may not have variant codes, while some may have ten.

When a color code has variant color codes listed, the person mixing the paint will always supply the paint from the prime formula if the paint is intended for a complete paint job. If the paint is for a repair, color chips from each of the variant colors must be compared to the vehicle to be repaired to obtain the correct color.

A second method of determining the paint formula for virtually any color found on an automobile involves the use of a color spectrometer. This is an expensive tool that the average paint retailer will not have but may be able to gain access to through their paint distributor. If you're trying to match a color that can't be found through available paint codes, the extra effort of finding a color spectrometer may be the answer.

A portion of the vehicle with the desired paint color is scanned, using the color spectrometer. The information gathered by the spectrometer is then downloaded into a computer, which deciphers the color and displays the appropriate paint formula. Although paint matching cannot be 100 percent accurate all the time, this process is extremely accurate on single-stage or two-stage paints. However, it is not designed for nor capable of determining the formula of tri-stage paints or finishes that include special-effect additives, such as pearl or metallic.

Auto body paint and supply stores can match almost any color of automotive paint. However, if you want a specific color not displayed in any color chart or paint chip catalog, it will have to be made by hand using trial and error. Expect to pay a lot more for this service than for stock colors because of the added labor involved.

This situation arises when you request a color match with a repainted car and have no idea what color was used or who did the work. In those cases, jobbers will simply ask you to search through volumes of color chips until you find the closest match. Then they work with specific tints until they produce a suitable color. Unless you find a paint chip that perfectly matches that car, they mix paint by hand until they find a match, which may require hours. This is why special, hand-matched colors cost a lot more than standard quantities of those colors whose formulas are stored in company computers.

SELECTING THE NEW

Selecting a new color for the complete repaint of a vehicle might not be quite as easy. Valspar Refinish already has 100,000 different automotive paint colors on file, and its engineers are kept busy using computer science and experience in graphic arts to develop new hues. The days of walking into a paint store and simply asking for a quart of red paint are gone. Today, there are easily over 600 different shades of red, so customers must be a lot more specific. They need to pick out a certain color chip from any number of color catalogs or have a particular paint code number available. Most other colors have as many variations.

One way to decide on a new paint color is to visit local automobile dealerships. When you find a car or truck with a paint scheme you like, copy the vehicle's numerical paint code and take it to your local auto body paint and supply store. In lieu of paint codes, proper paint mixing formulas may be located on computer files with just the year, make, and model of most newer vehicles. Customers can confirm colors by comparing that information with corresponding color chips from paint color catalogs.

CUSTOM FINISHES

Along with color selection, you may want to investigate special custom paint additives. Metallics have improved since their heyday in the 1960s. Now,

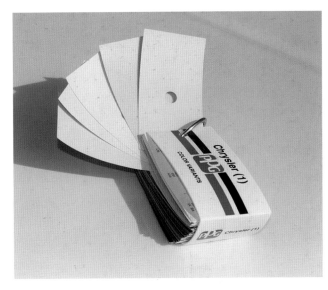

Although difficult to distinguish in the photo, all five variant chips are slightly different but are all for the same paint code. You place the card on your car and compare its color to the surrounding shade through the hole in the middle. After determining that the vehicle you're painting is the prime color or a variant thereof, make note of it for future reference, in case you need to purchase additional paint for that vehicle at some other time.

instead of large, bold flakes loudly accenting a car body, you can add specific doses of tiny microflakes to make an otherwise bland color light up to a magnificent and brilliant finish. A good number of newer car paint finishes include tiny metallics. You can see them firsthand on automobiles at almost any new car dealership or on color chips at your local auto body paint and supply store.

Pearl additives are another means by which you can make a solid color look custom. In years past, fish scales were used to give stock colors a pearlescent appearance that made them look different shades when viewed from various angles. In essence, a vehicle that might appear white when viewed straight on may offer a bright pink or blue shade when seen from a lower angle or from the front or back.

Today's pearl additives are made by applying oxide pigments to micaceous iron oxide (mica) or aluminum. These tiny chips may be painted on one side while remaining clear on the other. Depending on the pearl color selected and the angle of light reflection from your viewpoint, these paint jobs can offer unique perspectives.

It used to be that for spot repairs, manufacturers of these products would advise repainting the entire affected side of the vehicle, from headlight to taillight. This is so each part of the full side will display iden-

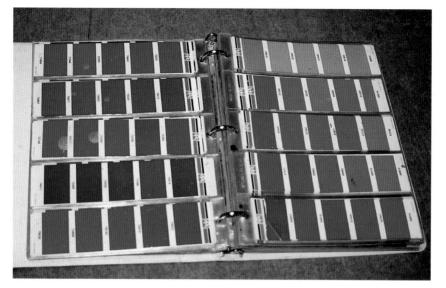

If you're not looking to match an OEM color or for a metallic or pearl, you may decide to go with a fleet color for your repainting project. This is a sample book of virtually every color of vehicle paint imaginable, although they're all solid colors—no pearls, metallics, or other "custom" additives. This is just one page of predominantly red paints, with a few more pages of reds in the book and several other pages of predominantly yellows, blues, and shades of gray.

Body filler and primer sufacers must be allowed to dry fully before you apply additional fillers or topcoats. Painters often use heat lamps to speed up the process. This GM truck has had some sheet metal straightened, some body filler added, and some primer sufacer applied. The current coat of primer sufacer is being dried with a heat lamp.

tical tints from all directions and not cause clouds of varying degrees between panels or parts of panels. With improvements in pearl products and stricter standards, these paints are now easier to blend for spot repairs than just a few years ago. Today, the only real drawback to a pearl finish is that it absolutely must be clearcoated for long-term color stability.

Special paint systems using metallics and pearls can be satisfactorily applied by novice painters who follow all label instructions and tips from application guides. Take advantage of this wealth of information at your fingertips to make your paint job progress as expected.

CONSULTANTS

Besides choosing what color to paint your car or truck, possibly the biggest decision is whether to paint it yourself or pay someone else to do the work. Before

you simply jump in (and possibly get in way over your head before you know it), first find out what your choices are and what they will cost. If you want to get your daily driver painted but don't have the proper equipment or the necessary time, you may be better off to have the work done by a reputable shop.

TALKING WITH A PROFESSIONAL AUTO PAINTER

Automobile owners with little or no knowledge of the auto body repair and paint business are frequently surprised at the cost of a quality paint job. They have no idea of the amount of work involved during preparation stages before painting, nor of the cost of materials such as primers, sealers, reducers, hardeners, and paint. Uninformed car owners have a difficult time understanding why some companies can paint cars for as little as $99.95 while other shops might charge around $5,000 or more for a top-notch, complete paint job. Of course, the price of a paint job has no real ceiling because the labor involved will vary greatly, depending on what you need done.

If you decide to have a professional paint your car, remember that you get what you pay for. Outfits that specialize in cheap paint jobs cannot afford to spend a lot of time preparing or masking cars. Their business relies on volume. The more cars they paint, the more money they make. Therefore, sanding and masking work is normally minimal.

Close inspection of vehicles that have been repainted by inexpensive paint shops generally reveals overspray on fenderwells, leaf springs, emblems, badges, window trim, spare tires under pickup truck beds, and the like, due to minimal masking. Rough surface spots may receive a quick pass or two with sandpaper, but extra time cannot be allotted for definitive sanding and feathering. These shops are not going to remove the bed from your pickup truck to paint the back of the cab, either.

If you want a much more thorough paint job than the one just described, and most people do, these shops can provide better-quality service. This will, of course, cost you more, with the price of "extras" quickly approaching that of a more thorough, lower-volume shop. Inexpensive paint shops are forced to use bulk supplies. Color choices are usually limited to the colors on hand in 55-gallon barrels. Frequently, shops like these will buy out paint manufacturers' supplies of discontinued colors at huge discounts. They pass this savings on to you. In many cases, enamel-based products are used because they cover in one or two coats and don't require rubbing out or polishing afterward.

Auto paint shops that specialize in overall quality and customer satisfaction are vastly different from high-volume shops. You'll have to pay more for their service, but your car or truck will be meticulously prepared and then painted with a high-quality, durable paint. All exterior accessories will be removed, including bumpers and grille. Masking will be complete, and work required after spraying will be accomplished professionally.

Once the surface has been meticulously smoothed, coats of sealer are sprayed on, to protect undercoats from absorbing potent solvents included in paint. Sufficient drying time must be allotted. Professionals often use high-intensity heat lamps to speed this process. These lamps use a tremendous amount of electricity, which must be figured into estimates as part of the overhead costs.

After that phase has been completed, color coats are applied and then cured with assistance from heat lamps. Depending on the type of paint system used, clearcoats might be sprayed over the entire vehicle. Normally, three coats are enough. When the clear has dried, painters carefully inspect car bodies for imperfections. Then 1200 to 2000-grit sandpaper is used to smooth blemishes, as needed, and additional coats of clear may be applied.

Satisfied that their job has turned out correctly, painters buff entire vehicle bodies with fine polish and a soft buffing pad. After all of that has been done, parts still have to be replaced. Again, this takes time, as gaskets and seals must be perfectly positioned to function as intended. Care must be taken so that parts are not bumped against newly painted finishes to cause nicks or scratches.

As if that weren't enough, each vehicle is then detailed to perfection. I doubt many customers would pay their paint bill if glass, wheels, tires, weatherstripping, and other parts were dirty and covered with sanding dust when they arrived to pick up the car. Most quality body shop owners insist that their customers' cars be detailed before delivery. Their customers enjoy a freshly painted car and can relish the fact that it has been cleaned to perfection. The car stands out, looks crisp, and is a pleasure to drive.

When shopping for a professional auto painter, be sure to ask if your car will be detailed before delivery. Ask if all exterior accessories will be removed for painting and whether overspray to fenderwells and suspension assemblies will be removed or painted over. Be certain that maximum attention will be given to masking and that quality paint products will be used throughout the job.

Finding a professional auto paint shop with a reputable track record should not be too difficult. Word-of-mouth recommendations are generally reliable. If a friend or neighbor has recently had a car painted, ask how he or she feels about the quality of service. You can also talk to your auto insurance agent, fellow car enthusiasts, a local detailer, or your mechanic.

You might even ask the owner of a local specialty auto sales business. These folks are true auto enthusiasts—they have to be, to stay up to date on the latest classic car trends and make the best deals when it comes to the sale of classic and vintage automobiles. To them, a less than professional auto bodyshop is a

This small portion of the stock room at the paint store contains just about everything you could possibly need for painting your vehicle—sandpaper, masking tape, paint spray guns, respirators, paint, and primer.

Virtually any color you could imagine can be mixed from the toners on these shelves. After choosing a color, you could decide to have it in a base/clear system, a single-stage urethane, acrylic lacquer, or acrylic enamel. Few colors are actually stocked in a ready-to-use mix, as shelf space would quickly be depleted.

nightmare. They expect to pay higher prices for quality work, but in return, they demand that work be of the highest caliber. Dealers in this business get a lot of money for the cars they sell. They know that quality $5,000 paint jobs can easily raise values of special automobiles by $6,000 or more.

Your telephone book's yellow pages are loaded with auto body repair and paint shop advertisements. Call a few of the shops to get a feel for their professionalism over the phone. As you cut your list to three or four, take time to visit selected facilities, to see firsthand what kind of operation they conduct. You should expect courteous and knowledgeable estimators and organized, well-lighted, tidy work areas. Talk to estimators and ask direct questions. Get estimates from each shop before committing to one. At the end of the day, compare

prices and select the shop that offered the best service for the most equitable price.

AUTO BODY PAINT AND SUPPLY STORE

Auto body paint and supply stores are in business to keep body shops adequately supplied in paint products, body repair materials, and tools for both types of work. The jobbers who work in these stores are constantly updated with product information from manufacturers of paint and body repair supplies. Although some jobbers may never have actually painted cars, their technical knowledge of paint product use is second to none.

Novice auto painters can learn a great deal from jobbers when both parties fully comprehend the paint project at hand. Be up front and honest with the jobber. If possible, bring your car to the store's location so the jobber can see your project firsthand. This way, he can best recommend a proper paint system to use and supplies you'll need to complete the job.

Don't expect jobbers to drop everything just to give you lessons in painting cars. Their primary job is to serve professional body shops, not teach auto painting. For the most part, Mondays and Fridays are their busiest days. Shop owners generally call in orders on Monday for supplies they'll need for the week's work. On Friday, shops may need special deliveries of materials to complete jobs that customers expect to pick up that afternoon. So plan to visit an auto body supply store during midweek, when jobbers may have more time to converse with you.

In addition to stocking everything from paint guns to sandpaper, auto body paint and supply stores carry information sheets and application guides on almost all of the paint-related products they sell. Paint manufacturers provide this material. You can get sheets on the use and application of primer sufacers, sealers, and tri-stage paint systems, as well as just about every other product you might ever put on your car's body. They're free, so take one for every product you intend to use.

Unless you have experience painting cars, you might ask your auto body paint and supply jobber how much sandpaper of which grit you'll need to properly prepare your car's finish for new paint. Sanding chores are different with each job, and fine-grit paper doesn't last as long as you might expect. Along with sandpaper, buy plenty of automotive paint masking tape and paper. Two-inch tape works great for some chores, while 3/4-inch and 1/8-inch works better for more detailed tasks.

By and large, your auto body paint and supply store jobber can be a fountain of information. Take advantage of this person's knowledge by being polite and courteous and by asking intelligent questions. Be aware of the store's busiest hours and plan to visit during slack times.

SPECIAL CONSIDERATIONS

Automotive painting has become a high-tech business. Not only do painters have to be concerned about the finished product, they must also be keenly aware of personal safety hazards involved with potent chemicals used in paint bases and hardeners. Where filter masks proved to be health-conscious aids a few years ago, positive-pressure respirators are state of the art now. Be aware of fire hazards, especially pilot lights on hot water heaters and home heating systems. Thinners and reducers are highly flammable, so be sure cigarettes and other sources of ignition are kept far away from your project.

LAYING DOWN THE
BASE COAT

BY DENNIS PARKS

How you apply the paint is every bit as important as the quality of the paint itself. Before you start spraying on your carefully prepped vehicle, get a used door, hood, or trunk lid and practice the art of laying on paint smoothly and evenly. You're not just developing your own skills, you're also learning how your equipment performs its job. Leave the runs, drips, and irregularities on your practice panel and shoot your vehicle like a pro.

Another thing to consider before mixing the paint and filling your gun is to highlight certain time recommendations and other important data that came with your paint system, so you can refer to them during your job. If you prepare a small outline, including all the painting and drying steps in sequential order, you can check off each step once you've completed it. If you like to multitask or have kids, a cell phone, or other distractions, this approach will help you remember what you've done, what you need to do, and how much time you have to do it. Try using something other than a typical sheet of paper for this, such as an off-size piece of light cardboard or a colored sheet, and you'll be able to distinguish it quickly among any other notes or papers.

Mix your paint products according to label instructions and apply them at the recommended air pressure. Try painting with different fan patterns and pressure settings to see which combinations work best for intricate work in confined spaces and which perform better on large panels. Practice holding paint guns at perpendicular angles to work surfaces; see what happens when you don't. Use cans of inexpensive paint, and practice until you become familiar with the techniques required for good paint coverage. When the paint has dried, practice wet sanding, rubbing out, and buffing.

Practice with your new dual-action sander to remove those coats of paint. Put a deep scratch in your practice panel and repair it, instead of practicing on your favorite car or truck. Become proficient with the tools and materials you expect to use while fixing your special car before attacking its precious surface with power tools and harsh chemicals. Practice, practice, and practice some more. Once it looks good on your practice panel, you know you're ready for the big time.

PAINT MIXING

Because there are tens of thousands of different automotive paint colors, mixing the correct shade for your car is a precise science. Following stock vehicle color codes or those selected from paint chip catalogs, auto body paint and supply personnel measure drops of color tint to the tenth of a gram to create the prescribed colors. They do this work for you as part of your paint system purchase.

Paint materials are shipped in concentrated form, which helps keep the heavy pigments and other solid materials from settling. Painters then add solvents to make those products sprayable. Remember that the atmospheric conditions at which you spray the paint also affect the thinners or reducers you need to add. By shipping the paint in concentrated form and allowing end users to mix and dilute it as necessary, according to suppliers' instructions, manufacturers help ensure that painters in any region and climate can get precisely the paint and mixture they need for best results.

In most cases, you'll have to dilute concentrated paint with solvent (thinner or reducer) to yield a sprayable mixture. You must also add specific quantities of hardener to those products that call for it. Be careful—once you mix in hardener, the hardening process begins. Catalyzed paint has a limited shelf life, which your paint system's instructions will explain.

Take the following steps to be sure you get the right paint mixture. First, read the instructions that came with the paint system. Next, read the instruc-

Before spraying paint, you need a suitable area for mixing, reducing, and then pouring the paint into your spray gun. This spacious, stainless-steel-topped table provides plenty of room and is relatively easy to keep clean. A wooden workbench will provide the same results for the hobbyist, but this is a glimpse of the ideal setup. At the middle of the photo are two stands for holding gravity-feed spray guns while paint is poured into the paint cup. At the back of the table are the various reducers and cans used for mixing. At the far end is a selection of pearl additives.

Also located in the mixing room is a 55-gallon drum that serves as a receptacle for excess paint, reducers, and other solvents. Any time a spray gun is cleaned, additional solvents are added to this. The body shop then has to have these products disposed of on a regular basis. For the hobbyist, disposal may present more of a problem, depending on where you live. Many paint distributors will accept small amounts of solvents from their customers, sometimes for a small fee. If it's not convenient to return the waste solvents to where you bought them, check with your local authorities to determine proper disposal methods.

tions that came with your spray gun and air compressor. These two sources should give you a strong sense of the mixture ratio you'll need. Then, before you mix, run any questions you may have past the paint supplier from whom you got your paint. By checking and crosschecking in this manner, you'll be sure you have just the right mixture for your application, climate, and equipment.

For the mixing process itself, paint manufacturers have designed calibrated mixing sticks. According to the mixing directions, pour an amount of paint into a clean, empty can with straight sides (not a spray-gun cup), up to a certain number located along one vertical column on that paint system's designated mixing stick. Then pour solvent in until the fluid level in the can rises to a corresponding number on the next

column over on the same stick. Clear mixing cups with calibrations printed on them are used in the same manner as mixing sticks.

If you need a one-to-one ratio of paint to solvent, for example, pour paint into an empty can up to the number one. Then add reducer until the mixture reaches the number one on the next column over. If you need more paint for a large job, simply mix the ingredients up to a higher number—again, following the ratios your particular system and circumstances indicate.

If your paint system requires mixing paint, solvent, and hardener, it will use a mixing stick with three columns instead of two—one for each ingredient. Pour paint up to the desired number on the paint column, solvent to the appropriate number in that column, and hardener to its corresponding number.

Not all paint systems are based on a one-to-one ratio. By looking at a paint-mixing stick, you'll see that sometimes the numbers on the reducer or hardener are not twice as high up the stick as those in the paint column. Measuring sticks provide an accurate way of mixing paint, solvent, and hardener. Follow the manufacturer's recommendations and instructions to be assured of a quality blend.

Once you've blended your paint product, use the stir stick to swish the contents around in the mixing can. Pointed tools, such as screwdrivers, don't work well for stirring. You want something flat-bottomed and rather wide—hence the stir stick. Stir for at least 2 minutes. Then place a paint filter over the opening of your spray-gun cup and pour in the mixture.

Never, repeat, *never*, pour paint into your spray-gun cup without using some type of filter. An impurity passed into your gun could cause it to misspray or clog, creating a lot of extra work fixing the paint surface and your spray gun.

Your paint product is now ready for spraying. Be sure to put the caps back on containers of solvent, hardener, and paint. This will prevent unnecessary evaporation or accidental spillage.

In the paint booth, tack off your car or truck's surface immediately. Then start painting. Some paint products and colors are designed with a lot of heavy solids that could settle to the bottom of paint cups in just 10 to 15 minutes. If you were to take your time tacking and get distracted while your paint gun sat idle, solids could settle, possibly causing the color to change. This would be a catastrophe, especially with spot paint repairs.

Custom paint mixing (when a formula is available) has always been done by weight. The paint formula provides a starting amount of base color, which is poured into the appropriate-sized paint can. The second toner is added until the weight matches the given total for the two parts. Third and successive toners are added in the same manner, until the sum of the parts equals the total amount. An electronic digital scale is much easier for this process than an old-fashioned beam scale. Kevin Brinkley mixes a pint of paint that he will eventually pour into a spray can for a customer who simply needs some touchup paint.

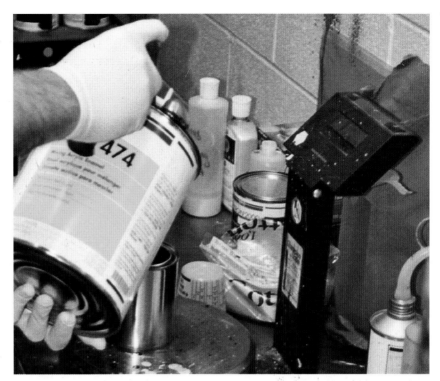

Once the various toners specified in a paint formula are combined, they must be mixed sufficiently by vigorous agitation in a paint shaker. It will also be necessary for you to stir the paint prior to use because the solvents will settle to the bottom as it sits on the shelf.

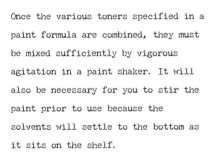

SPRAY-GUN CONTROLS AND TEST PATTERNS

Paint companies recommend specific spray-gun setups for applying their products. A sample recommendation for the DeVilbiss JGV-572 base coat spray gun is "Fluid Tip—FW (0.062 in.); Air Cap #86." This would indicate a specific fluid tip and air cap that should be used with this particular paint product and would be available from the dealer of the spray gun. This is another reason to purchase your spray gun from a paint supply outlet, rather than a tool store that sells a variety of tools without servicing any of them. A similar recommendation would apply to primer and clearcoat spray guns by the same manufacturer, Sata or Sharpe. These settings are available from information sheets and application guidelines or from your auto body paint and supply jobber.

Most full-size production spray-paint guns have two control knobs. One controls the fan spray, while the other manages the volume of paint that exits the nozzle. They're located at the top rear section of most models. About the only way to achieve proper spray patterns and volume is to practice spraying paint on a test panel. Various paint products and their reduction ratios will spray differently, especially with different recommended air pressures.

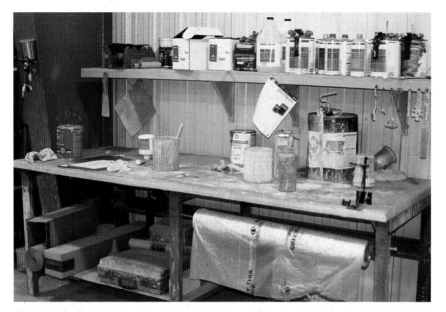

This mixing table at an auto body shop is comparable to what the hobbyist painter might have. At the left, we see some body filler and catalyst, along with some spreaders and a mixing board. To the right are some mixing cups and reducers. Above the bench is a shelf where the various primers, primer sufacers, sandpaper, and other supplies are stored. At the far right is a 55-gallon drum for waste primers and solvents.

Technological advances make today's paint products very user friendly. If you prepare the surface correctly, mix the products correctly, and apply them correctly, they will yield a good paint job. Proper mixing ratios are included with the product information sheets, and calibrated mixing cups or measuring sticks are available from your paint store.

Many painters keep test panels in their spray-paint booth. Usually, these are nothing more than sheets of wide masking paper taped to a wall. They can spray paint on the test panel and then adjust the gun's control knobs to get the right pattern and volume. At that point, they begin painting.

Periodically during paint jobs, painters may notice a flaw in their gun's fan pattern. To check it, they turn to the test panel and shoot a clean section with a mist of paint. If it looks off, they check the controls and air pressure. If the pattern is still flawed, they disconnect the paint gun from the supply hose and clean it. Chances are, a small port or passage has become clogged and must be cleaned before they can continue the job.

As the surface to be painted becomes more confined or difficult, such as on some front-end sections, painters must reduce pressure or change fan sprays to hit a smaller area. They make these adjustments with the help of the test panel.

SPRAY-GUN MANEUVERING

You've secured two essential components for your project: good paint and a quality spray gun. But those essentials alone won't get you a great paint job. How you apply the paint is just as important. Spray-paint guns typically work best when held perpendicular to the surface being sprayed, at a distance of 6–10 inches; check the recommendations for your gun.

PPG's *Refinish Manual* has this caution for painters: "If the gun is tilted toward the surface, the fan pattern won't be uniform. If the gun is swung in an arc, varying the distance from the nozzle to the work, the paint will go on wetter (and thicker) where the

Most body shops have special dispenser caps that allow them to pour the desired amount of paint into the mixing cup. These are a convenience, but not necessary. You will undoubtedly find that pouring from a quart can is much easier than from a full gallon can, however. Enough sealer (in this case) for the next application is poured into the mixing cup to a predetermined line on the mixing cup. Reducer is added until the total mixture comes to the same numbered line in the next column marking the appropriate ratio.

nozzle is closer to the surface and drier (and thinner) where it is farther away." If the outer layers of the thick, wetter paint dry before the inner layers, the solvent evaporating from within will cause defects in the finish. At the far end of the arc, the paint will go on too thin to provide adequate coverage or may be too dry by the time it hits the surface, resulting in something more like overspray than a proper coat of paint.

About the only time painters do fan the paint gun is on small spot repaints. These spots call for full coverage in the center and less paint around their feathered perimeter, where it blends with existing paint. This is done with wrist action to lightly blend edges only. Practice this technique on a test panel before attempting it on your car or truck.

Because automobile roofs, hoods, and trunk lids lie in a horizontal plane, hold the paint gun at a horizontal angle and make smooth, even, uniform passes. To prevent paint from dripping on the body, many painters tie an old tack cloth or other absorbent and lint-free rag around the top of the cup, where it makes contact with its support base. Even with paint guns that are reported to be dripless, this is not a bad idea.

Holding the paint gun so the nozzle is perpendicular to the surface is important. Lock your wrist and elbow, then walk along panels to ensure a right-angle position. Do not rely solely upon your arm to swing back and forth. Move your body with your arm and shoulder anchored. Again, this takes practice, especially when you have to move from one panel to another in a smooth, steady, even walk.

The mixture is then stirred for a couple of minutes, using a paint stir stick. Don't attempt to use a screwdriver for this. The blade isn't wide enough to stir anything, and it ruins the screwdriver. Stirring sticks are available where you purchase your paint, so make sure you ask for a few when you pick up supplies.

Even fan spray should overlap the previous spray by half. In other words, the center of the first pass should be directed along the masking line: half of the paint on the masking paper, the other half on the body surface. The second pass should be directed in such a way that the top of the fan rides right along the masking line. Then, each successive pass should overlap the previous one by half. Maneuver each pass with the same speed and at the same distance away from the surface: 6–10 inches.

Look at your painting results. If you have practiced with your equipment on an old hood or trunk lid, chances are good that your efforts are proving worthwhile. If not, you might be experiencing runs or other gross abnormalities. Runs are generally caused by too much paint landing on the surface at one time. You may be holding the gun too close or walking too slowly. Whichever, you have to adjust. Keep practicing until the paint appears to go on smoothly and evenly without running.

SPOT PAINTING

Whether your project involves a minor body repair or complete repaint, the rules of right-angle application and controlled spraying remain in effect. The difference is in the amount of paint needed and the technique for blending new paint into old finishes.

What you want to avoid when spot painting is a raised line separating the section you painted from the old surface. One way to get around this problem is to mask along a definite edge, groove, vinyl graphic, or stripe. Depending on the type of paint you use and the prominence of the lip or raised paint edge, some delicate wet sanding could make the scar almost invisible. Professionals opt for a different method. First, they mask an edge or stopping point with tape rolled over on itself.

Let's say you want to spot paint a ding repair near the driver's side taillight on the quarter panel. You've masked along a piece of bodyside molding on the

With the gravity-feed gun securely supported in the stand and a paint strainer in place atop the paint cup, the sealer can be poured into the paint cup. For most suction-feed guns, the stand isn't necessary because the bottom of the paint cup is large enough to stand on its own. No matter what you're spraying, make sure you use a paint strainer when pouring it into your paint cup. Also, make sure you put the cap back on the spray-paint gun and secure it properly. With the air pressure involved when spraying paint, an unsecured paint cap can make a mess.

The two knobs on the back of the spray-gun housing are for adjusting the paint material and the airflow. Material control is usually adjusted by the knob in line with the air nozzle, while the airflow is adjusted by the opposite knob. Refer to the literature included with your spray gun or ask your salesman if you have any questions regarding adjusting or cleaning your spray gun. This is all the more reason to purchase a spray gun from an auto body paint and supply store rather than a discount store. When adjusted properly, most spray guns will give great results and, if cleaned and maintained correctly, will last indefinitely.

This parts-holding rack is designed to tilt and adjust as necessary for the parts being painted. These are common in body shops but are probably too expensive for the hobbyist painting his first car. Although not actually the case in this photo, it appears as though the upper portion of the rack would interfere with the spray gun while the painter sprays this bumper. This is something you must consider when laying out or hanging parts to be painted. They must be situated so that you can access them completely. Anything that cannot be adequately covered will require repositioning after the part has dried, to allow you to paint the opposite side or anything that was not accessible.

Attempt to position parts to be painted so that as much of the part as possible can be painted from a comfortable position. This won't always be possible, but make it easy on yourself when you can.

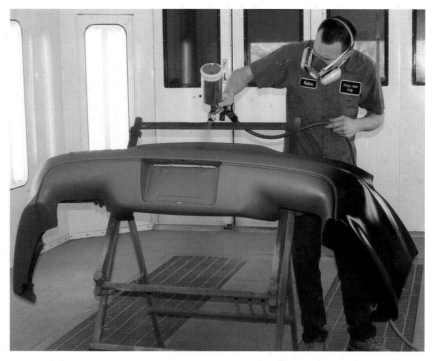

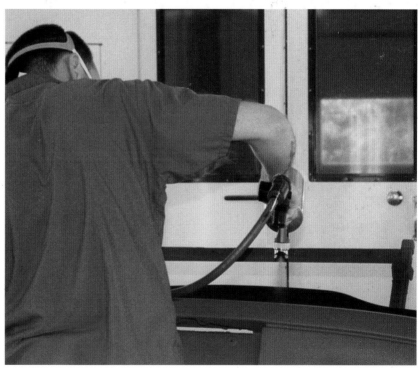

bottom of the panel and a design groove on the top. But toward the front and back, there are no definite break points. To solve this problem, lay a piece of masking paper at both the front and rear ends of the repair area, as if they were going to cover more of the paint surface than needed. Affix the front tape edge of the piece toward the front and the rear tape edge of the piece toward the rear.

Now, roll the paper over the tape edge so that only the sticky side of the tape is exposed. In other words roll the front section of paper toward the front of the car, over the secured tape edge, and roll the rear section of paper toward the rear of the car. This leaves the repair area clear and both the front and rear areas masked with a strip of tape that has been rolled back over itself.

The purpose of this technique is to create a curved section of tape that paint can bounce off of and become overspray, with only a portion of it actually adhering to the surface. This prevents the paint from forming a well-defined line along the tape and helps it feather into a great blend.

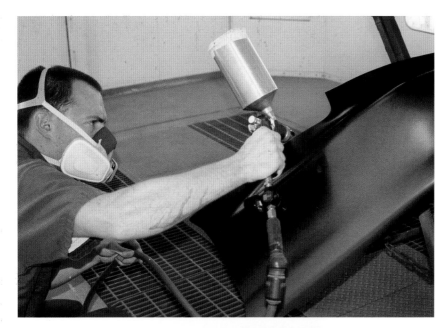

Unless you're painting a very small part, you'll need to move around to see and paint all surfaces. When you think you have all surfaces covered, it's a good idea to walk around the pieces or parts again, looking from different angles to make sure you have indeed covered all you intended.

To help that kind of situation even more, painters like to reduce paint to about a three-to-one ratio for melting. Once they've painted the spot, they remove those rolled-over strips of paper and tape and then empty their paint gun cups to about 1/4 inch full. To that, they add 3/4 inch of reducer. This makes for a very hot mixture, a blend that will loosen old paint and allow just a tint of the new paint to melt in. The results are great because it's difficult to find where the new paint starts and the old paint leaves off. If any nibs remain, you can wet sand them smooth, unless you've used uncatalyzed enamel paint.

The most important thing to remember about spot painting is that a valley has to be filled where you removed the old paint and sealer. It might only be 1–3 mils deep, but nevertheless, it has to be filled if the overall surface is to be flat, even, and smooth. New sealer and primer sufacer will fill up most of the valley, with paint filling in the rest and then blending with the adjacent surface.

The reducer-rich paint mixture literally opens up the existing paint to let a touch of new pigment fall into place and blend with the old. This is the last step of a paint job, after the appropriate flash (drying) time has passed for the final spray-paint pass for the center of the repaint.

Warning! Before attempting this kind of spot repair technique on your car, confirm its value with your auto body paint and supply specialist. It works great for some urethanes and lacquers, but it may not fare so well with certain enamels. It all depends on the brand and type of product you use, the paint currently on your car, the color, and what additives, such as metallic or pearl, are involved. There is no clear-cut rule to follow—each case is unique.

FULL-PANEL PAINTING

Automobile and paint manufacturers advise auto painters to repaint complete sides of certain cars, even if the only problem area is minor body repair on a single panel. As ridiculous as this sounds, there is a method to the madness. This type of overkill repaint involves vehicles factory painted with pearl or other special additives. Tricoat or candy finishes are also extremely difficult to match with new paint because of

When spraying a large, flat area, it should be either horizontal or vertical rather than at an angle. When spraying the side of a vehicle, it will basically be vertical, while the top, trunk, and deck lid will be horizontal. Depending on your stature, you may have difficulty reaching the middle of some large panels, such as the hood or deck lid from some of the land barges of the 1950s and 1960s. In that event, you may want to remove the panel, to be sure you get an even coat.

the complex interplay of coatings that produces the finish's unique look.

To find out whether your finish is amenable to spot painting—new-style paint schemes are more likely to be difficult—check with your local auto body paint and supply store.

Painting just a panel or two is generally no big deal with noncustom paint products. Masking can begin and end on definite body design breaks. You can see what has to be painted and know that virtually everything else has to be masked. But what if your car or truck is a little on the old side and you're concerned about matching the new color with the old? Who wants a door and fender to look like new while the quarter panel, hood, and roof look old and oxidized?

Many times, a complete buff job on old paint surfaces makes them look just like the new paint that was just sprayed onto doors and fenders. In other cases, you must spray a blend to feather in between the new paint and the old.

Feathering in is similar to the melting-in process described earlier—melting-in describes this process on a single panel, whereas feathering is blending surrounding panels to match the one that was repaired or refinished. After a panel is completely painted, you remove the masking and spray a light coating of heavily reduced paint and reducer onto the existing paint. This works well for certain products but not at all for others. Check with your auto body paint supplier to see if your new paint can be feathered into the existing paint in this manner.

To blend in panels with compatible paint finishes, painters complete their main job and then take off strips of masking from adjoining panels. With a heavily

reduced paint mix, they gently melt in a feathered edge. These edges may extend out to 6 inches. When the paint finishes are incompatible for melting, painters must rely on a perfect color match between adjacent panels.

FLASH TIMES
Paint dries as its solvents evaporate and its pigments cure. You cannot spray additional coats until the solvents from the first coat, and each successive coat, have had adequate time to evaporate. This is critical! If you spray a new coat of paint over one that has not had time to flash (dry), you will be trapping solvents underneath the new layer. They will not remain harmlessly in place but will pass through the overlying material, causing blistering, checking, crazing, cracking, dulling, lifting, sagging, or other such imperfections on the topcoat.

Flash times are clearly indicated on all information sheets and application guides for all paint products. Second and final coats may require longer flash times than initial coats. Read and follow the directions for the paint system employed. They are not all the same. This goes for undercoats, topcoats, and clearcoats.

CLEARCOAT FINISHES
Along with offering better protection for metallics and other paints, clearcoats reduce the amount of color material needed for a good finish, thus reducing some of the overall solvent needed and helping manufacturers stay within governmental guidelines. Clearcoat finishes are also good for smoothing out sharp paint lines left behind along custom graphic paint edges. Additionally, painters

Whether you're painting something as small as a gas filler door or as large as a truck bed or complete vehicle, remember to use wax and grease remover before every application of anything in the paint system. This includes sanding, body filler, primer sufacer, sealer, basecoat, and clearcoat. Then also spray off the entire surface with an air nozzle, to make sure no wax and grease remover or moisture of any kind is left on the surface.

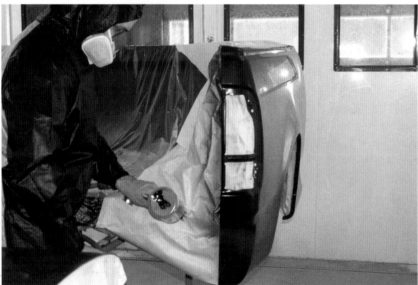

Paint the edges of an area first, then the main surface. That way, overspray helps cover the main area, and you can apply less paint there. If you get the main area painted to the appropriate thickness first, then do the edges, the extra paint from the overspray may cause blemishes on the main surface.

use clear to help feather in repaints along adjacent panels and old paint perimeters.

Applying clear is no different from applying other paints. You have to maintain a close eye on your work, so that each pass is uniform. Exterior body parts, such as door handles and key locks, can be masked for clear paint applications without as much concern about overspray blemishes as with color coats. This is because clearcoat dries to a clear, invisible finish. Beware not to spray clear until the last color coat has dried for the recommended period. Spraying clear too early will trap the color coat's solvents and lead to the same finish problems described above.

TRI-STAGE FINISHES

Originally reserved for custom jobs or high-end vehicles, tri-stage paint systems are becoming more common. Whether custom or original, tri-stage finishes include a base coat, color coat, and clearcoat. The base coat gives the color coat a compatible base and also influences its appearance. For example, a purple coat sprayed over a silver base will have a different tint than the same color sprayed over a white base.

As you would with any other paint, you apply base coats to cover all intended new paint surfaces. After the recommended flash time has elapsed, spray on color coat using the techniques described earlier. When you've sprayed the correct number of color coats and the proper flash time has passed, proceed to the clearcoat stage.. Be sure to clean your spray gun according to the methods described earlier and the paint and spray-gun manufacturers' instructions.

Once the final coat of clear has dried for the recommended period, you'll be able to wet-sand blemishes and buff areas that need extra polishing. The clearcoat finish will prevent wet sanding or polishing from distorting the blended color achieved between the base coat and color coat.

PLASTIC OR FLEXIBLE ASSEMBLIES

A great many different kinds of plastics are in use today on all types of automobile parts and assemblies. They range from acrylonitrile butadiene styrene (ABS) to thermoplastic olefin (TPO) and sheet molded compounds (SMC) to reaction injection molded plastic (RIM). Each has its own place, from rigid grillework sections to flexible bumper covers.

If you're using lacquer or enamel paint, such as on a vintage restoration, any flexible components should be sprayed with paint containing a special additive that allows it to flex along with the part. You may also have to use special undercoats in addition to topcoat additives. The only way to be certain that the products that you use are compatible and designed for painting the parts you intend to spray is to check with your auto body paint and supply specialist. If you're using a basecoat/clearcoat paint system, however, flex additives are no longer necessary because of the flexible characteristics of today's urethane products.

The same caution applies to rigid plastics. Some materials are compatible with normal painting systems, while others may require specific undercoats. By using the designed paint system and proper additives, along with the recommended preparation techniques, you will be assured that newly applied paint coats will not peel, crack, or flake off. In rare cases, you cannot repaint certain solvent-sensitive plastic or urethane parts when the factory primer seal has been broken. In those situations, you have to replace the parts.

AFTER SPRAYING PAINT

Once you've painted the vehicle to your satisfaction, you need to complete several further tasks to ensure the overall quality of the job. Once the paint has dried sufficiently, wet-sand nibs smooth and carefully

Even when painting the subtle wheelwell flare, position the spray-paint gun so it's perpendicular to the area that bulges slightly from the main panel. The flare varies in width from about 1 to 2 inches wide, so it's not large, but it's still important to apply the paint evenly. Remember that when using a basecoat/clearcoat paint system, the basecoat should be applied only to achieve complete coverage. Gloss will come from the clear.

Kneeling helps this painter see where he's applying the clear. Notice how he took the time to mask the inner wheelwell and the inside of the bed of this pickup truck.

remove the masking tape to prevent unnecessary paint-edge peeling or other accidental finish damage. Read the sections on wet sanding and buffing before removing any masking material.

Uncatalyzed enamels cannot withstand wet sanding or polishing. With this kind of paint system,

It's much easier (less work), faster (again less work), and less expensive (less material) to thoroughly wash the area to remove contaminants than to take the chance you'll have to strip and repaint it. This entire bedside will be washed and dried before it's scuffed.

With the edges covered, the rest of this bedside can be coated with clear. After each coat of clear has had sufficient time to flash, all the dust, dirt, and nibs can be lightly sanded out if necessary prior to the next coat. In collision repairs, two or three coats of clear would typically be applied, with little to no sanding between coats. Custom show-car painters do lots of sanding with extremely fine sandpaper between coats of clear to achieve those mirror-finish paint jobs that cost tens of thousands of dollars. Sanding between clearcoats is what makes the difference between a good paint job and a great one. You decide what best suits your needs.

what you see is what you get, unless you later decide to sand a completely cured but blemished panel down to the substrate and repaint it to perfection.

Certain lacquer and urethane paint finishes can be wet sanded and polished to remove nibs, flatten orange peel, and otherwise smooth small blemishes. This work is normally done on clearcoats, as opposed to color coats, and may require additional light applications of clear. For this reason, professionals seldom remove masking material until they're pleased with the entire paint job and are satisfied that they've remedied all imperfections.

DRYING TIMES

Automotive paint has to dry. If not allowed to do so in a clean environment, the wet finish can be contaminated by dust, dirt, or other debris. Professional painters always leave freshly sprayed vehicles in paint booths until enough time has elapsed for the material to cure completely, according to the paint manufacturer's recommendations.

For example, PPG recommends their DCC acrylic urethane paint systems be allowed to dry 6–8 hours at 70 degrees Fahrenheit or forced dried for 40 minutes at 140 degrees. Force drying requires portable infrared heaters or high-tech paint booths equipped with heating units. For its Deltron basecoat and clearcoat systems, PPG lists specific drying times for air drying or force drying each of the system's components. As stressed earlier, proper drying is essential to prevent future coats from being damaged by trapped solvents.

To ensure good paint adhesion, the freshly washed bedside is scuffed with 400-grit sandpaper. Since basecoat will be applied to approximately half the panel and clearcoat will be applied to all of it, the entire panel must be scuffed. After the panel is scuffed, it will be cleaned again with wax and grease remover and masked completely before it's painted.

Factory paint jobs with urethane paint products and those that are suitable for force drying are baked on body surfaces at temperatures around 450 degrees Fahrenheit. This can be accomplished only while cars are stripped. Otherwise, plastic, rubber, and vinyl parts would melt. Cars still equipped with these items cannot be force dried at temperatures above 160 degrees. Excessive heat can also damage the vehicle's computer.

There are other factors to consider when using heat lamps and other force dry methods. Initial flash times are extremely important. Most paint products must air dry for 15 minutes or longer on their own, to let the bulk of the solvent material evaporate. Too much heat too soon will evaporate this solvent too quickly, causing blemishes.

Some paint finishes have a window of time during which you must wet sand or recoat. Wait beyond that period and you may have to scuff sand and clean the surface again before applying touchup coats, to get proper adhesion.

WET SANDING

Confirm ahead of time that the paint system you use is compatible with wet sanding. Your auto body paint and supply jobber can do this while you're discussing your paint needs at the time of purchase. Each automotive paint manufacturer has its own set of guidelines. What may be good for PPG's Deltron system may not be so good for a BASF or DuPont system. In fact, you might even be advised to completely disregard wet sanding and opt instead for polishing to guarantee a perfect finish with the type of product you've chosen.

With the body repaired, this pickup truck is moved to the paint preparation area. primer sufacer has been applied to about the rear third of the bedside. To blend the color, basecoat will be applied from the very rear edge to about the front of the wheelwell, with full coverage centering over the repaired area and feathering out from there. Clearcoat will cover the entire bedside to further blend the repaired area into the old.

Not every type of paint system can be wet sanded. Enamels, for example, cure with a sort of film on their surface, which will be damaged if broken by sandpaper or harsh polish.

Lacquers and some urethane products can be sanded with fine sandpaper soon after they have cured. Although wet-sanding color coats is not recommended, you might be able to lightly sand off nibs, providing you're prepared to touch up the spots with a

light color coat. Wet sanding yields its best results on clearcoats that are then polished.

Basecoat/clearcoat paint systems generally call for a number of color coats and then clearcoats. Especially with candy finishes, sanding directly on the color surface will distort the tint and cause a visible blemish. Wet sanding for them is done on clearcoats only. Your wet sanding efforts should be concentrated on clearcoats, so as not disturb the underlying color coats. Wet sanding clearcoats will bring out a much deeper shine and gloss when followed by controlled buffing and polishing.

Painters use very fine 1500 to 2500-grit sandpaper with water to smooth or remove minor blemishes on cured paint finishes designed to allow wet sanding. Only sandpaper designated wet-or-dry should be used. Those that are not waterproof will fall apart.

As with all other sanding tasks, use a sanding block. Since nibs of dirt or dust are small, fold sandpaper around a wooden paint-stir stick instead of using a large hand block. Their 1-inch width is great for smoothing small spots. Use only light pressure for this type of delicate sanding. Be sure to dip sandpaper in a bucket of water frequently, to keep the paint surface wet and reduce the amount of material buildup on the sandpaper. Add a small amount of mild car-washing soap to the water bucket, to provide lubrication to the sandpaper. The sandpaper should

also be allowed to soak in water for 15 minutes before wet sanding.

If certain blemished areas need a lot of sanding, you may need to apply new coats of clear. This is why you should leave masking material in place during wet sanding.

In some cases, such as on show cars, the entire car body may be wet sanded to bring out the richest, deepest, and most lustrous shine possible. Because they anticipate extensive wet sanding and polishing operations, painters of these cars make sure they have applied plenty of clearcoats.

REMOVING MASKING MATERIAL

To many enthusiastic automobile painters, removing masking paper and tape to reveal a new paint job or quality spot paint repair is like opening birthday presents. It's always a pleasure to see a finished product, especially after viewing it in primer for any length of time. However, unlike the wrapping paper on presents, masking materials must be removed carefully, to prevent finish damage.

As we've discussed, paint has solids in it that build up on car bodies. Especially on jobs where numerous color coats and clearcoats were applied, the thickness of the paint can bridge the lips along masking tape edges. What will occur, in some situations, is the formation of a paint film on a car body that continues over to include the top of the tape. If

If epoxy primer has been applied to keep moisture from penetrating through to the metal surface below, parts may be wet sanded to achieve the ultimate in smoothness before spraying color coats and clear. You can also wet-sand painted parts. (The paint serves as a sealer to keep moisture from the metal below.) Using progressively finer sandpaper, 1500 to 2500 grit, soaked in water, and sand in a circular motion, using light pressure on the sanding block. A slight amount of car-washing soap added to the water lubricates the sandpaper. It is critical not to sand through the paint.

you pull the tape straight up, it could tear flakes of paint from the body surface.

To prevent paint flaking or peeling along the edge of masking tape strips, painters pull tape away from the newly painted body area, as opposed to straight up off the panel, and back upon itself, to create a sharp angle at the point where it leaves the surface. This sharp angle can cut extra-thin paint films, so they don't cause flakes or cracks on the finish.

When they've applied several color and clearcoats along a masked edge, meticulous painters often use a sharp razor blade to cut the paint film between the panel surface and tape edge. If you damage the paint while removing the masking material, you'll have to sand and repaint as needed.

RUB OUT AND BUFFING

As with wet sanding, not every type of paint system can stand up to vigorous polishing or rubbing out. With single-stage urethane, for example, buffing with a gritty compound will only dull the surface and ruin the finish. In contrast, polishing a catalyzed urethane (basecoat/clearcoat) or cured lacquer can make the finishes much more brilliant, lustrous, and deep shining.

A wide variety of polishing compounds is available for new paint finishes. Auto body paint and supply stores carry the largest selection. Some are designed to be used by hand, while others can safely be

polished with buffing machines. Foam pads work best with prescribed compounds and buffing machines limited to slower rpm, while pads made with cloth are better suited for other compounds and machine speeds. Be sure to get what is appropriate for your paint.

PPG manufactures its own brand of rubbing and polishing compounds for its paints. In addition, companies such as 3M and Meguiar's produce several varieties of polishing products, all of which carry labels with instructions for their intended use and application.

Basically, rubbing compounds include relatively coarse polishing grit material. They are designed to quickly remove blemishes and flatten paint finishes. Because these compounds contain grit, they leave behind light scratches or swirls. Therefore, after using compound to flatten orange peel or produce a higher surface luster, you'll need to buff or polish the paint finish with a fine grit material. This may involve, especially with dark colors, exceptionally soft-finish buffing pads and wax.

As refinish products have changed over the years, some ideas that seem like common sense are no longer valid. Manufacturers of the new urethane paint products often suggest polishing with 2,000-grit compound using a foam pad. This should minimize swirls and yield a satisfactory finish the first time around. If swirls are still present, you go back to a

Rubbing compound will "rub out" minute imperfections or orange peel in the final layer of paint. Available in different formulas, it works like extremely fine sandpaper. Even though a vehicle with orange peel in the paint can be shiny, it will have a much higher gloss if the orange peel is buffed out and the surface is that much flatter.

Buffers with maximum speeds of about 1,450 rpm are best for novices. Machines with faster revolutions require more experience. Be aware that even the slower, 1,450-rpm buffers are quite capable of causing paint burns if you don't pay close attention to what you're doing.

To use a buffer, first spread out a few strips of compound parallel to the floor, about 4–6 inches apart. Cover an area no bigger than 2 square feet. Operate the buffing pad on top of a compound strip and work it over that strip's area, gradually moving down to pick up successive strips. The idea is to buff a 2-square-foot area while not allowing the pad to run dry of compound. Keep buffing on that body section until compound is gone and all that remains is shiny paint.

Buffing pads can be operated back and forth as well as up and down. Always keep them moving. Just as with power sanders, a buffer left in one spot can rub through the paint. Be exceptionally careful buffing near ridges, gaps, and corners. If you hit those surfaces with the buffer, all the buffing force is expended on a small, focused area and will quickly burn through the paint. Instead of running the buffing pad on top of ridges, run it just up to their edge and stop. Some painters prefer to mask edges, ridges, and corners with strips of masking tape, to protect them against accidental buffing burns, then remove the tape and buff them by hand. This might be a good idea for the novice.

If you have to buff in tight areas, such as near door handles, throttle the machine on and off to lower the rpm speed. Slowing the pad in this way will help reduce the possibility of paint burns. Be sure plenty of compound is spread over the area. For extra-confined spaces, apply compound by hand with a soft, damp cloth.

Make sure you don't drag power cords for electric buffers and air hoses for pneumatic models over the paint finish. A good way to keep them under control while buffing roofs, hoods, and trunk lids is to drape them over your shoulder. To prevent buckles, zippers, snaps, or rivets on your clothing from scratching the car as you move alongside it, wear an apron. A long sweatshirt may also work. If possible, simply avoid clothing with these hard, sharp features.

Power buffers will throw spots of compound all over your car, clothes, and nearby surfaces. Be prepared for this kind of mess by covering adjacent cabinets or workbench items with tarps or dropcloths. Always wipe buffing compound thrown by the buffer

slightly coarser compound to remove the swirls, then use the finer 2,000-grit again. With older technology, painters would start with the coarse rubbing compound, then work up to the finer stuff, instead of this seemingly backward procedure.

Although paint finishes may appear dry, especially those that included a hardening agent, they may not be ready for buffing right away. Allow sufficient time for all solvents to evaporate before smothering them with polishing compound. Application guides and information sheets generally list the recommended time. The information sheet for PPG's polyurethane clear, for example, states, "Allow 16 hours before polishing either air dried or force dried DCU 2021."

By hand, use a soft, clean cloth for rubbing out and polishing, and follow directions on the product label. Many auto enthusiasts apply polish in straight back-and-forth movements from the front to back of vehicles, instead of circular patterns. They profess that polishing panels in this manner greatly reduces their chances for creating swirls.

You need experience practicing with a buffing machine before using it on your car's new paint job. Practicing will help you avoid a paint burn—polishing through the paint finish down to primer or bare metal.

Polishing products come in a wide variety for many applications. You can apply them by hand, or by machine with a wool buffing pad or a foam pad. Polishing products are available in a variety of compounds, or grits. If you're polishing by hand, you would typically use a coarser compound than with an electric or pneumatic buffer.

off the paint as soon as possible because it can damage the new paint if it's allowed to dry.

As cloth buffing pads become covered with compound, or every three passes, whichever comes first, use a pad spur to clean them. With the pad spinning, gently but securely push a spur into the pad's nap. This will break loose compound and force it out of the pad. You'll be surprised at how much material comes off pads, so be sure to do your pad cleaning away from your car and anything else that you don't want covered with compound or pad lint. You can't clean the buffing pads too much.

OVERSPRAY

Polishing and buffing efforts usually work well to remove light traces of overspray from hoods, roofs, and trunk lids. Extra-heavy overspray residue may require a strong polishing compound for complete removal. For severe problems, consult your auto body paint and supply jobber.

If you've been meticulous with your masking, most overspray problems, if any, will involve items like tailpipes, fenderwells, horn units, and other lowdown pieces. You could spend a lot of time removing overspray from painted items, like fenderwells, or spend a lot less by simply covering overspray with black paint or undercoat. If this won't work for some reason, such as a show car with matching-color fenderwells, you'll have to sand, polish, or possibly even repaint affected areas.

Overspray on chrome might be easily removed with a chrome polish, such as Simichrome. Heavy concentrations may require number 0000 steel wool with polish. Chrome items commonly prone to overspray include tailpipes, wheels, bumpers, grille pieces, and trim. The best way to avoid overspray problems on these accessories is to mask them properly, with plenty of tape to secure paper edges, so puffs of paint spray can't infiltrate the masked space.

Remove paint overspray from glass using the solvent appropriate to the vehicle's paint system. Dab some solvent on a clean cloth and rub off overspray. If that doesn't work, try using number 0000 or finer steel wool and solvent. (**Caution:** Some newer windshields are made with acrylic ingredients that even fine steel wool may scratch. If you aren't sure whether your car's windshield is solid glass or acrylic, check with a dealership service department, auto glass business, or your auto body paint and supply jobber.) In extreme cases, you might have to use a razor blade and a delicate touch to scrape overspray off glass.

CHAPTER 4.3

PAINT F/X:
THE GRANITE EFFECT

BY CRAIG FRASER

In this world of radical paint jobs and mind-numbing graphics, it has become the general consensus that man cannot live by single color alone. It used to be that if you had graphics, or anything with four or more colors, your paint job was considered radical. But now, colors aren't enough—we need F/X (effects).

One of the newest concepts to hit the shops in the last few years is the return of the airbrush to the automotive painting scene. Drop shadows, highlights, marbleizing, and Van Halens are terms that are becoming all too familiar to the painter and striper. With just a little ingenuity and a few stolen sign-painting tricks (not to mention some vintage Hot Rod magazines), painters can spice up their graphics with their own bag of F/X.

In fact, the techniques described here are similar to those popular back in the 1960s and early 1970s—the height of the custom painting genre. The only difference between then and now is not the tricks but the way painters present them.

Popular with sign painters for years, the "granite" or "stone" effect has had a successful run in the mini-trucking and Harley industries. "Granite" serves a dual purpose as a graphic effect and as a neutral backdrop. Its medium gray value coordinates well with any color and acts as a good background canvas for multiple color graphics. Neutral grays and silvers are important as backdrops to many graphic designers because of their ability to tie in the individual colors without competing with the design itself. (Plus, if used as a bottom graphic on a car or truck, the granite effect successfully hides rock chips.) The effect works well with silvers, by the way, and gives a pretty funky reflective look when done with pearls incorporated into the colors.

For this demo, we've used a power-coated metal sign blank. For practice, use any power-coated or previously painted metal panel. I highly recommend practicing and experimenting on sign blanks when airbrushing. First, you can clearcoat and keep them as graphic examples; second, it's better for your health than experimenting on a client's car or Harley.

I mention a number of House of Kolor products only because they're what I currently use in the studio and in our shop at Kal Koncepts. But the techniques and demos remain the same, no matter what products you use. I do, however, recommend the use of automotive urethanes, primarily transparent toners. Our shop has used different brands during the past six years, but our use of transparent toners has remained constant.

1.

Prep the sign blank with 600-grit wet/dry sandpaper. To create a nice border for the piece, mask the edges with 2-inch-wide masking tape; the tape will prevent the graphics from running off the edge of the sign blank. (On an actual vehicle, the border would be the masked graphic. Be sure to mask a large area off to protect the surrounding paint.) Using the same 2-inch tape, mask off the bottom half of the sign blank and draw a few "breaks" in the stone with a fine-point marker.

2.

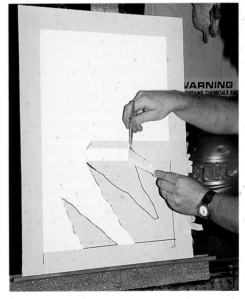

With an exacto knife, cut and peel off the area to be painted, leaving the breaks masked. On a vehicle, take great care when cutting tape, so as not to score the surface. This can cause lifting later on when you unmask. A good trick for getting a rough broken surface is to tear the masking tape before laying out the breaks.

3.

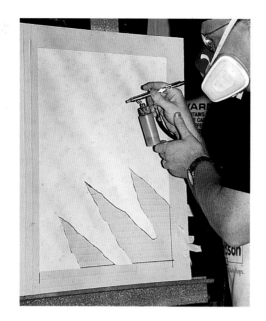

Using a mixture of black and white urethane basecoat, create a medium gray color with which to base the stone effect. HoK BC 25 and 26 baseboats work well for this, since they bite into the surface of the paint and won't wipe off while working. Using solvent-based urethane is also the best way to prevent reaction problems while clearcoating later. Spray the medium gray onto the surface using an Iwata Eclipse bottom-feed airbrush. To give the stone a natural uneven appearance, allow the airbrush to streak the surface instead of applying an even coat. Make sure to follow the direction of the breaks to emphasize the grain direction of the stone.

4.

Keeping the gray basecoat in the airbrush, I use a little T-shirt airbrush trick to give the speckled texture of the stone. Using half of a clothespin (a popsicle stick works just as well) place the stick under and against the airbrush's tip. When spraying, the paint will now load up on the end of the stick and flick off, giving the speckled effect. When using a larger, fan-tipped gun, a piece of cardboard laid over the top will create the same effect.

5.

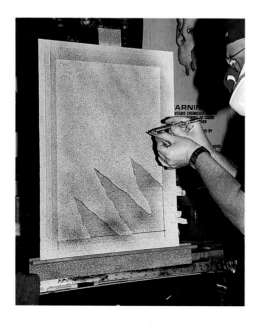

With the entire surface covered in the gray stippling, switch over to the black. It's usually a good idea to practice on a sample board, so as not to ruin your graphic. By varying the angle of the stick against the tip, you can vary not only the quantity of stippling but the size. (The shallower the angle, the finer the stippling, and so on.) Be careful at this stage not to get "clothespin-happy" and obliterate your gray; the stone will get dark fast when spraying black.

Switch to pure white basecoat and apply the final touches to the texture. Not much white is needed to create a good stone effect, so remember the old airbrush rule: less is more. Again, remember to mask the surrounding area well. This may be a good time to look around your shop to see how many vehicles and clients are starting to take on the appearance of stone. If you can't seem to get the hang of this effect, don't worry. Speckling can also be achieved by other methods. For example, you can lower the air pressure of your brush until it starts to split. On the tip-feed models, you can flick the trigger before spraying to load up the needles, thus creating a stipple. And if this doesn't work, don't forget the good ol' toothbrush flick.

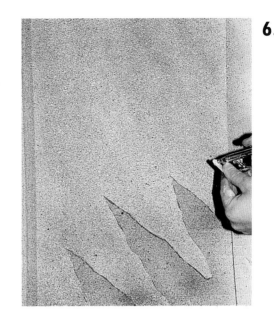

6.

When the stippling is finished, airbrush the cracks and inclusion in the stone, using a thinned-down solution of black urethane and Iwata HP-C. You can create this weak black by over-reducing your existing black basecoat about 1:1 (1 part paint: 1 part reducer). Use the weak black to sketch the cracks. If you make a mistake, the transparent black won't cover up the stone's texture. Nothing ruins a good stone effect faster than too much opaque. Keeping everything transparent will also give the effect more depth after you finish the painting and the clearcoat reactivates the basecoat.

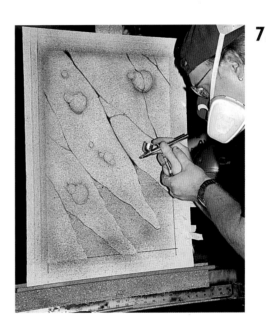

7.

After the sketching is complete, continue laying to darken the cracks and drop shadows. (You can thicken your black solution if you find it's too watery.) Add water streaks to the surrounding areas of the stone, to give them an aged look. Always make sure to paint in the direction of the grain, and with gravity, for water streaks. (Just like in nature!) The third element of the stone is the shadows. To oppose grain direction, choose a light source of the design. Always consider these things before you start painting; you wouldn't want them to conflict with other areas of your paint job.

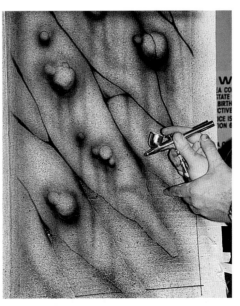

8.

9.

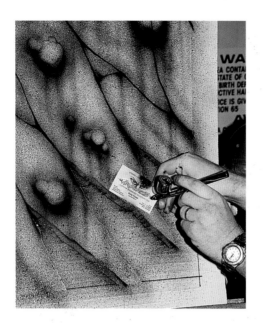

Create the broken edge of the stone by using a movable mask and following it with the airbrush. You can use something ordinary, such as a business card or torn piece of masking tape, to mask the edge. After completing the stone's edge, you can soften it with a little freehand fogging if necessary.

10.

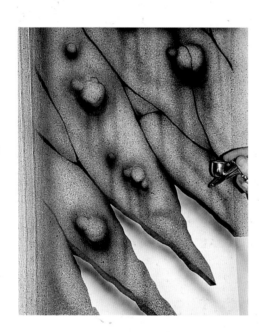

When you've finished applying black to the surface, remove the masking of the stone's breaks (being careful not to lift the border). Following the light source, add drop shadows to the lower left of the breaks. This will separate the stone from the background and add a sense of depth.

11.

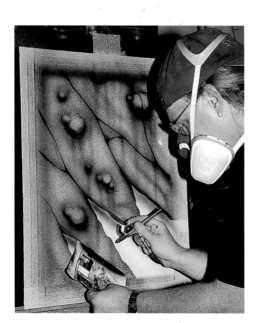

Switching to white and using a freehand shield, spray in a few light reflections across the surface. Again, it's important to keep the white as thin as possible, to maintain transparency. Nothing will muddy a surface faster than opaque white.

Continue with white to trace the side of the cracks where the light would fall, giving them a very thin, highlighted edge. Also add a few reflections and hot spots off the outcroppings and inclusions. Though the hot spots may not be completely authentic, they create a nice effect and make the stone punch out more.

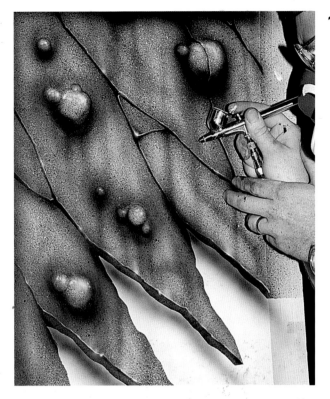

12.

The final step is the clearcoating and buffing. The only drawback is that because of the stippling, the surface may require a few extra coats of clear before it will flow out. This is also a good reason not to stipple too heavily; it can haunt you later in the expensive multiple clearcoats.

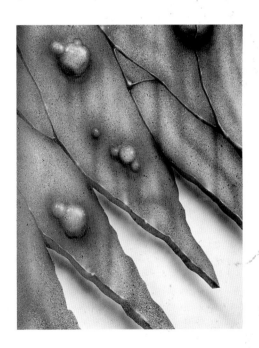

13.

PAINT FX:
RIPPED METAL
&
BRAINS

BY CRAIG FRASER

ontinuing with the faux effects theme, we've thrown in a little metal effects demo. And where you have metal, you have rips, tears, and exposed brains in the background, of course.

Actually, it's a good way to combine effects, and rendering brains is a good way to practice negative/positive-space drawing techniques.

1.

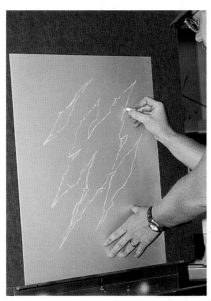

Prepare the sign blank with 600-grit sandpaper and spray the entire surface with a medium-grade silver basecoat. Before picking up the airbrush, it's a good idea to sketch out the ripped area in chalk. This will help center the image and, in more complicated designs, will serve as a massing study. Chalk is a better sketching tool than pencil, since it's easily removed from the surface and is inert, unlike Stabilo or other grease-based pencils.

2.

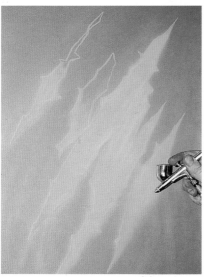

Airbrush the sketched area with SG-102 Chromium Yellow. The yellow acts as a base for the "brain" effect behind the torn metal. Though I prefer to freehand the background on small projects, you can use frisket or masking tape on larger designs to prevent overspray problems. Before going on to the next color, wipe the surface down with a pre-cleaner. Besides eliminating oils and contaminants, the pre-cleaner removes any overspray from the surrounding silver area that may be locked down by later airbrushing.

3.

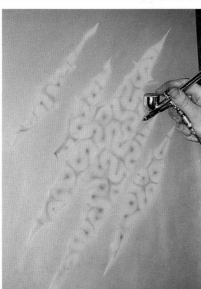

Mix equal parts of HoK Tangerine and Root Beer KBC Kandy basecoats to create a transparent red oxide toner. (You can also add intercoat clear to this mixture to increase the transparency and improve the flow characteristics.) Lightly sketch the outline of the brain tissue. This is tricky because you have to deal with the design in the negative form by drawing the seams between the folds. It's important to keep the spacing equal between the folds, or it will lose its pattern and won't look like a brain.

4.

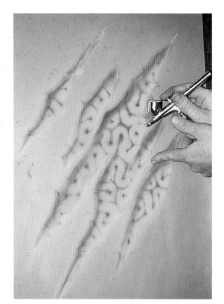

With the red oxide kandy, darken the design and include a drop shadow under the top edge of the rips, to increase the sense of depth. The best characteristic of a true kandy is that you can continue to layer with the same color. And unlike an opaque, which will eventually reach its primary hue, the transparent kandy will continue to darken until almost black but will retain the depth of a transparent. If you're using frisket to mask the area, this would be a good time to remove it. The overspray of the red oxide on the surrounding area will add to the illusion of distressed metal.

5.

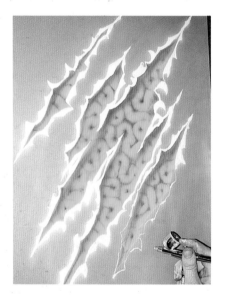

Using opaque white and .2 mm Iwata HP-C, begin sketching the ripped curls of the metal. The previously made notches in the yellow areas are the starting points for the rips. At this stage, you'll have to work close to the surface to reduce overspray and will have to be precise with the airbrush. I suggest using a detail brush here, instead of masking. This eliminates the sharp, raised edge that normally results from masking.

6.

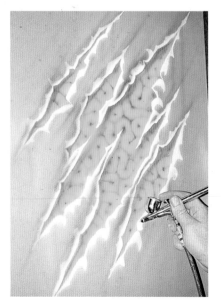

Create a phthalo blue by combining equal parts HoK Oriental Blue and Cobalt Blue KBC Kandy. Fog in the top of the metal rip on the silver side. Keep the blue overspray away from the yellow area; otherwise you'll end up with green because of the transparent nature of the toners. Use the blue to create water streaks and discoloration effects in the metal surface.

7.

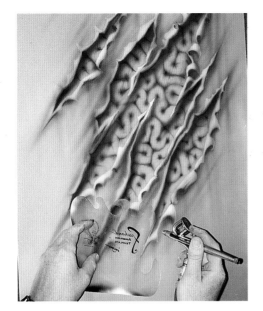

Switch to the .2-mm detail gun and go back over the brain details with deep violet toner. The violet becomes a reddish brown when sprayed over yellow. It also helps continue the discolorations in the metal surface and helps shadow the underside rips. To protect the white edge of the rip from overspray, use one of Artool's freehand shields while darkening in the drop shadow.

8.

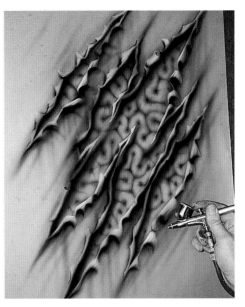

To punch out the details, stay with the fine-line airbrush, using a weakened solution of black. Don't overdo the black—although it's necessary in this design. Too much can deaden or even kill the depth.

9.

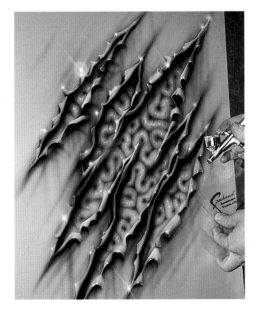

Returning to opaque white, use the Artool shield with the Iwata Micron-C to outline the edges of the rips and to put in the hot spots. With a random squiggling motion, lightly add the highlights on the brains, to give them a wet look. Keep the white over-reduced and transparent at this stage, or the overspray will decimate the underlying detail.

10.

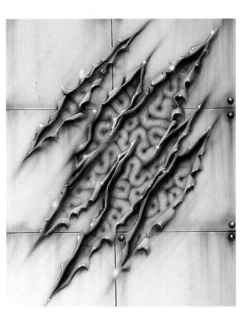

Finish the design either by adding some seams and rivets to the background, as I did, or just leaving it plain, as brain-ridden metal. It's all up to your own sick imagination!

PAINT F/X: FLAME JOBS

BY CRAIG FRASER

Since the first known custom hit the streets, the flame job has been the ultimate poster child of the hot-rod era. While there are a number of ways to do a flame job correctly, there are just as many ways to do it badly. For that reason, entire books have been written on the subject. A good book to check out, and one of my personal favorites, is Rod Powell's *Flame Painting Techniques.*

Flames are somewhat misleading. The trick to flames is to realize that they must occupy negative and positive space simultaneously, to balance out the design. In other words, the flames should appear as flames in the positive sense, but in the negative sense they should resemble drips. If the drips don't appear balanced, aren't symmetrical, or don't look like drips at all, your flames are going to suffer as well. The design should also have continuity. Look at the f lame in this demo as if it were a body. There's a neck, then a torso, then two final licks coming out of the top, which could become the neck of a continuing flame. Like juggling, it's a lot easier to demonstrate than to describe.

1.

Using a red Scotch-Brite pad, scuff a powder-coated sign. On an actual vehicle, if a paint job is fresh enough, you can use Scotch-Brite for total prepping, but I suggest 600-grit wet/dry sandpaper because it does a more thorough, even job.

2.

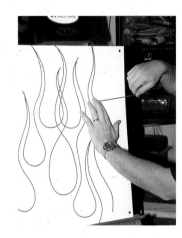

Using blue fineline vinyl tape, begin laying out the general pattern of the flames. Working from left to right, focus on the even balance between the body and the licks, or tongues, of the flames. Keep an eye on the negative and positive space, to balance the overall design on the board, as well as on the flames themselves.

3.

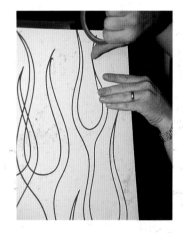

When using blue vinyl tape, work both hands in unison to pull and place the design. This tape is pressure-sensitive and repositionable, but you can burnish it down to increase the adhesion. Make sure to press especially hard on the ends when they overlay, to prevent paint bleeding.

4.

With a roll of 3/4-inch masking tape, begin masking off the flames, butting the tape against the blue fineline. Be sure not to leave any gaps that can allow paint to work its way under the tape.

5.

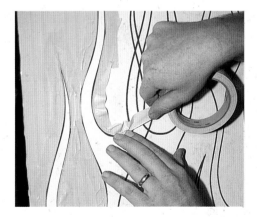

The tape can roll on an inside curve but not an outside curve. By spinning the tape around the design, you can mask the flames off quickly without having to cut different sections out. Press the folds down because they can channel the overspray to the masked-off areas like the tunnels.

6.

Using an exacto knife, cut out the overlapping areas of the blue fineline tape. (The crossover section of the flame will be sprayed with the rest of the design, and overlap will be drop-shadowed later with the airbrush.)

7.

Mix a batch of HoK Hot Pink Pearl and use the RG-2 to spray the design. On a full-sized vehicle, a larger gun would be better, but for this panel and small helmets or tanks, the RG-2 is just right.

8.

Using a mixture of violet kandy and intercoat clear, spray the fades onto the tips. Use the freehand shield to help create the weaving effect of the flames while you drop-shadow the corresponding licks. The intercoat clear not only improves the flow of the paint but also acts as a structural binder to the violet kandy toner.

9.

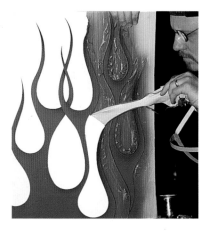

Being careful not to peel the paint, remove the masking design. Always pull the tape back against itself. This will prevent it from lifting and chipping the tape edge.

10.

Using a dry, red Scotch-Brite pad, scuff off any tape residue and eliminate any overspray that may have sneaked through the tape. A little pre-cleaner on a damp towel can also help with this.

11.

With the HP-C, mix up a batch of transparent HoK Basecoat Black and lay in the drop shadow of the flame. Create the transparent black by over-reducing the paint. Masking isn't necessary, since the transparent black won't discolor the flames too much. (But be careful!)

12.

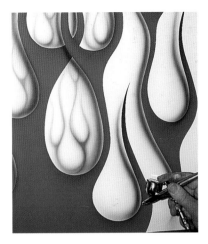

To fill in some space, use the transparent Violet Kandy to airbrush in some freehand flames. Not only does this look good, it's a great way to hide any imperfections you couldn't eliminate with the Scotch-Brite.

13.

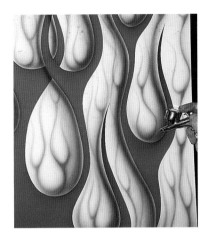

Use the violet to go back over the drop shadows too. Remember, always think on your feet when painting. If something doesn't look right, fix it!

14.

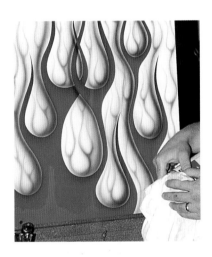

Before pinstriping, wipe the entire surface down with a little PPG DX-330 pre-cleaner. You can use any pre-cleaner to remove overspray or tape residue-just be sure it's not too strong, or it will take off all your fades and freehand flames.

15.

Mix a batch of lime green striping urethane by combining HoK Green and a small amount of lemon yellow. Carefully pinstripe the outside edge of the flame with a 000 (sword) striper brush. If this were a car, you'd clearcoat the flames first, then pinstripe them between clearcoats. This buries the edge of the flame, so that it doesn't peek through the pinstripe. Pinstriping designs on small panels is the best way to build up your pinstriping chops.

16.

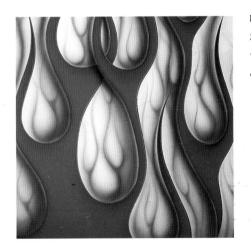

Now your flame job is just itchin' to be put on a street rod. Practice is the only way to pick up this technique. Remember, there's no correct style. If the paint doesn't fall off and small children don't cry when they see it, you've done your job. Flame on!

PAINT F/X:
TRIBAL FLAMES

BY CRAIG FRASER

Tribal graphics have been getting a lot of attention lately, especially the tribal flame design—a hybrid of the classic flame and tribal patterning. This design became popular with the resurgence of the flame job and the popularity of tribal tattooing. Tattoos and tattoo flash art have always been a good source of inspiration for automotive graphics and vice versa. I decided to kick this fairly simple design up a notch with a little lizard-skin airbrushing. Any graphic can be souped up with this type of airbrushing.

1.

We painted the sign blank for this demo black to show a flame design over a darker surface, and we masked the border with masking tape. This isn't necessary for the flame design, but it looks nice for a presentation piece.

2.

Lay out the initial flame design, using blue fineline vinyl tape. This step is the same as laying out an ordinary set of flames. It's much easier to lay out the standard classical design of the flames instead of adding the tribal licks first. Since you're going to add the tribal licks and spikes, make the flames a little more open and spaced farther apart.

3.

After the flames are laid out, burnish the tape down, to keep it from creeping back, and begin adding the licks and tongues of the tribal patterns. For now, stick to a conservative Polynesian pattern, to keep the design less busy. After you get used to the tribal patterning, you can go wild. The vinyl tape is handy for this, since it's repositionable, allowing you to make a lot of layout mistakes without wasting tape.

4.

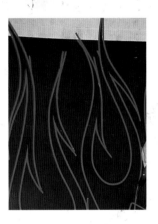

With an exacto knife, remove all of the tape overlaps. The inside of the tape line is what you're trying to keep clean, not the outside edge. Cut into the original flame to allow the added lick to become part of the flame body.

5.

In the previous flame demo, you learned how to mask out the flames in the traditional way using 3/4-inch masking tape and paper. For this design, you'll use another technique that's one of my favorites and is good on large, flat areas that have few or no curves. Using some Gerber transfer paper, which is used to transfer vinyl lettering, roll and flatten out the transfer tape onto the surface. By rolling and pulling, you can apply the paper with few or no bubbles. The transfer paper is much like contact paper but less adhesive.

6.

With the exacto knife, follow the underlying blue tape (you can see it easily through the paper). Carefully cut through the paper, using the blue tape as a buffer to the metal surface. Make sure you don't cut through the paper and tape into the metal surface. This mistake would allow a ghost line to bleed through, possibly damaging the underlying surface, which can cause problems when clearcoating.

7.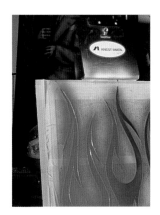

Using the Iwata RG-2 spray gun with the fan tip, spray an even coat of HoK Shimrin Limetime Pearl Green. The benefit of the Shimrin designer pearls is that the metallic/pearl within the basecoat gives the paint a high level of opacity and covers well, as you can see over the black. For this same reason, I don't use them for spraying details later on, since the opaque overspray is devastating to the details of a design.

8.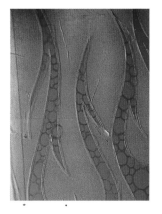

With a top-feed airbrush, mix up a batch of HoK Kandy Organic Green Basecoat Koncentrate. This kandy is transparent, which allows you to build up layers, steadily increasing the detail, depth, and darkness of the design. The snakeskin (as I like to call it) is a conglomeration of differing sizes of circles intertwined within one another. Although labor-intensive to apply, it is definitely a unique space filler for graphics.

9.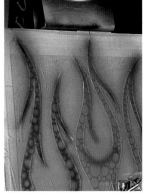

After sketching in the faint design, go back over the flames and darken the design, adding shading and shadowing between the circles to emphasize the texture and add depth. Use the same transparent green kandy, just apply it more heavily. The sign of a true kandy is its ability to turn almost black when applied in multiple layers.

10.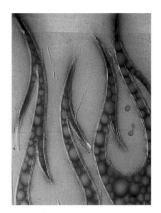

For the final layer, shadow the undersides of the circles to give them individual depth and a slight 3-D appearance. This gives the snakeskin the illusion of having a pebbled surface. To bunch out the larger circles, add a drop of black in the green to speed up the layering process (but not enough black to kill the hue).

11.

Give the paint an hour to set and then pull the tape off slowly. Carefully pull back to prevent the paint from lifting. By pulling the tape back against itself, you create a knife-type edge that cuts the paint as you pull, instead of chipping and lifting the paint. Another nice thing about the transfer tape is that you can usually lift the entire masking system with one careful pull (which is a lot better than pulling for a few hours).

12.

Even the most careful masker has problems with blowouts and bleed-throughs. The difference between good painters and bad ones is not in how few mistakes they make but in how they repair them. In this case, use a little piece of red Scotch-Brite to scuff off the blow-throughs. Sometimes a rag with a bit of pre-cleaner is all that's necessary to wipe off these annoying overspray demons.

13.

Add a small teaspoon of Lazuli dry pearl to some HoK transparent marbleizer. Marbleizer is a substrate or binding medium used as a carrier of dry pearl. It dries slowly, which gives you time to manipulate the surface of the sprayed area.

Though you can use anything to manipulate the surface, I decided to use the classic "old-school" technique of plastic wrap. While the marbleizer is still wet, place the plastic wrap on the surface. The plastic wrap gives an effect similar to that of veins in marble. The effects can vary, depending on the amount of time the plastic is on the surface or whether it's shifted. If there's a problem with the surface texture, respray the area with marbleizer, which will reactivate the surface and allow you to create another effect.

14.

15.

Allow the marbleizer about half an hour to dry, then spray the entire surface with a protective layer of SG-100 Intercoat Clear. Remove the masking, and the piece is ready to be pinstriped. The protective clear is necessary if you have to wipe the pinstriping off without damaging the underlying design. Combine HoK light blue and white striping urethanes and begin striping the flame.

Using light blue, begin striping the border edge with a standard Xcaliber 000 sword striper and add a panel effect to the flames. I used a phone book as a palette for the striper, to work the paint into the brush. This gives a constant line, and when working on a vehicle, allows you to pull a solid line down the entire length of a car.

16.

17.

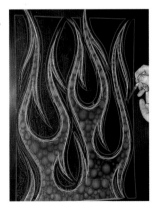

This is a good example of a tribal flame with a little bit of the old-school patterning and some airbrushed goodies. Knowing how to modify a flame design will make your designs stand out as your own.

PAINT F/X:
STRETCHED FACES

BY CRAIG FRASER

W hat F/X demos would be complete without one on painting warped faces pressing through toxic green plastic wrap? If you don't find these images frightening, picture them poking through your wallpaper or bathroom mirror at 3 A.M.!

I've painted this effect several times, but recently I've had a number of requests for it. This demo is a bit tricky because you're creating a positive element by airbrushing in the negative space. In the finished piece, the lightest areas of the image that appear closer to you are actually the underlying green color.

To create the illusion of depth, you can make these colors appear lighter and bring them forward by airbrushing-in the surrounding shadows of the stretched fabric. It follows along the depth theory that light colors come forward and dark colors recede. If you've got an existing light-colored area and you bring it forward by darkening the surrounding areas, you're airbrushing-in the negative space to create design depth.

Use the demo as an example, but also try to render different objects with this stretched effect, including lettering.

1.

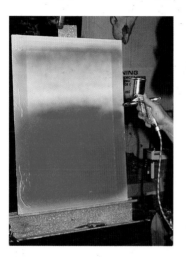

First, sand your sign blank and mask the border. To create the toxic green background, spray with a good coat of HoK Limetime Shimrin urethane. These Shimrins have a cool pearlescent effect that changes color, depending on the light source. You can also use other colors; just remember that if they're too dark, the detail work is hard to see.

2.

I don't recommend stretching plastic wrap over a friend's face as a reference source, but you can obtain a similar effect with wet cheesecloth. For this demo, I used a photo of a face behind a sheet and a model skull. Lightly sketch the design on the sign blank with white chalk.

3.

Using HoK BC-26 Basecoat White and the Eclipse, freehand-spray all the highlights of the faces, fingertips, and folds. Don't go overboard with the white at this stage; if you do, it could clutter the piece. Also, make sure the white is thinned enough so that it still covers but doesn't leave any grainy spray. Very little chalk was used in the sketch because of the transparent nature of this design.

4.

With Limetime Shimrin and the RG-2, fog over the white high-lights with metallic green. This not only blends the design into the background but also mutes the white, so it doesn't stand out as much. Keeping the light source to the right, fog the left side of the images more, to give the illusion of cast shadows.

5.

Allow the Shimrin half an hour to dry. Using the HP-C, begin defining the shadows and folds with Kandy Organic Green Koncentrate mixed with SG-100 intercoat clear. This highly transparent solution has enough pigment to color but still allows the metallic to show through. The trick to airbrushing shadows is that you must visualize the design in the negative to airbrush around the highlights.

6.

Moving to the HP-C .2-mm detail gun, darken the solution with a bit of black toner. This speeds up the layering process and adds more depth, especially around the teeth and fingertips, where more contrast is needed to punch them out. A movable photo-paper mask gives a cleaner, hard line to the dark sides of the folds and wrinkles. Keeping the shield slightly off the surface prevents the line from appearing too hard and masked.

7.

With the transparent green, soften the shielded lines and finish any final details and touchups. At this stage, highlights and hot spots can be added to increase depth and give the green a wet look. I decided to leave white out of the final step, giving the piece a dark, eerie look. I've seen many pieces ruined by too many highlights and last-minute touches. Remember, when it comes to highlights, less is more.

8.

9.

10.

Strip off all the tape, then add a slight drop shadow to the edge for a floating-off-the-surface illusion. While this design can be used as a standalone mural on a tank or hood, it's also a good effect to include in a graphic or on a T-shirt, to attract attention. The final step is to apply a clearcoat of HoK UFC-40 urethane. The clearcoat not only protects the surface but adds a whole new dimension of depth that's impossible to obtain with non-cleared surfaces. Besides penetrating the layers of urethane tones, the clear reactivates and brightens the colors and acts as a light transport to provide that "reach-in-with-your-arm" depth that custom automotive paint jobs are known for.

PAINT F/X:
THE ART OF
SKULLING

BY CRAIG FRASER

Where would the custom paint business be without the art of airbrushing skulls? An alternative to freehand skull airbrushing is movable mask and freehand stencils.

We highly encourage the use of freehand shield systems. I use them often because they provide a softer edge than masking tape and a cleaner, harder edge than you can get from freehanding, without the fear of overworking the area.

I first learned about freehand shield systems from Radu Veru's *Complete Studio Handbook*, which, in my opinion, is the finest airbrush book ever written. I've been making these stencils/shields for the past 10 years out of anything from acetate to photo paper, even x-ray film. Artool has saved me a lot of exacto cutting and layout work by making a number of shield shapes available, not to mention how much more convenient it is to have a shield that is urethane-proof. So if you're a purist and you feel that shields are evil, don't knock it till you've tried it!

1.

Pictured here are a passel of freehand shields to play with. These particular shields are from the Artool Skullmaster series, designed by yours truly.

2.

These stencils are identical. Soak overnight in lacquer thinner and the one on the left will look as new as the one on the right. Before using any commercial or homemade stencil, be sure it's solvent-proof. All it takes is a little solvent to convert an ordinary stencil into a potato chip!

3.

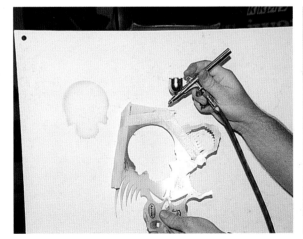

Mix a batch of HoK Violette Kandy. Using the frontal skull stencil, spray the positive element of the skull outline with the Iwata Eclipse-C. Be careful not to brush the stencil across the wet paint when lifting it, otherwise you'll smear your work.

4.

Choosing the evil eyes on the stencil, position and spray the eye and nose area. If you were to choose the normal eyes on this particular stencil, you'd mask off the second set of eyes. The masking is important, since overspray can wreak havoc when working with stencils.

This chapter shows how to use stencils and free-hand airbrushing to complete the design. The trailer example at the end shows how these stencils work without freehand and how they can save quite a bit of time and sanity. However, no stencil system is a magic wand. Stencils are merely tools. They can be under-used and overused. When properly used, they can improve the overall design and shave time off any job.

5.

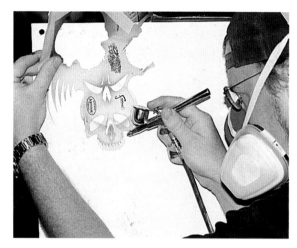

Move the stencil back into position, to align with the positive area already sprayed, and lightly fog in the gum line for the teeth. The bottom edge of the teeth was already laid out with the positive area. The image of the stencil in front of you can play a nasty negative/positive game on your perception!

6.

After removing the stencil, you can see how the image starts to take shape. Use the small crack design in the Screaming Skull stencil to spray in a crack in the head. Though the three skulls in the pack are separate entities, you can use them together quite often.

7.

Sorry, for those of you who thought there was only going to be stencil work; it's time to freehand! Freehand sketching with the airbrush not only softens the mask lines but adds a lot more depth. In this case, you should add a drop shadow and some streaks running underneath the skull image.

8.

Just to be different, go ahead and add a melted candle on top of the skull. By incorporating more and more freehand airbrushing into the piece, it becomes difficult to differentiate the stencil areas from the freehand areas.

9.

Switching over to white basecoat, apply slight high-lights to the skull, to punch it out more. Because of the white basecoat on the panel, the effect is not as dramatic in this demo. Your highlights will stand out only as much as the contrast of the surroundings allows. A little highlight in the center of the eye sockets adds a ghoulish touch.

10.

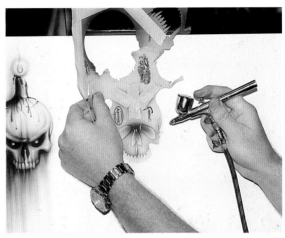

Using the same stencil, create a similar skull with alternative eye design. This eye design is the classic blank-stare look reserved for most skulls. (Usually the angry eyes are reserved for characters who have skin.)

11.

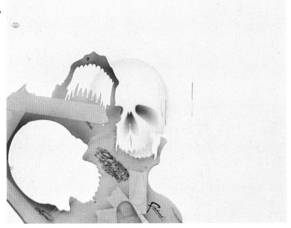

With the lower-jaw section of the stencil, add a different bottom jaw to this skull. Note the masking tape throughout the stencil, necessary to prevent overspray into the surrounding pattern areas.

12.

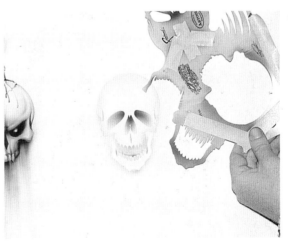

Here you can see the negative and positive elements of the lower jaw in the stencil. By repositioning the lower jaw, you can also alter the opening of the mouth itself. To simplify the design, have the mouth shut for this one.

13.

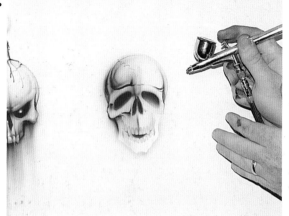

Using freehand, shade and shadow the contours of the skull to give it shape and depth. As in this case, you can give a hard horizon reflection to the skull, for a polished or chrome effect.

14.

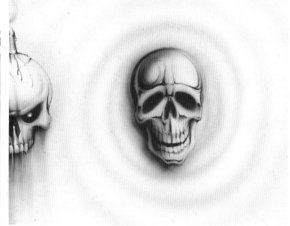

The freehand airbrushing of the skull is necessary to complete the image. The stencil acts merely as a template for the completed image. A faded spiral surrounding the skull adds a "twilight zone" touch to the image.

15.

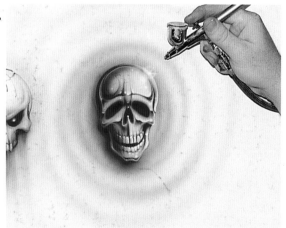

Using HoK White Basecoat, punch out the highlights and emphasize the light source. The highlights add a nice touch to the chrome effect. Normally, you would use a multiple-color rendering for chrome, but the point comes across in monochrome.

16.

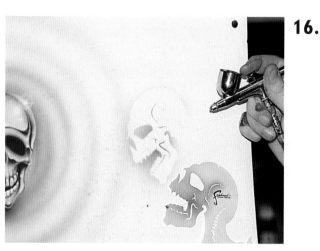

For the third skull, switch to the side profile screaming skull stencil. The side profile skull has the jaw already attached, as can be seen in the positive relief airbrushed on the board.

17.

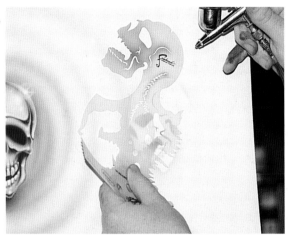

Use the same stencil for the crack as used on the first skull. Like the other stencils, this one has a selection of circles and half circles for the eyes, just in case you want your skulls to have a little more personality.

18.

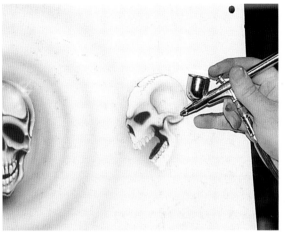

More freehand! Again, this is necessary to give the skull realistic depth and to cover the unnatural shield edge of the design. Good freehand skills will dramatically improve your overall work, so practice as much as you can.

19.

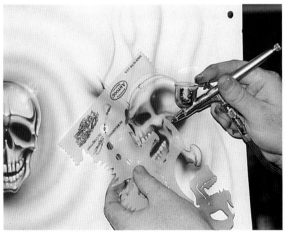

Using the negative section of the stencil, sharpen the edge of the teeth and redefine the positive image. You can also try adding a few freehand flames in the background, to change the design a little.

20.

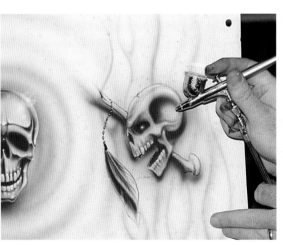

By throwing in a single bone and a feather attached, the skull suddenly takes on a tribal look. Any design should be allowed to progress as you paint. If you stop the creativity of your work at the sketching phase, you'll bore yourself to death (and usually your audience).

21.

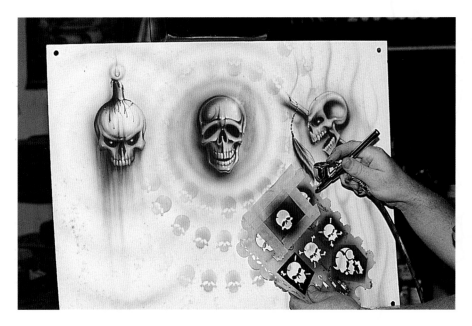

With the third stencil, the multiple, you can add a background design of spiraling
mini-skulls. Again, mask off the skull you want to spray.

22.

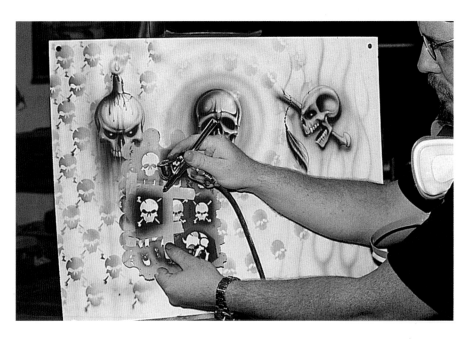

Switching to the skull-and-crossbones stencil, add another pattern to the first skull
design. This type of close patterning is pretty cool because it takes on a dual
image. From a distance, it looks like a paisley pattern; the skulls appear only as
you approach the image. This is a great automotive attribute.

The part of the multiple stencil I've used the most is the section with the "screamy faces." They're little screaming faces, some with hands, some without. They're quite effective when combined with a flame or smoke effect in a mural. They also make great graphic filler.

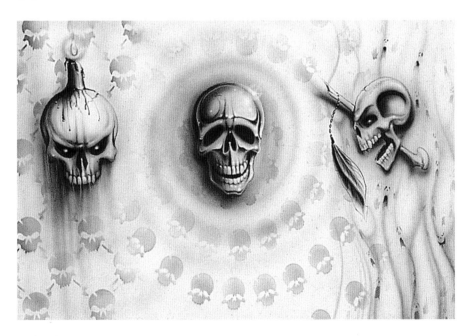

While these skullmaster stencils have a number of other applications, this panel demonstrates a good sampling of some of the things you can do with them.

PAINT F/X:
HOMAGE POUR GIGER

BY CRAIG FRASER

Although the biomechanical style has become popular recently among many automotive artists, few give credit to the originator, H. R. Giger, who pioneered this macabre blend of the living and the mechanical. He is the innovator and Oscar award–winning genius behind the movies *Alien* and *Species.* Giger has done for the macabre and gothic art of this century what H. P. Lovecraft did for literature. Giger's dark fantasy art is disturbing in many ways, but most disquieting is his blending of recognizable objects and anatomy.

You can interpret another artist's style without copying it. Giger pioneered the biomechanical style but not the gothic undertones and influence he used to create it. Always try to expand a style and experiment to bring something of your own to the design. While I used a number of reference pieces from Giger's book series *The Necronomicon*, I also added quite a bit of my own goodies to give it a unique twist.

Biomechanical not only makes a nice mural style but a great background landscape piece.

Sand the surface of your powder-coated sign blank with 600-grit sandpaper, then mask off the border. To obtain a metallic look, spray the sign blank with HoK Orion Silver Shimrin using the Iwata RG-2 gun with the fan tip.

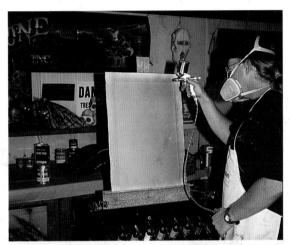

1.

Using one of Giger's art books or other reference material, sketch the rough design with white construction chalk. When rendering a biomechanical design, try to maintain balance in the layout, with implied symmetry. If you study Giger's work, it has balance; yet, when observed closely, it has no true mirror-image symmetry. To quote Giger, "Symmetry is a sign of insanity."

2.

Using a weak (over-reduced and transparent) mixture of black urethane toner, begin laying in the rough outline of the design, using masking tape and straightedges to give faint but sharp edges to the border. For this demo, I used a masked-off circle template to airbrush rivets and screwheads with the bottom-feed Iwata Eclipse. The transparent black allows the silver to show through, giving the black a ghost image.

3.

4.

Using a movable mask cut from photo paper, I defined the random images before freehanding the details. Although I used a Giger book as reference, the design is an interpretation of Giger's biomechanical style and not a duplication of an existing image. You can learn more from an artist by breaking down and analyzing his style than by just copying an image.

5.

Setting aside the freehand shield, I switched to the top-feed Iwata HP-C to start freehanding in the details. This is the fun part. Just let your imagination go. Keeping yourself in the same biomechanical mindset, be sure to step back and look at the work often, to make sure you're not overworking or crowding a particular area.

6.

When the majority of the image is laid out, go over the whole surface lightly with a worn red Scotch-Brite pad and water. Not only does this knock off any high spots and eliminate overspray, it also removes the last of the chalk lines. Be sure to scuff the surface in only one direction, so that if you accidentally scratch the mural, the metal will have a damaged or aged look.

7.

Using the 0.2-mm HP-C detail gun and the same mixture of HoK black toner, finish the details and make the background recede by darkening it and casting shadows. The transparent toner is perfect for shadowing and can become opaque by layering.

A trick when working on small panels or shirts is to turn
the design upside down to finish the detail. This is helpful
for reaching the lower areas and improves the balance of the
final design, by tricking your brain into seeing it as a
group of shapes and not your intended design.

Switching to a combination of HoK Tangerine and Root Beer
Kandy Koncentrate, create a red oxide kandy and use it to
airbrush a rust pallor and water-damage streaks into the
design. This not only breaks up the monotony of the black
and silver but adds depth to the piece and gives it a
sickly, neglected look.

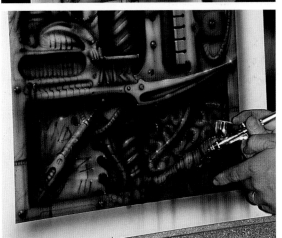

After removing the tape border, use the Micron-C for the
razor-fine highlights along the metal edges. Hot spots are
also added to the skull and curved surfaces, to emphasize
the light source and shadows. Note the added rust streaks
and the drop shadow on the bottom right of the image in the
photo. Even though this is just a demo piece, this gives it
a framed 3-D touch.

10

The result: a good conversation piece for anyone's port-
folio. This high-profile biomechanical style can be tied in
with graphics as a background landscape or as a standalone
mural for any Harley, hood, or jacket mural.

THE FLAMED-OUT:
BRAIN BUCKET

BY CRAIG FRASER

One of the fastest-growing fields in customizing is the aftermarket helmet-painting industry. Ranging from motorcycles and Indy cars to sports like hockey and cycling, the market for individualized helmets has doubled in the past few years. If you have a little motivation and a well-ventilated garage, you can make a sizable dent in this industry.

Helmet costs range from $100 to over $1,000 for a custom-made helmet, and the cost of customizing is fairly high, too. Although many helmet owners are happy with their factory sticker kits, nothing is quite as expressive as a custom-painted helmet. In all the motorsports arenas, the rider is considered practically naked if he's not sporting a full-blown custom-painted helmet. This market has grown so large that many automotive painters and airbrush artists have begun specializing solely in spraying helmets.

For this demo, we'vel picked a rather simple helmet, so that the process was not lost in all the airbrush tricks. This particular helmet was done for Steve Stillwell, editor of *Hot Bike* magazine. Steve wanted something unique on his brain bucket. He wanted it to be a classic design but also wanted to have some airbrushing in it too. The helmet also had to match the kandy color of his bike and the flames. Nothing like a little challenge.

The helmet we used is known in the industry as a half-helmet, or beanie. Be aware that beanies aren't legal in all states.

Although Steve's helmet was used, even brand-new helmets should be prepped, which involves removing stickers on or under the gelcoat clear. For durability and quality of finish, we used only urethane-based products.

Although the techniques covered in this chapter were applied to a little peanut helmet, remember that 90 percent of all helmets are made in the same manner, with gelcoat skins. These same techniques also apply to hockey helmets, baseball helmets, NASCAR helmets, skiing helmets, and even bicycle helmets.

1.

Disassemble the helmet, mask off the underside, and sand the black gelcoated surface with 220-grit sandpaper. It's necessary to sand and reseal the gelcoat, due to mold-release waxes in it that can reactivate later, causing lifting or bubbling of the clear if not sealed properly.

2.

After the entire surface is sanded, it is sprayed with a catalyzed polyester sealer. This sealer/primer locks in the mold-release waxes and gives a good, sandable foundation for the upcoming paint. Any nicks or scratches are taken care of at this stage with a catalyzed polyester filler.

3.

Give the primer a few hours to fully dry. Then spray on a combination of HoK Orion Silver Basecoat and HoK Solar Gold. This base gives the Kandy Apple a deep metallic look.

4.

Notice the slight gold shimmer of the metallic. The gold is necessary in the painting of a true Kandy Apple paint job. It decreases the brightness of the red kandy and gives it a richer glow than if it was solely shot with a silver base.

5.

Starting with a tack coat first, dust the plate and helmet with HoK UK-11 catalyzed Kandy Red. The tack coat provides an important tooth for the subsequent wet coats to adhere to. Without the tack coat, it's common for any additional coats to run, especially on curved surfaces such as this helmet.

6.

After applying three additional wet coats of kandy, the true color of the helmet begins to show through. It's important not to give the helmet too many coats of kandy. Besides the obvious running and sagging problem, the kandy will also continue to darken. A true kandy will darken until it appears black. This may be desirable for some effects, but not if you're trying to match a lighter shade of kandy already on the bike.

7.

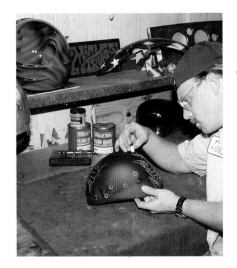

A protective coat of clear is applied after the previous color coat. Then let the helmet set for 24 hours before sanding in preparation for the airbrush work. Using 600-grit wet/dry sandpaper, knock down the shine to provide a good surface to work on. The design is then lightly sketched using pure white chalk. This is the same inert chalk I use for all my design work. It wipes off easily and leaves no residue to interfere with the clearcoat.

8.

With HoK Basecoat White, I continue the sketching process using an airbrush. The brains and breaks in the helmet are retraced and detailed over the chalk sketch. (The nitride rubber gloves are great for artists who are sensitive to reducers. Personally, I feel claustrophobic with them, so this is the only demo where you'll see me wearing them.) Of course, the aluminum skull support for the helmet is an absolute necessity.

9.

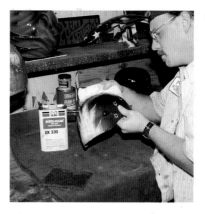

After finishing the white, I wipe the entire surface with a damp rag and pre-cleaner. This removes any of the excess chalk as well as overspray. I do this wipe-down process after every color change, giving me a clean surface for every step and preventing buildup of dry areas caused by overspray.

10.

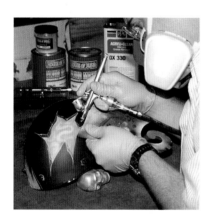

Donning my Superman gloves, I come back to battle crime with some HoK SG-101 Lemon Yellow Basecoat. An Artool freehand shield allowed me to control the overspray and give the area a sharp, soft edge without the buildup a taped edge would give—not to mention that the freehand shield is a heck of a lot faster and leaves no tape residue.

The darkest areas of the details were done with a mixture of transparent violette and cobalt blue kandy koncentrate and intercoat clear. This creates a deep purple that appears as red/brown when layered over the red oxide and yellow. Continuous layering gives the illusion of black in the detail without killing any of the colors.

11.

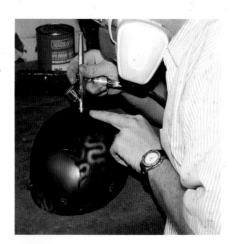

Next, build up the detail using a mixture of tangerine, root beer, and pagan gold kandy koncentrates mixed with intercoat clear. The result is a transparent red oxide that works nicely in sculpting the brains.

12.

13.

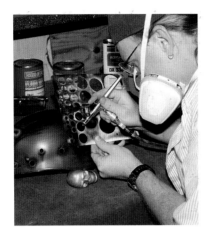

To create the realistic holes in the sides, use an architectural circle template. The purple kandy mixture is used with a few drops of black added to it. The black makes the bullet holes stand out from the details in the brains and give them more depth.

14.

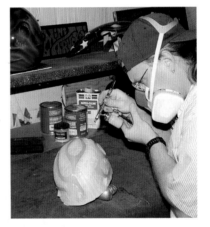

Last but not least, the highlights and rising smoke from the holes is airbrushed in white. To get the extra-fine detail in the broken-edged highlights and thin wisps, I used the Iwata Micron-C airbrush. The white is even further reduced, to prevent spitting and clogging at this detail range.

15.

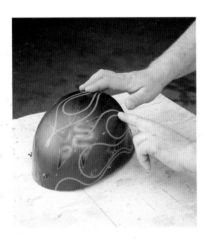

With the airbrushing done, the helmet is given a light coat of clear to protect it from the masking. Noncatalyzed intercoat clear is used because it has a drying window of only one hour. The surface is then scuffed to prepare for the flame layout. The flames are laid out using 1/8-inch blue fineline tape. Fineline tape is perfect for helmets, since it can turn a radius without bunching and is repositionable.

16.

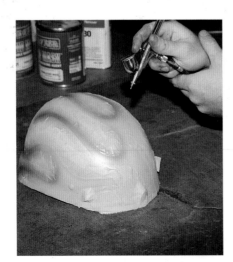

After the blue fineline tape is applied, mask up to the edge with 3/4-inch masking tape to cover the surrounding area of the shell. With the previous batch of SG-101 Lemon Yellow Basecoat, paint the flames with the Eclipse airbrush. The Eclipse not only has a wider spray pattern, but the bottle allows me to spray longer without refills.

17.

Mixing up more of the red oxide concoction, spray a light orange fade on the tips of the flames. A little lavender dry pearl added to the red oxide kandy gives a deep red color when layered over the yellow.

18.

After the tape is removed and the surface is wiped down
with pre-cleaner again (tape residue!), use a freehand
shield to help lay in the drop shadows under the flames.
The drop shadow is sprayed using a transparent over-
reduced mixture of Basecoat Black.

19.

Then switch to an Xcaliber 000 sword striper brush. With a
little HoK light blue urethane striping paint, carefully
pull a line around the flames. Practicing striping on
an old helmet is an excellent way to build up brush control
and mastery.

20.

The helmet is then taken into the booth and clearcoated.
Dion uses his trusty Iwata LPH-95 to lay down a tack coat
and three good wet coats of HoK UFC-35 Komply Klear.
While a helmet normally needs one final clearing session,
this one may need to be sanded and cleared again to
eliminate the pinstripe edge.

CHAPTER
4.11

DETAILING YOUR MONSTER

BY DENNIS PARKS

After spending considerable hours, maybe even days, cleaning, polishing, painting, and waxing exterior body parts, you may think your car is detailed to the highest degree. But have you looked at the vents on your car's dashboard? Are they dusty? If you spent any time at all sanding the body of your car or truck, chances are that more sanding dust than you had imagined has infiltrated the interior, trunk, and engine compartment. That stuff is amazing. It seems to find its way into just about every nook and cranny.

Since the outside of your automobile looks so good, why not spend a little time on the interior? Your vacuum cleaner with a soft brush attachment will work well to remove large accumulations of dust on and around the dashboard. Use a soft cloth, toothbrush, or cotton swab to clean corners and confined spaces. The vacuum cleaner's crevice attachment fits into tight spaces around seats and center consoles to remove dust and debris.

Mix a small amount of a cleaner such as Simple Green in a bucket and dip cleaning cloths into it periodically to help clean sticky steering wheels, stained sun visors, dirty door panels, and vinyl seats. You'll be amazed at how much dirt gathers on your cleaning cloth.

Next, vacuum the trunk thoroughly. If yours is an older American car that features an open metal space with no cardboard or carpet siding and it's been neglected for far too long, detail it. Remove scale, rust deposits, and other debris with a wire brush. Use a vacuum to remove residue. Then consider applying a couple of coats of a rust-inhibiting paint as a sealer. To really make the trunk space look new and original, apply a quality coat of trunk splatter paint. Two cans are generally

By the time you've fully prepped a vehicle for repainting, a vast amount of dust will have engulfed it. Using a heavy-duty shop vacuum or one at the local car wash, vacuum all this dust and dirt from everywhere you can. It will be in the air conditioning and heat vents, on and between the seats, under the seats, and in the carpet. An accessory nozzle with a narrow tip will be helpful. Also, clean the seats with the appropriate upholstery cleaner for your vehicle.

Even though it isn't fancy, this vinyl door panel looks much better after being cleaned. Some of these specially treated wipes work well for cleaning the dash and door panels, but since they contain silicone, be careful not to get them on painted surfaces. The silicone won't really affect the cured paint, but it could cause fisheye blemishes if the affected area needs to be repainted.

4.11

Other than needing some mild cleaning and minor detailing, this trunk is not in bad shape. For the most part, some soap and water, a scrub brush, and some elbow grease could have it looking brand new. Many older vehicles have severe problems with rust in the trunk. As wheelwell or fender panels begin to rust, they allow moisture to gain access to the trunk. This moisture gets trapped under the spare tire and carpeting. Since it's hidden, you usually don't notice it until it's a major problem.

Although it may not look bad in the photo, this engine compartment could use some major cleaning. An all-purpose cleaner and a small brush would work wonders for cleaning the multitude of plastic and rubber parts. Some car-wash soap and water applied with a towel, then rinsed and dried, would clean up the painted surfaces, such as the shock towers and inner fenders. Some aluminum cleaner and a brush could be used to clean up the valve covers and engine components.

If any paint overspray is found on the window glass, a paper towel with a bit of reducer will usually remove it. If it's excessive, you may need to use a fine Scotch-Brite pad or even a razor blade first. Once you've wiped it with paint reducer, remove any traces of the chemical with a window cleaner.

Thoroughly washing the vehicle by hand with soapy water and rinsing with plenty of clear water provides the body shop one last chance to find any blemishes.

After washing, the car is thoroughly dried. Preferences differ when it comes to the best material for drying a car. Some people use clean cloth baby diapers, others use bath towels, while still others use "special" car-drying towels. The best bet is a chamois, but these work their best only if the car is sporting a good coat of wax, which is a great idea.

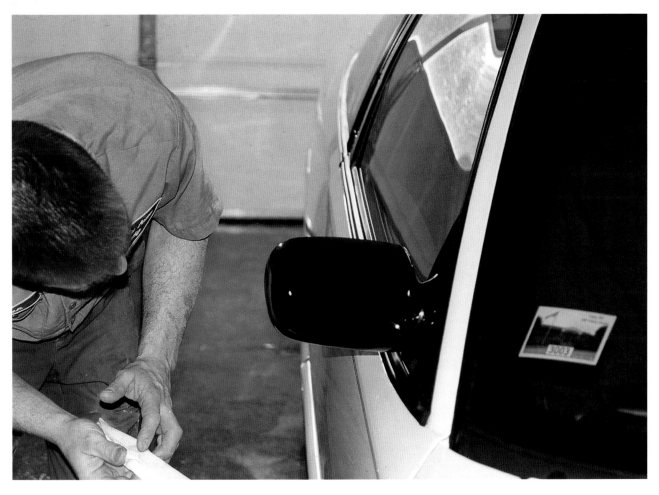

If you find small blemishes during detailing, touch them up with some of the same paint and a small brush. If there are small dabs of dirt on the freshly painted surface, a small dab of rubbing compound on a clean cloth can usually remove it.

enough for normal-sized, 1950–70 vintage American car trunks.

Trunk splatter paint comes in a few different colors. The unique part about splatter paint is that three colors are generally spit out. The base color might be gray, highlighted by spots of white and black, just like an original finish. Don't apply this material to the back of the rear seats, and make sure the entire space is clean before application.

Engine compartments can present detailers with more than just sanding dust. Years of accumulated grease and oil may make cleaning seem like an impossible chore. But an engine cleaner, such as Gunk, and pressure from the wand of a self-serve car wash can easily remove the bulk of those accumulations. Be sure to cover newly painted fenders with large towels or other soft material, and keep the water wand away from the distributor and carburetor.

After that, some time with a stiff paintbrush and an all-purpose cleaner can make the engine compartment on your automobile look almost as good

as the new paint job. You can take more time to make the engine compartment look better by painting the engine block and polishing all items that need it. The more you do, the better it will look.

LONG-TERM PAINT CARE

Automotive paint jobs can last for years as long as their finishes are maintained, protected, and not abused. Frequent washing, maintaining effective wax protection, and limiting exposure to ultraviolet rays will add greatly to almost any paint job's longevity. Although the new catalyzed paint systems are more durable than most paint products employed before them, gross neglect will cause their shine and luster to fade and oxidize over time. It's up to you to maintain them in clean condition and prevent the penetration of lingering dirt, tree sap, bird droppings, airborne pollution, and mildew.

Although newer, catalyzed paint products are much more durable and longer lasting than the materials used before them, you can't expect their finish to

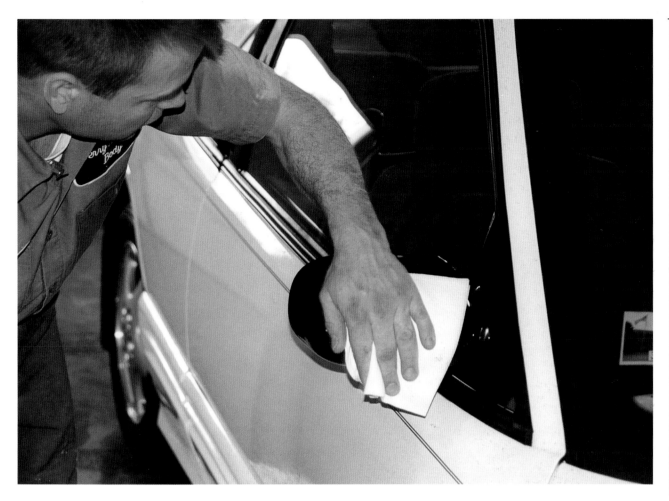

Make sure you wipe off all the residue of the rubbing compound.

shine forever without a minimal amount of routine maintenance. Basically, this entails washing, polishing as needed, and scheduled waxing.

Even though some paint products may be advertised as never having to be waxed, many auto enthusiasts and professionals believe that good coats of wax not only help provide great paint longevity but also make washing car bodies a lot easier. It almost seems like dirt and road debris float off waxed surfaces instead of having to be rubbed off.

Unless yours is a show car that will seldom, if ever, be driven, sooner or later, nicks or small chips will appear. Along with regular maintenance, repair these minor paint problems as soon as possible. If not, exposed metal will oxidize, and that corrosion will spread under paint to affect adjacent metal areas.

WASHING, POLISHING, AND WAXING

Auto parts stores, some variety outlets, and even a few supermarkets sell car-wash soap products. For the most part, almost any brand should be well suited

for the finish on your vehicle. Many auto enthusiasts prefer to use liquids, as opposed to granular types because they believe that just one undissolved granule on a wash mitt could cause scratches. Be sure to follow the mixing directions on labels of any product.

The best way to prevent minute scratches or other blemishes in the paint is to wash the car in sections. Wash the dirtiest parts first, such as rocker panels, fenderwell lips, and lower front and rear end locations. Then thoroughly rinse your soft cotton wash mitt and wash bucket. Mix up a new batch of wash soap to clean the vehicle sides. If they were relatively clean to start with, you can continue with that bucket of sudsy water to wash the hood, roof, and trunk areas.

This process rids your wash mitt and bucket of dirt and other scratch hazards, such as sand and road grit, so they don't get picked up and rubbed into the finish. Likewise, anytime you notice that your wash mitt is dirty, or if it falls to the ground, rinse it off with clear water before dipping it into

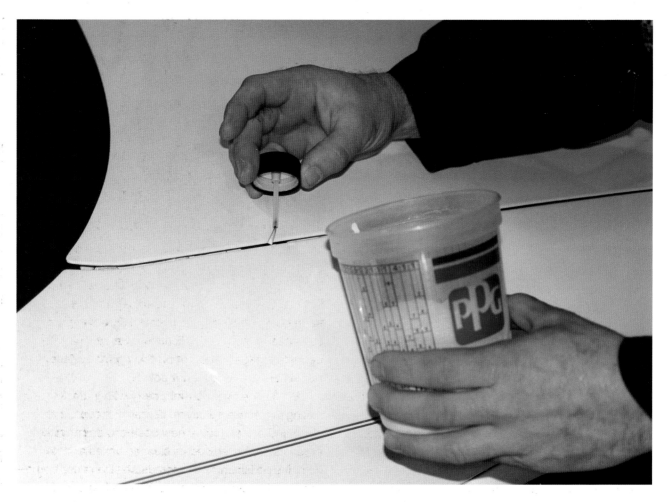

A small scratch is being touched up with a bit of paint and a small brush. Since this is a new paint job and the paint used to touch it up is from the same can, it should match with no problems. Paint from actual touchup bottles will sometimes differ slightly.

the wash bucket. This helps keep the wash water clean and free of debris.

Soft wash mitts, soft cotton towels, and soft waxing applicators and cloths go a long way toward keeping paint finishes in pristine condition. Operating any mitt or cloth on your car's surface in a straight back-and-forth movement will also greatly reduce the formation of swirls or spiderwebbing. Always read the labels of any car wash soap, polish, or wax product to determine just what it's intended to do.

To clean inside tight spaces, such as window molding edges and cowl louvers, use a soft, natural-hair floppy paintbrush. Don't use synthetic-bristled paintbrushes because they could cause minute scratches on paint surfaces. In addition, wrap a thick layer of heavy duct tape over the paintbrush's metal band. This will help guard against paint scratches or nicks as you vigorously agitate the paintbrush in tight spaces, possibly knocking the brush into painted body parts, such as around headlights and grilles.

Let's talk a moment about polish and wax. Although both are designed as paint-finish maintenance materials, each has its own purpose. Polishes clean paint finishes and remove oxidation and other contaminants. Wax, on the other hand, does no cleaning or shining. It does, however, protect paint finishes that have already been cleaned and polished. Simply stated, polish cleans; wax protects.

Auto body paint and supply stores generally carry the largest selection of auto polishes and waxes, although many auto parts stores stock good assortments. Every polish should include a definitive label that explains what kind of paint finish it's designed for—for example, heavily oxidized, mildly oxidized, and new-finish glaze. Those designed for heavy oxidation problems contain much coarser grit than those for new-car finishes.

The labels also note whether the product is intended for machine (buffer) use. Those with heavy concentrations of coarse grit are not recommended for machine use. Their polishing strength, combined with the power of a buffer, could cause large-scale paint burning problems.

Carnauba wax is perhaps the best product for protecting automobile paint finishes. Meguiar's, Eagle 1, and other cosmetic car-care product manufacturers offer auto enthusiasts an assortment of carnauba-based auto wax products. Other paint protection products profess to work like wax but contain different chemical bases, which you must clearly understand before applying them to your new paint job.

Some of these (typically, they have "poly" or "polymer" in the product name) are loaded with silicone. Although they may protect your car's finish for a long time, professional auto painters advise against them because the silicone can saturate the paint right down to the metal and create fisheye problems if you need another repaint down the road. In some cases, silicones can even become embedded in the sheet metal itself.

If you find yourself in a quandary when it comes time to select a polish or wax product, seek advice from a knowledgeable auto body paint and supply jobber. This person should be up to date on the latest product information from manufacturers and the view professional painters and detailers in the field have of the products.

WHEN TO WASH NEW PAINT FINISHES

Allow plenty of time for your paint's solvents to evaporate or chemically react before washing the vehicle. For uncatalyzed enamels, this may entail a few days or a week. You can generally wash newer paints with hardener additives after one or two days, as long as you use mild automotive soap products and a gentle approach.

Because auto painters have such a wide selection of paint products to choose from, and because each brand or system may react differently from others, it's always best to confirm appropriate paint drying times with a professional auto body paint and supply jobber before washing, polishing, or waxing any new finish.

HOW LONG BEFORE WAXING?

The rule of thumb is to wait 90 to 120 days before waxing your freshly painted vehicle. This varies according to weather conditions. During summer months, while temperatures are warm and humidity low, 90 days should allow plenty of time for paint solvents to completely evaporate. Cool, wet weather reduces solvent evaporation activity and therefore requires a longer waiting period.

Light coats of quality auto wax form a protective seal on top of the paint finish. Even though it is quite thin and by no means permanent, this wax seal will prevent solvent evaporation. Should that occur, those vapors that need to exit paint would be trapped. As a result, they slowly build up pressure within the paint, which will eventually damage it, frequently in the form of blistering. So waxing too soon after new paint applications can cause unexpected damage instead of protecting the surface. Remember, this is wax, not polish.

Polish does not normally carry with it any long-lasting protective additives. Its main function is to clean and shine. A lot of new cosmetic paint finish products are advertised as cleaner-waxes and do combine polish and wax ingredients. Don't use combination polish-wax products until paint has cured for at least 90 to 120 days because the wax ingredients in these products will form a light seal over surfaces and trap solvents, just like dedicated wax-only products. If you need to polish a new catalyzed or lacquer paint job, be absolutely certain the polish contains no wax ingredients. Read labels to be sure, and don't be afraid to consult with an auto body paint and supply store jobber.

CAR COVERS

Quality car covers made of materials that breathe provide an excellent means of overall paint protection, especially when your car has to sit out in the sun for days on end. The sun is your paint finish's enemy. The more you can do to prevent it from suffering through endless days of baking under harsh sunlight, the longer its shine will last. If a quality car cover is not within your budget now, try parking in the shadow of a building. Alternatively, park head first in the parking lot one day and then back in the next, to alternate sunlight exposure between your car's sides.

PHOTO CREDITS: Unless otherwise credited, photos are courtesy of Discovery Channel

Aeroquip, 108 top, 104 middle & top
Craig Fraser, 173-213
Dennis Parks, 141-172, 215-222
Deuce Factory, 72 middle & lower, 84 lower & middle, 90 top, 104 bottom, 108 top
ESAB Welding and Cutting Plastics, 128 top, 133 bottom
Jim Richardson, 23-68

Lee Klancher, 101 bottom
Lincoln Electric Company, 115 bottom
Miller Electric Company, 131 bottom, 132
Pete & Jake's, 90 bottom, 98, 99
Richard Finch, 115-134
Sellstrom Manufacturing Corporation, 115 bottom
So-Cal Speed Shop, 77-80, 88, 89, 94 bottom
Super Bell, 71 lower
Tim Remus, 71-76, 83, 85, 87, 101-109
WAG Aero Group, 134 middle

INDEX